The Reminiscences of
Rear Admiral Odale D. Waters, Jr.
U.S. Navy (Retired)

Interviewed by
Dr. John T. Mason, Jr.
and
Paul Stillwell

U.S. Naval Institute • Annapolis, Maryland

Copyright © 1994

Preface

For a variety of reasons, the oral history of Rear Admiral Odale "Muddy" Waters has remained incomplete far too long. The first interview was conducted nearly 25 years ago. The interviewee himself has been dead since 1986. Finally, however, the transcript is now done and available for use by students of naval history. It is worth the wait, because Admiral Waters covered a wealth of interesting and valuable topics in the course of discussing his more than 40 years of service in the Navy.

After his graduation from the Naval Academy in 1932 he served in the heavy cruiser _Augusta_. He told of serving in that ship under one commanding officer, Captain Chester Nimitz, who later became a fleet admiral and served as Commander in Chief Pacific Fleet during World War II. Later, after destroyer duty and postgraduate education, Waters was sent to England, where he was trained in the art and science of mine disposal. Armed with his new-found expertise, he returned to this country to set up the Navy's first mine disposal school. Mine warfare remained a strong interest throughout his professional life.

During the latter part of the war, he was associated with the colorful Admiral Jonas Ingram in South America. Admiral Waters's recollections help explain just what was so colorful about Ingram. At the end of the war, Waters took command of the destroyer _Laffey_, a tour of duty he looked back upon with great satisfaction. He was her skipper during the Operation Crossroads atomic bomb tests at Bikini Atoll in 1946. Later he was involved in research at the Naval Ordnance Laboratory and served in the Operational Development Force. In the 1950s he commanded the deep-draft attack transport Glynn during arctic research and spent a productive period on the staff of the Supreme Allied Commander Atlantic, Admiral Jerauld Wright.

In the late 1950s Waters enjoyed commanding the Naval Mine Depot at Yorktown, Virginia, and succeeded in having the command's name changed to the more fitting Naval Weapons Station. His enjoyment was enriched when he was selected for flag rank and went on to a series of billets, including command of Destroyer Flotilla One, Mine Force Pacific Fleet, and Naval Base Los Angeles. The culmination of Admiral Waters's career came during an unusually long five-year tenure as Oceanographer of the Navy. During that time the office grew in stature as the oceanographer began reporting directly to the Chief of Naval Operations. His service as oceanographer was honored when the Navy named the survey ship USNS Waters (T-AGS-45) for him in 1992.

Thanks go to my predecessor, Dr. John T. Mason, Jr., for initiating this oral memoir as one of his first projects after beginning the oral history program at the Naval Institute in 1969. He interviewed Admiral Waters for a series of oral histories related to Admiral Nimitz and then began a full-length memoir about Waters's career as a whole. After the first four interviews were completed, Admiral Waters moved from the Washington area to Florida, and the project remained dormant for a decade and a half.

Fortunately, I was able to resume the project and conducted the final interview only a few months before Admiral Waters's death. I found him to be a friendly, gracious man--the epitome of the southern gentleman. At the age of 75 he was still trim, straight, and distinguished looking. He looked like an admiral. In addition, I remember his dark brown eyes as being a particularly striking feature of his appearance.

Admiral Waters did not offer any corrections to the transcript prior to his death, so I have done some editing on his behalf. I have made changes in the interest of clarity and smoothness but have not changed the substance of his remarks. My thanks go to Linda O'Doughda, formerly of the Naval Institute's oral history program, for her careful proofreading of the finished transcript. It is better because of her efforts.

                              Paul Stillwell
                              Director, History Division
                              U.S. Naval Institute
                              February 1994

REAR ADMIRAL ODALE D. WATERS, JR.,
U.S. NAVY (RETIRED)

Odale Dabney Waters, Jr., was born in Manassas, Virginia, on 13 July 1910, son of the late Mr. and Mrs. O. D. Waters. He attended the Swavely School and Strayer Business College, Washington, D.C., prior to entering the U.S. Naval Academy, Annapolis, Maryland, on 9 July 1928. As a midshipman he was a member of the track team, was managing editor of the *Lucky Bag*, and was battalion commander his first class year. Graduating with distinction, ninth in the class of 1932, he was commissioned ensign on 2 June 1932 and subsequently advanced in rank to that of rear admiral, to date from 1 October 1960.

After graduation from the Naval Academy in June 1932, Waters was assigned to the USS *Augusta* (CA-31), in which he had junior officer duties in gunnery and fire control. During part of that period the cruiser served as the flagship of the Commander in Chief Asiatic Fleet. He then returned to the United States and in September 1936 joined the USS *Downes* (DD-375) as torpedo officer. Detached in June 1938, he was a student in ordnance engineering at the Naval Postgraduate School, Annapolis, Maryland, until October 1940. After that he served for six months as assistant naval attaché at the American Embassy, London, England, also serving as technical observer in mine recovery operations. This resulted in his establishing the first U.S. Navy mine disposal school, after his return to the United States in 1941. In June of that year he became officer in charge of that school and operated it during the early part of the war, until January 1943.

Ordered next to the USS *Memphis* (CL-13), he served aboard a year. From February 1944 until October of that year he served as fleet gunnery officer and assistant chief of staff to Commander Fourth Fleet. For five months thereafter Waters was assistant operations officer and war plans officer on the staff of the Commander in Chief U.S. Atlantic Fleet. He was awarded a Bronze Star Medal, "For meritorious service as Gunnery, Training, War Plans Officer and Assistant Chief of Staff to Commander FOURTH Fleet from March 18 to November 15, 1944, and as Assistant Operations Officer and Officer-in-Charge of War Plans on the Staff of Commander in Chief, United States Atlantic Fleet, from November 15, 1944, to April 27, 1945. . . . Commander Waters contributed materially to the success of the anti-submarine campaign in the South Atlantic by his persistent prosecution of the training program of the FOURTH Fleet.

After keen analysis and studies of past operations and of current and probable future situations, he prepared operational plans which further contributed to the success of the Atlantic Fleet in the prosecution of the war."

In June 1945 Waters assumed command of the USS Laffey (DD-724) and after the close of hostilities of World War II in August 1945 remained in that command until October 1946, participating in Operation Crossroads, the atom bomb tests at Bikini in the Pacific during the summer of 1946. In November of that year he reported to the Naval Ordnance Laboratory, Washington, D.C., for duty as senior technical officer and mine development project officer. There he was also engaged in the design of atomic weapons. Detached in January 1950, he spent five months as a student at the Armed Forces Staff College, Norfolk, Virginia, finishing the course in July 1950.

Commander Waters served as ordnance and gunnery officer on the staff of Commander Operational Development Force from July 1950 until May 1952, after which he commanded the USS Glynn (APA-239) in sub-arctic waters. During the three years to follow he served on the staff of the NATO Supreme Allied Commander Atlantic, concerned with strategic applications and policy. In September 1956 he assumed command of Destroyer Squadron Two, which operated during the Suez Canal incident as a unit of the Middle East Force.

On 31 December 1957, Captain Waters assumed the duties of Commander U.S. Naval Mine Depot, Yorktown, Virginia. During his tenure, the name of the command was changed to U.S. Naval Weapons Station Yorktown. In July 1960 his selection for the rank of rear admiral was approved by the President of the United States, and in December of that year he reported as Commander Destroyer Flotilla One. From 5 March 1962 until February 1964 he served as Inspector General and Assistant Chief for Administration of the Bureau of Naval Weapons. He then became Commander Mine Force Pacific Fleet, with additional duty as Commander Naval Base, Los Angeles, California. In September 1965 he reported as Oceanographer of the Navy, Office of the Chief of Naval Operations, and Commander Naval Oceanographic Service, Suitland, Maryland. He was awarded the Distinguished Service Medal for his "exceptionally meritorious service" in that billet. The citation states in part:

"At a time when the Navy's oceanographic effort was widely distributed among various elements of the Naval Establishment, Rear Admiral Waters was chiefly responsible for carrying through a program to bring all oceanographic efforts under centralized direction. As a result, the Oceanographer now supervises all of the oceanographic efforts from planning phases to final execution. This has included the work of twenty-seven field activities, more than thirty survey and research ships, and such other platforms as submarines, deep research vehicles, helicopters, buoys, fixed towers and manned bottom habitats. [His] centralized direction has made it possible to provide the Navy and its Fleet with a more efficient support program and to cooperative actively with other government agencies and civilian interests in the oceanographic field. By his professional skill and resourcefulness, along with his dedication and effective leadership, he has enhanced the scientific and military posture of the Navy while making the most effective utilization of limited resources of men and money."

Rear Admiral Waters was relieved as Oceanographer of the Navy on 23 September 1970. The following month he was assigned to the Office of the Assistant Secretary of the Navy (Research and Development) and was detailed on loan as an adviser in the National Oceanic and Atmospheric Administration of the Department of Commerce. He served as such until relieved of active duty, pending his retirement, effective 1 February 1971.

In addition to the Distinguished Service Medal and the Bronze Star Medal, Rear Admiral Waters had the American Defense Service Medal with star; the American Campaign Medal; European-African-Middle Eastern Campaign Medal; Asiatic-Pacific Campaign Medal; World War II Victory Medal; the National Defense Service Medal with bronze star; Korean Service Medal; and the United Nations Service Medal. He also received the Navy League's Parsons Award for outstanding contributions in the field of science and the Public Relations Society of America's Silver Anvil award for his outstanding programs in institutional public relations.

Rear Admiral Waters was married in 1936 to Miss Lucile Elizabeth McGehee of Washington, D.C. They had four daughters: Martha Lane Waters Philipps, Carol Weir Waters Waldron, Lucile Dabney Waters Schmitt, and Ann Elizabeth Waters Scott. The admiral died at Indiatlantic, Florida, on 7 May 1986.

Authorization

The U.S. Naval Institute is hereby authorized to make available to individuals, libraries, and other repositories of its choosing the transcripts of five oral history interviews concerning the life and career of the late Rear Admiral Odale D. Waters, Jr., USN (Ret.). The interviews were recorded on 6 August 1969, 7 April 1971, 27 May 1971, and 4 June 1971 in collaboration with Dr. John Mason, Jr., and 4 December 1985 in collaboration with Paul Stillwell for the U.S. Naval Institute.

The undersigned does hereby release and assign to the U.S. Naval Institute all right, title, restrictions, and interest in the interviews. The copyright in both the oral and transcribed versions shall be the sole property of the U.S. Naval Institute. The tape recordings of the interviews are and will remain the property of the U.S. Naval Institute.

Signed and sealed this ___24th___ day of ___April___ 1990.

Martha W. Philipps (Mrs. George Philipps)
Mrs. George Philipps
for the estate of Rear Admiral O. D. Waters, Jr., USN (Ret.)

O. D. Waters, Jr. #1 - 1

Interview Number 1 with
Rear Admiral Odale D. Waters, Jr., U.S. Navy

Place: Admiral Waters's office in Alexandria, Virginia

Date: Wednesday, 6 August 1969

Interviewer: John T. Mason, Jr.

Q: Admiral, I'm delighted that you've consented to tell me about your own naval career, because it has been and continues to be a very significant one.* Would you begin in the proper fashion by telling me something about yourself, about your background, about your family, your early education.

Admiral Waters: Well, I'm a native Virginian. My whole family have been in Prince William County, Virginia, for a long time.

Q: One need only to know your middle name, Dabney, to know that you're from Virginia.

Admiral Waters: Yes, that's sort of strange in that most people, when they have a name like that, it's from their own family. Actually, this name got into my family during the Civil War when my ancestors were refugees. Prince William County contained Bull Run battlefield, and a lot of

---
*The interview was conducted while Waters was still on active duty as Oceanographer of the Navy.

that land had belonged to my ancestors, so they had to vacate it when the war came along. They were taken in by some friends of theirs down in the northern neck--some friends named Dabney. That's how the name crept into the family. So it isn't really a blood relationship.

Q: No, but it's a very legitimate kind of entry.

Admiral Waters: I grew up in the town of Manassas, which was then a small, sleepy county seat, a dairy farm community.

Q: Yes, yes, Admiral.

Admiral Waters: Of course, Manassas is now sort of a far-out suburb of Washington and not very far at that. But I went to the local public schools, and at that time there weren't nearly as many restrictions as there are today on when you can go to school and when you can't. When my older sister started to school, I refused to stay home, so I ended up entering school when I was only five years old. Therefore, I graduated from high school just before I was 16.

Q: I share that experience.

O. D. Waters, Jr. #1 - 3

Admiral Waters: So there I was, really too young to go away anyplace. But, fortunately, in my last year in high school I took an examination and won a scholarship to Strayer Business College in Washington for the next year, which was 1927. I commuted into Washington and became a full-fledged secretary, which I never worked at. In other words, I graduated with a capability of typing and taking shorthand.

Q: You've never regretted the typing, have you?

Admiral Waters: I never have. I've lost a lot of the shorthand, although I still recall a bit of it. Every now and then I can confound a yeoman by telling him he's transcribing something incorrectly. But the typing has been a tremendous help to me. Then, during that year, I succeeded in getting a promise of an appointment to the Naval Academy. Actually, I got interested in both service academies, because I found out that they paid you to go there, and these were sort of hard times.

Q: And scholarships weren't very readily available, were they?

Admiral Waters: No. I thought at first that I would like

to go to West Point and ride a white horse like General Lee.* Then, when I was told by our congressman that he had promised his West Point appointment and that he had his Annapolis appointment available, I took it, and I've been very glad that it worked out that way.

Q: Who was your congressman?

Admiral Waters: It was Judge R. Walton Moore of Fairfax, who was later on, I believe, an Under Secretary of State.** He was a fine old man. I always did as I think most midshipmen do; they usually correspond with the congressmen that appointed them, send them Christmas cards and that sort of thing.

Q: I had the pleasure of knowing him casually.

Admiral Waters: So, having this appointment promised, I then went for a year to a prep school which was located in Manassas. It moved there several years before from Washington. It had been called Army-Navy Prep in

---
*General Robert E. Lee, a graduate of the U.S. Military Academy, commanded the Army of Northern Virginia for the Confederacy during the Civil War.
**Robert Walton Moore, a Democrat from Virginia's 8th district, served in the House of Representatives from 1919 to 1931. From 1933 to 1937 he was Assistant Secretary of State and from 1937 to 1940 Counselor of the State Department, a position coequal to that of Under Secretary of State. The title "judge" was an honorary one.

Washington. When they came down into Virginia and acquired more land and buildings, the name was changed to the Swavely School for Boys. And it was a very fine school. A good percentage of the boys they prepared got into the Naval Academy, but the record they were proud of was that once there, they stayed there.

Q: Whose wisdom was this, sir, that you went to the prep school? Was it your own or your parents'?

Admiral Waters: Well, it really was more or less happenstance. The dean of the prep school, Mr. Robert Walter, was my Sunday school teacher in the Episcopal Church in Manassas, and he sort of got interested in me. That's how I first got interested in going to one of the service academies, and then all of these things happened.

Although Manassas High School was a good and an old accredited high school, the science they offered there at that time was chemistry, and the Naval Academy, of course, required physics. So even though I had done very well in chemistry in high school, I still needed to have physics. It was one of the reasons I went to Swavely. That and my age too, because I was only 17 then, you see.

Q: I referred to it as wisdom. Really, in light of experience, many men who are quite capable intellectually

O. D. Waters, Jr. #1 - 6

go the academy ill-prepared for it.

Admiral Waters: Yes, I think it was a very wise move, and it wasn't mine. I was well-advised, I think. By going there, I not only got the physics that I required, but I took a lot of other courses too. I took many of the courses that were included in the first year of the Naval Academy--practically the whole math course, for instance--so that I was well prepared. Mr. Walter, who was sort of my adviser and guide in this, was also one of the best English teachers that I've ever had. I had a very fine course in English at Swavely. As a result of that, I stood number one in English at the Naval Academy--sort of a reflection on his teaching ability.

Q: It wasn't a frenetic experience as it has been for some men.

Admiral Waters: I think that one of the requirements for naval officers is that they be able to both write and speak the English language pretty well. This, I think, served me in very good stead.

At that time there were two ways to get into the Naval Academy. One was to take the whole spectrum of regular examinations. But if you had a certificate from a recognized school and certain credits, you could get in on what they called substantiating examinations. They took one day and included one exam in math, as I remember, and one in English, and that was it. So it was much simpler then.

Q: Just a sampling of your ability.

Admiral Waters: Yes.

Q: You had the principal appointment, did you?

Admiral Waters: Yes, I had the principal appointment, and so after one year at Swavely I entered the Naval Academy in July of 1928. By that time I had two more years on me from finishing high school, and I was at the exact average age of my class. I was 18 years, zero months.* I was just sort of in the middle.

Q: Were your parents pleased with this development in this direction that you were taking?

Admiral Waters: Yes, yes, they were very much so. Although there had been nobody connected with the Navy in my family for quite a few generations, they thought it was a great thing. Of course, my mother had a few qualms about

---
*Waters was born 13 July 1910.

O. D. Waters, Jr. #1 - 8

my going away from home so far. But I think she sort of resigned herself to the fact that this would happen sooner or later anyway.

Q: Well, tell me about your years at the academy.

Admiral Waters: Well, I thoroughly enjoyed it. Of course, everyone thought they were having a bad time plebe year, but I think we had fun. I suppose I was a pretty diligent student. I worked pretty hard. I did make pretty good grades, but I wasn't the type of genius that could make them without working at it.

I also had some extracurricular activities. I was on the soccer team and track team, which, because of those two seasons, pretty well filled up my time. They sort of slide into each other, particularly if you go out for winter track. I also was on the editorial board of our class annual, the Lucky Bag.

Q: This was your prowess as an English major coming up.

Admiral Waters: My title was managing editor, but we didn't seem to stick to our job descriptions. Sort of everybody did everything, I think. Everybody wrote bits and pieces for it.

O. D. Waters, Jr. #1 - 9

Q: Well, at least it gave you some extra experiences.

Admiral Waters: Yes, yes.

Q: What type of cruises did you go on? Were they limited by the Depression years?

Admiral Waters: No, they were very good cruises.

Prior to that time, there had been a cruise each summer: after the first year, second year, and third year. While I was there, that changed. I think ours was the second class that had what they called the second-class summer, where you didn't go on a cruise but stayed at the Naval Academy and underwent familiarization with aviation in the old patrol planes they had there. We stayed at the Naval Academy and had various drills and exercises, but it was mainly devoted to familiarization of the midshipmen with aviation.

Q: And that was a real innovation, wasn't it?

Admiral Waters: Yes. I think the class of '31 was the first one that started that their second-class year, and then ours was the second class to do it.

Q: One can term it a kind of watershed in terms of naval

O. D. Waters, Jr. #1 - 10

education.

Admiral Waters: Yes, and, of course, there have been various changes since then. But I think they still maintain some sort of a substitute for a cruise in this way.

Q: Of course, during the Twenties naval aviation was in its infancy and not in the best of standing with the powers that be.

Admiral Waters: That's right. The surface battleship was still the major weapon of the Navy, and the aviators were having a hard time fighting to the fore. But I think this is one sort of a milestone in their progress, in that midshipmen were exposed to this sort of familiarization with flying. Of course, we didn't do any flying. We were just taken up and exercised in gunnery and navigation and that sort of thing.

Q: What sort of an impact did this make on the boys as a whole? I mean, were more of them then of a mind to become naval aviators?

Admiral Waters: I think so. I think so. Some of them found they got airsick and didn't want any part of it. I

O. D. Waters, Jr. #1 - 11

wasn't particularly impressed one way or the other. I wasn't alienated away from aviation or particularly attracted to it. I decided that when I graduated, I would go ahead to sea and then make up my mind later on.

Q: You didn't know that your ultimate destiny was the depths rather than the heights.

Admiral Waters: Our youngster cruise and our first-class cruise were both very good ones. Youngster cruise we cruised in the Arkansas, Wyoming, Florida, and Utah, the oldest battleships we had then. I was in the Arkansas that year and also my first-class year.* In the youngster cruise we went to the Mediterranean--Gibraltar, Naples, Barcelona--and up to a stop in England and home. On our first cruise, which I think was confined to the Arkansas and the Wyoming, I was again in the Arkansas. That year we went up to Scotland, to Glasgow, and then across to Copenhagen. So I had one cruise to southern Europe and one to northern Europe.

Q: Did these cruises include any stops and a look-see at naval installations like Scapa Flow or that sort when you were in Scotland?

---

*USS Arkansas (BB-33) was commissioned 17 September 1912. She had a standard displacement of 26,100 tons, was 562 feet long, and 106 feet in the beam. She had a top speed of 20.5 knots and a main battery of 12 12-inch guns. After service as the oldest U.S. battleship in World War II, she was sunk 25 July 1946 in atomic bomb tests at Bikini Atoll.

Admiral Waters: No. I suppose the different navies of the world weren't that close together in those times. Of course, we were entertained by the Royal Navy and that sort of thing, but there wasn't so much sight-seeing to naval installations as there were Cook's tours that you paid for. For instance, when we were in Naples, we had Cook's tours up to Rome, which were run by Thomas Cook & Sons, Limited. They laid on the hotels, the sight-seeing buses, and then the sight-seeing tours around Naples when we went to Vesuvius and Pompeii and so forth.

Q: It was more of a cultural education than anything else.

Admiral Waters: Yes. One of the things that we did in Rome that was rather noteworthy at the time was that we had an audience with the Pope.* At the conclusion of the audience, the Navy cheerleaders got up and led all the midshipmen in a four N, one Navy, and three great big "Pope, Pope, Popes." He seemed to like it.

Q: How did he react?

Admiral Waters: He thought it was great. He was a great fan of mountain climbing as a sport and told us about it. Of course, it had to be translated.

---
*Pius XI was Pope from 1922 to 1939.

Q: Would you comment on the course as a whole at the academy in that time: the direction, the intent, the preparation, and that kind of thing.

Admiral Waters: Well, it certainly wasn't nearly as good then as it is now, not nearly as thorough. Certain parts of the engineering course were very good, particularly mechanical engineering and steam engineering. The hard-core sciences--physics, chemistry, and mathematics--were all pretty good. I thought that of the science parts of the curriculum at that time, the weakest part was electrical engineering. I came away feeling that I knew less about electrical engineering than the other kinds. That may well have been partly my fault and partly the faculty's fault.

The liberal arts parts of the course left a great deal to be desired. The language instruction was good. I took French, and we had a lot of Frenchmen there teaching this subject rather than amateurs, although there were some naval officers who taught that were pretty good. I thought the English course was particularly weak when I was there. One reason, I suppose, was because I had had excellent instruction before I went to the Naval Academy. At that time it seemed, at least to us midshipmen, that most of the officers ordered back, if they really didn't know anything else to teach, were put in the English Department. It was pretty obvious at times that you knew a great deal more about English grammar than the guy who was teaching it. I thought that part of the course was weak, and the technical parts were more or less memory courses. They were pretty good, but they didn't have much imagination. So that, really, when you finished the Naval Academy, you were prepared to go out and start learning to be a naval officer.

Q: But with a good basic.

Admiral Waters: Yes, yes.

Q: Well, some of the men I've talked with seem to feel that the general intent of training at the academy was to train a young man for command and to be a gentleman as he commanded.

Admiral Waters: That's right. I think I agree with that viewpoint. Some of the things that we were taught to do in order to be gentlemen were a little bit humorous at the time, such as the basketball coach teaching everyone to dance: midshipmen pairing off on the gymnasium floor going through the fox-trot with each other.

O. D. Waters, Jr. #1 - 15

Q: So you'd be adequately prepared for the hops.

Admiral Waters: For the hops and socially being an acceptable gentleman of the time.

Q: I suppose there's a real problem with a school like the academy, where young men come from all walks of life and from all parts of the country with a vast difference in their backgrounds.

Admiral Waters: Yes, that's true, and that sort of thing is necessary. We just used to laugh about the way it was done. I'm sure that part of the curriculum has been changed drastically since then.

Q: Probably has.

Admiral Waters: The wife of a deceased classmate of mine is the social director there, Mrs. Emmy Marshall.* From what I hear, she has done a very fine job helping out with the teaching of midshipmen social amenities.

Q: I would think that element would be an essential one to have.

---
*The widow of Captain James G. Marshall, USN, who died in 1951 while on active duty, Mary Emma Marshall was Naval Academy social director from 1959 to 1980. She is an honorary member of the Naval Academy Alumni Association.

O. D. Waters, Jr. #1 - 16

Who was superintendent in your time?

Admiral Waters: When I first went there, it was Admiral Samuel Robison, one without the "n" in his name.* And then in the latter part of my time it was Thomas C. Hart.**

Q: Oh, he was there then?

Admiral Waters: Yes. The commandant of midshipmen--the main one I remember was C. P. Snyder.***

Q: Well, Admiral Tommy Hart told me that his intent was to train youngsters for leadership.

Admiral Waters: Yes, and they made a pretty good attempt at doing it. As I say, some of the liberal arts courses could have stood improvement, and I'm sure they have been improved since then, particularly with the new curriculum, where they put much more emphasis on it.

---

*Rear Admiral Samuel S. Robison, USN, was Superintendent of the Naval Academy from June 1928 to May 1931.
**Rear Admiral Thomas C. Hart, USN, was Superintendent of the Naval Academy from May 1931 to June 1934. As a four-star admiral, he was Commander in Chief Asiatic Fleet, 1939-42.
***Captain Charles P. Snyder, USN, was commandant of midshipmen from 1928 to 1931. As a four-star admiral, he served as Commander Battle Force, 1940-41.

O. D. Waters, Jr. #1 - 17

Q: In his regime the discipline was fairly strict, wasn't it?

Admiral Waters: Yes, yes.

Q: There were no infractions of the rules.

Admiral Waters: Oh, there were plenty of infractions, but there was strict and sudden punishment. At that time, you know, we still had the Reina Mercedes as the prison ship.* For a class A offense you drew your hammock and did your time on the Reina Mercedes, only getting off of it to go to classes, and that was pretty effective punishment. That was a pretty hard regime, living down there aboard that ship.

Q: Did you know it from the inside?

Admiral Waters: No, I was fortunate. I was never caught. But at one time we had an awful lot of my friends on board. We had a sort of a scandal. It wasn't really scandal, because nothing scandalous happened, but the rules were badly broken. It was during our second-class summer, when

---

*The USS Reina Mercedes (IX-25), a former Spanish cruiser captured in 1898 during the Spanish-American War, served as station ship at the Naval Academy from 1912 to 1957. Until 1940, midshipmen serving punishment slept and took meals on board the ship but continued to attend classes ashore.

O. D. Waters, Jr. #1 - 18

we had the summer at the Naval Academy.* Part of the relaxation in the ordinary academic year of discipline was that we were allowed weekends off from time to time. Most of us would go to Washington or Baltimore, and we used to have to be back on Sunday evenings in time for evening meal formation.

After one of these weekends, there were a couple of midshipmen whose girls brought them back in their cars. Someone got the brilliant idea of dressing the girls up in white works and taking them into the mess hall to dinner. This was found out somehow or another, and the whole thing was investigated. There were two girls in, I believe, and each one at a different table. The boys who brought them in got the worst punishment, but the two whole tables were put on the ship for the rest of the summer, and I think they lost their September leave.

Q: Guilt by association.

Admiral Waters: Because they didn't report it. Those suffering particularly hard were the ones that happened to be the midshipmen in charge of the tables. I can recall that two of them who were involved in that escapade became flag officers. That was Francis Foley and Magruder

---
*The incident described here took place on 13 July 1930.

O. D. Waters, Jr. #1 - 19

Tuttle.*

Q: When it came to graduation, you graduated with distinction, I notice, ninth in standing in the class. How large was the class?

Admiral Waters: We started off with around 650 plebe year, and we graduated 421.** It was a fairly large class for those days--not huge like '27 was but a fairly good-sized class for that time.***

Q: The Depression was being felt in the Navy, and they had begun to cut down funds.

Admiral Waters: Yes. My first ship was the Augusta.**** It was in San Pedro Harbor, and I reported to her the first of July. I think that the next couple of months we got under way one time to go alongside the tender inside the

---

*Midshipman Francis D. Foley, USN, who retired in 1972 as a rear admiral; Midshipman Magruder H. Tuttle, USN, who retired in 1967 as a rear admiral. Foley's Naval Institute oral history discusses the incident in the mess hall and the punishment on board the Reina Mercedes.
**The Naval Academy Register of Alumni indicates that there were 157 non-graduates in the class of 1932, indicating that 578 midshipmen started with the class.
***The class of 1927 comprised 579 graduates.
****The heavy cruiser Augusta (CA-31) was commissioned 30 January 1931. She had a standard displacement of 9,050 tons, length of 600 feet, beam of 66 feet, and top speed of 32.5 knots. Her armament consisted of nine 8-inch guns and four 5-inch guns. Following World War II service in the Atlantic, she was decommissioned 16 July 1946.

breakwater. That was because the funds for Navy fuel oil had been cut back so much we just had to be that parsimonious with fuel.

Q: How were you occupied during that immobile time?

Admiral Waters: Shipboard drills.

Q: Some of the glamour of service at sea was not there.

Admiral Waters: The first time we really got under way was a couple of months later, when we went to San Francisco, which took some of the sting off of it. All the young ensigns enjoyed San Francisco, of course, but it wasn't a very long cruise.

Q: Did the low state of the Navy at that time cause any of the graduates to think in terms of another kind of a career rather than staying with the Navy?

Admiral Waters: No, there wasn't much of that kind of thought, because at that time the pay of an ensign in the Navy was $125.00 a month. That was before Mr. Hoover put a 15% reduction on that.* But 15% of $125.00 was not very much, so we didn't notice that. The pay that you got in

---
*Herbert C. Hoover was President of the United States from 1929 to 1933.

in those days, plus having a place to sleep and a fairly interesting life and good surroundings, was pretty much an inducement to stay in the Navy, particularly when you compared it with your friends back home who had gone to college and gotten a degree of some kind and then came back and found that the only place they could get a job was working in somebody's garage. There wasn't much rushing for the exit, because times were so tough.

Also, even though we were in an economy phase and an austere budget, as they say, the state of the Navy was pretty good also. Because of the Depression, the caliber of enlisted men in those days was very high. There were no jobs available, and a lot of very good young men, even college graduates--lots of college graduates--enlisted in the Navy as a means to subsist.

Q: And I suppose the Navy could be highly selective.

Admiral Waters: We were highly selective, and I can remember back being a division officer where all of these young fellows were just really head-and-shoulders people, top-notch young men. Of course, a lot of those people that enlisted in the Navy and stayed in became commissioned officers when the wartime expansion came.

I had a particularly large number of them, because I

was in the F division, the fire control division. We usually got a larger proportion of the smarter boys, because we had to have smart boys to train them to run things that we thought were very sophisticated systems at that time. These were the rangekeepers, antiaircraft directors, and that sort of thing which were just starting to come into the Navy in a more sophisticated way.

Q: Your first assignment on the Augusta was a very happy one, as you indicated when you were talking about Admiral Nimitz.*

Admiral Waters: Yes. It was rather strange. I wanted to go to a cruiser. When we graduated, we could put in our choices of type of ship. Of course, we were limited. At that time, it was the policy to put freshly graduated ensigns into larger ships, such as battleships and cruisers. None of them went directly into destroyers. In order to learn, you'd do your first two years learning in the larger ships and then go to the smaller ships, where you had to be able to shoulder much more responsibility. So I asked for a cruiser in the Atlantic. I don't think we had an Atlantic Fleet at that time.

---

*Captain Chester W. Nimitz, USN, commanded the Augusta from October 1933 to April 1935. Admiral Waters did a previous interview with Dr. Mason as part of the Naval Institute's oral history series on Nimitz. Nimitz eventually became a fleet admiral, Commander in Chief Pacific Fleet during World War II and Chief of Naval Operations after the war.

Q: It was all in one.

Admiral Waters: It was the Scouting Force in the Atlantic and the Battle Force in the Pacific. The Scouting Force had only cruisers in it. But I asked for one of the newer cruisers. The Augusta, which was only a year old, was assigned to the Scouting Force, and I was assigned to it.* But just before then, because of the warlike intentions of the Japanese, the Navy had shifted most of the Scouting Force around to the Pacific; it was supposed to be a temporary measure. So I went ahead and joined the Augusta, thinking she would be coming back to the East Coast. Before I got back to the East Coast, I had spent three years on the Asiatic station.**

Q: One of the little surprises of naval service.

Admiral Waters: So that part of my planning didn't work out, but I didn't ever regret it at all. The Augusta was a very happy ship and a very fine ship. My first captain was

---

*In May 1931, the Augusta became flagship of Commander Scouting Force. In March 1932, she was transferred to the Pacific.
**On 14 November 1933, the Augusta relieved the USS Houston (CA-30) as flagship of Admiral Frank B. Upham, USN, Commander in Chief Asiatic Fleet. She remained fleet flagship until relieved by the Houston in November 1940.

O. D. Waters, Jr. #1 - 24

J. O. Richardson, who, as you know, later on became CinCUS, Commander in Chief of the U.S. Fleet.* Then he was relieved by Royal Ingersoll.** Then, as I told you when I was telling you about Admiral Nimitz, there was a swap between Captain Ingersoll and Captain Nimitz, and Captain Nimitz took us out to the Asiatic Fleet in the fall of 1933.

When we received those orders, the captain picked out a few of the junior officers--mainly the ones that had married on graduation and had families--and arranged for them to be transferred. But everyone else who wanted to go to the Asiatic station could. I think it was 100% of those that were permitted were taken out. There were some transfers, but a good number of those that went with the ship stayed with it for a three-year tour out there and then were transferred back by commercial ship.

Q: From someone looking on from the outside, it would seem that there was an unusual spirit of camaraderie on that cruiser.

---

*Captain James O. Richardson, USN, commanded the Augusta from her commissioning in January 1931 until May 1933. As a four-star admiral, he was Commander in Chief U.S. Fleet in 1940-41. His memoir, On the Treadmill to Pearl Harbor, was published by the Naval History Division in 1973.
**Captain Royal E. Ingersoll, USN, was commanding officer from May to October 1933, then left to put the new heavy cruiser San Francisco (CA-38) into commission as first commanding officer. As a four-star admiral in World War II, he was Commander in Chief Atlantic Fleet, 1942-44.

Admiral Waters: Yes, there was.

Q: Of course, the young officers have continued to know each other and . . .

Admiral Waters: Yes, we've had a number of old _Augusta_ reunions. I think the knitting of the whole group together goes back to Captain Nimitz and his great leadership ability, in that he was such a capable man and such a good leader too. It wasn't a sloppy ship, in that there was no mollycoddling of people. You did your job. He saw to it that you did your job, but he did it in a nice way, in the sense that he was not a driver; he was a leader.

Q: What specific training did you get from that experience on the _Augusta_?

Admiral Waters: I think the example that all of these were fine officers: Captain Richardson, Captain Ingersoll, and Captain Nimitz, whom I was with longer than the others, and also Captain Gygax, who followed, who was later a flag officer.* I think this sort of capability, particularly a man with such tremendous leadership capability as Nimitz, rubs off on you. You learn by example.

---

*Captain Felix Xerxes Gygax, USN. Gygax became a rear admiral shortly before World War II and retired in 1946 in that rank.

If you stop and think about it, you say, "Well, why does this man have such a fine ship?" It occurs to you that he is fair and impartial, he never loses his temper, never loses control of himself, so he never loses control of his people. If he has something to discipline you about, he calls you into the cabin, and it's between you and him. At the same time, if you do something well, he commends you on the spot. These are the little things that people write about in books all the time, but I think you have to see it yourself the first time to believe it, particularly when you are young. A man who's calm under stress on the bridge just creates that same feeling of calm capability throughout all the people working for him.

Q: Would you say that perhaps the kind of education you received at the academy made you very cognizant, very much aware of leadership qualities when you spotted them?

Admiral Waters: Yes, yes, that's true. Also, the basic training that you received at the academy made you capable of doing the technical parts of your job on the ship so that you knew that you knew how to do the things that you were required to do, and so you went ahead and did them. Under those circumstances, you would probably do them quite well. Such things as being assistant navigator; that was a fun sort of job. You were involved with the big job of navigating the ship safely, and you knew how to do these things and you learned how to do them better through experience.

I particularly enjoyed that, and I enjoyed being signal officer, because that got me up on the bridge where everything was happening. In those days, although the signal officer was usually a very junior ensign, in a lot of cases he was a pretty important fellow, because the visual signaling was so important. We didn't have voice radio then. Much of the signaling was done by flag hoist and semaphore and flashing light, and you prided yourself on a smart signal bridge. Of course, the first year we were the flagship for the Scouting Force, and that made it practically mandatory that you have the smartest signal bridge in the force. You were doing it for the admiral.*

Q: Also, your assignment on the Asiatic station, exposing you to the foreign countries and foreign peoples--there again I expect the kind of training, the direction of your training at the academy, prepared you to adequately represent our country.

Admiral Waters: Yes, I think it did for all of us. It gave you a little more self-confidence. In those days--it sounds like it's centuries ago--but a lot of changes have

---
*Vice Admiral Frank H. Clark, USN, was Commander Scouting Force, embarked in the Augusta in 1932-33.

O. D. Waters, Jr. #1 - 28

taken place since then.

Q: It was prior to World War II.

Admiral Waters: There have been changes in communications and transportation that make all these things so different, but then it sort of accentuated this business of a naval officer being really a diplomatic representative of the country. We were dealing with all of the foreign people we met, both the Navy and the consular people, as well as our own State Department consular officials. That was still in the days of the striped pants and high silk hats for dignitaries. So I think that the Naval Academy education stressing of these things paid off. Certainly, it was very beneficial.

Q: After the Augusta you came back. Then you were on a destroyer as torpedo officer.

Admiral Waters: Yes. Captain Nimitz came back and was Assistant Chief of the Bureau of Navigation, the forerunner of BuPers.* He had told us when he left the Augusta that when the time came for us to be detached to let him know

---

*Prior to World War II, assignments of naval officers were made by the Bureau of Navigation. In 1942, it became the Bureau of Naval Personnel (BuPers), a title that better described its function.

O. D. Waters, Jr. #1 - 29

what we wanted, and he'd try to get it for us. At that time, the building program for new destroyers had just started. Of course, we were all anxious to get into these new ships, and most of us wanted to go to destroyers anyway. We had been quite a long time in the big ships, longer than most of our classmates. So we all asked for new destroyer assignments, and I think we got them, practically 100%. We were spread all up and down the East Coast here in these new ships. That was a very fine experience. Of course, we were looked down upon by the old four-pipe destroyer sailors. They called us the gold-platers, because we couldn't hack it the way they could. We called them the bow-and-arrow Navy.

That was a very interesting cruise I had in the Downes.* We built down in the Norfolk Navy Yard at Portsmouth, Virginia, and went on a two-month shakedown cruise to South America. We went down as far as Buenos Aires and stopped off at Rio.

Q: You showed the flag.

Admiral Waters: Yes. This was the routine then for new ships, to take what was usually a foreign cruise to shake

---
*The destroyer Downes (DD-375) was commissioned 15 January 1937. She had a standard displacement of 1,500 tons, length of 341 feet, beam of 35 feet, and top speed of 36 knots. Her armament consisted of five 5-inch guns and 12 torpedo tubes. She was badly damaged in the 1941 Japanese attack on Pearl Harbor but rebuilt and restored to service.

the ship down and get her running well and get all the bugs out of her. These cruises usually lasted for about two months.

We were entertained by the chief of the naval mission in Rio and the naval attaché, so it was a fun cruise. It was a rather interesting one for me, because at that time there was a shortage of supply officers. We didn't have a supply officer for each destroyer the way we usually do now; there was just one for the division. But they would usually give you one when you went off on detached duty to pay the crew and buy the stores and the fuel and so forth.

But at that time there was a shortage of Supply Corps officers, and our captain was told to appoint one of the ship's officers as a special disbursing agent.* So he called me in and gave me a long speech about how much he valued my reliability and capability. I was waiting for the fast, low curve, which came when he said that he was designating me as a volunteer to be the special disbursing agent. Well, I immediately started charging over to the supply center to try to find out what this was all about.

But it turned out that it was a lot of fun, and I've always been very happy I had that experience, because it gives me one up on all supply officers. When they start

---

*The first commanding officer of the USS Downes was Commander Clifford H. Roper, USN.

O. D. Waters, Jr. #1 - 31

telling me their problems, it gives me a great deal of pleasure to tell them that I once had to do those duties, and I found it was the pleasantest and easiest job I ever had in the Navy.

It really wasn't a very difficult job, because they did assign, just temporarily for the cruise, an enlisted man who had had about ten years' experience in disbursing, and with his help we sailed right along. I did all the paying and bought all the supplies. We got back from the cruise, and about a year later I got my clearance from the General Accounting Office on a big sheet of paper. It said zero, zero, zero at the bottom. That means everything worked out. You don't owe them anything, and they don't owe you anything.

Q: That was the time when you were held personally accountable, weren't you?

Admiral Waters: Yes. I believe the regulations said that you were pecuniarily responsible, which meant that if somebody got in there and got the contents of that safe--as I remember, I think I had about $80,000 in cash--that it was up to me to get it back. But it really was a fun sort of job.

Q: And this involved food, too, didn't it? Everything?

Admiral Waters: Oh, yes, all supplies and paying the crew. All supplies including fuel. I remember my classmate Frank Brumby was in the Tucker, which was a sister ship, built side by side with us.* They went on a different cruise down around the Caribbean, but we met in Trinidad. We were in there at the same time to take fuel. Frank wrote out his check for the fuel to the name of the oil company that was on the side of the tanker instead of making it out to the name of the oil company that was on the bill submitted. So he had a check that was batting around the Caribbean for about two or thee months there that was no good. He was about six months later than I was getting cleared with the General Accounting Office, trying to run this check down.

Q: Somebody told me not so long ago--I guess it was Admiral Dyer--about some of his classmates who got into really bad trouble when they failed to insist upon a thorough accounting as they took over.** I mean, they just took the word of the departing officer that everything was all right, and then they found themselves at the short end of the stick.

Admiral Waters: Yes, if you got a bit relaxed and lazy in

---

*Lieutenant (junior grade) Frank H. Brumby, Jr., USN.
**Dr. Mason interviewed Vice Admiral George C. Dyer, USN, for a Naval Institute oral history.

O. D. Waters, Jr. #1 - 33

taking over. He was probably referring to not conducting a proper inventory of title B material.

Q: Exactly, that was it.

Admiral Waters: Title B was the one you had to worry about. If you took over a division or a department on a destroyer, you had a certain amount of title B which you were charged for. The only way you could get rid of that responsibility was to transfer it to somebody else to sign for it or survey it. If you weren't careful when you went around and checked the title B cards against what you actually had, this guy may have lost something, and he would stick you for it.

All these extra jobs were divided up, the way you particularly did on destroyers then, because we only had seven officers, counting the captain.

Q: And what sort of complement?

Admiral Waters: It would be close to 200, I guess, maybe a little bit less than that. Of course, you divided up all these extra jobs, such as commissary officer, stores officer, and one of my extra jobs was ship's service officer. At that time, ship's service was a separately run activity. It wasn't part of the supply system the way it is now. It was sort of privately funded by the Navy.

So I had this little ship store that I had to organize and start in this new ship. It was capitalized. I think we were limited to $1,500 worth of cigarettes, shaving cream, and that sort of thing. As the ship's service officer, I had to be bonded for this $1,500 worth of stock and the money I handled.

Well, when I took over this $80,000 or $100,000 worth of cash and the authority to write checks on the Treasurer of the United States and buy all these stores and everything, I didn't have to be bonded for that, because I hadn't volunteered to do it like a regular paymaster. A regular paymaster is bonded, but he volunteers to do it. But this special disbursing agent gets stuck with it, so the rule was and still is that he didn't have to be bonded. Also, since these were two different kinds of funds, according to the regulations, I couldn't keep both jobs. Another officer had to take the ship's service job, and I found out that the SDA job was a lot easier than the ship's service.

Q: Bigger amounts, for one thing.

Admiral Waters: Much bigger amounts, but it was much easier to handle because they had a beautifully worked-out system, cash books. You soon learned how to run a cash book and get a balance and count up after payday to make sure you hadn't overpaid anybody or lost any money.

Q: Do I understand that this system is changed now--that the personal responsibility is no longer?

Admiral Waters: I'm not sure. I haven't looked it up lately. The regulations have changed, but there certainly is still some measure of responsibility for disbursing officers. Of course, it was only temporary for me. They still do have special disbursing agents, I know, because a lot of times a detached unit such as a naval attaché may well have disbursing duties to do.

Q: Admiral, you were torpedo officer on this destroyer. I'm aware of the fact that within a very few years after that, at the outbreak of hostilities in the Pacific, our torpedoes proved to be most inadequate. Was there any experience of that when you were torpedo officer on the destroyer Downes?

Admiral Waters: Well, yes, there was a hint of things to come, not definite knowledge of this fact, but the things that contributed to that situation arising were pretty evident then. I don't think any of us were farsighted enough to see what was going to happen to us.

By late 1937, we had gotten around to the West Coast and had joined the Battle Force. We were based in San Diego. At Christmastime of '37, there was a flap in the intelligence community. We never knew this at the time--it came up later--but for a short while the intelligence people apparently lost track of a large part of the Japanese fleet. They didn't know where it was.

Of course, that was at a pretty tense time with the bombing of Shanghai and Manchuria and so forth.* So the fleet went on a special alert, and we had to keep one destroyer patrolling out offshore and one destroyer anchored right at the entrance of Ballast Point checking all vessels and all ships coming into the harbor. I distinctively remember it was Christmas of '37, because the Downes had the duty on Christmas Eve.

That was my first experience with Scripps Institute of Oceanography.** They came in, in one of their smaller craft that they were using for oceanographic work then. It looked sort of like a pleasure yacht, and I boarded it. They thought that this was the funniest thing in the world. I was the boarding officer aboard ship, and I came over in

---
*The Sino-Japanese War broke out in 1937. Referred to by the Japanese as the "China Incident," it wasn't really concluded until 1945. On 12 December 1937, Japanese aircraft attacked the river gunboat USS Panay (PR-5) near Nanking, China, later claiming it was mistaken identity.
**Scripps Institution of Oceanography and Marine Physical Laboratory, University of California, San Diego. Founded in 1946, the institute specializes in underwater acoustics, marine physics, geophysics, signal processing, and ocean technology.

a whaleboat all armed and accompanied by armed men and demanded to see their papers of identification. They said, "What's going on?"

I said, "I don't know."

They said, "Well, it's Christmas Eve, so come on in and have a drink." I thanked them very kindly but told them I was on duty.

But at that time, one of the things that happened was, we had our Mark XIV torpedoes on most of the ships. This was the newest torpedo, and we had the warheads for the torpedo, but we didn't have the exploder. That was because it was the new secret exploder that worked on the magnetic field of the ship it was fired against. When it got into close proximity to it, it went under it. This was brand-new and very, very secret, very hush-hush.

It was so secret that when we went into this special alert status, we were issued these secret things, but we weren't allowed to take them out of the box. They got all the torpedo officers over to the tender, and they had just a wooden mock-up outline of the exploder. We were shown steps one, two, three, and four of how to put it in the torpedo, but it was not explained how it worked. This was not explained to us.

Looking back on it, I think that that attitude of super-secrecy on the part of the Navy at that time was probably the main contributing factor to the fact that it wouldn't work. Someone should have taken those things out and tried them and shot them, but nobody in the operating fleet ever did. Only the people that were babying them along in the test phases in the ordnance establishment were involved. If we had been allowed to do it, we would have found out what the bugs were when the simple sailor tries to do it, which was what happened to us later on in the war when it wouldn't work.

Q: Yes, it was very costly.

Admiral Waters: It almost caused various submarine skippers to come back and assault the Bureau of Ordnance. Because these poor fellows would risk their lives to get into a torpedo-firing position on an enemy ship, fire the thing, and nothing would happen. The torpedoes gave your position away and they hadn't hit anybody. It was very bad. But we had that same exploder. It was never used; we didn't gain any experience with it.

The same thing applied to a lot of other little things like armor-piercing shells. We always had them in the turrets on the Augusta and kept them beautifully painted and cleaned up and scrubbed. When we fired target practice, we fired special old black iron target projectiles. I daresay an awful lot of the service ammunition in the early part of the war didn't work either, because it probably had too many coats of paint on it.

Q: But that practice of keeping things in wraps, as you comment on it, doesn't seem like the ultimate wisdom. Because very often the enemy or potential enemy has knowledge of this anyway, doesn't he?

Admiral Waters: I think we sort of get carried away with technical security at times. Of course, certainly when you have an obvious jump on the other fellow, you want to protect it from them and not have it all appear in Popular Mechanics and that sort of thing. But, on the other hand, looking back on World War II, we were very secretive about magnetic exploders on our torpedoes.

When the curtain rose on World War II, the Japanese had one, the Germans had one, the British had one. I guess the French and Italians had them too. I mean, everybody that was in the war had them, and most of them were better than ours to begin with. Also, we were very secretive at that time about sonar, which was just in its infancy. Again, when the curtain rose, the British had asdic, and they had a few features that were somewhat better than ours.* Their recorder, for instance, we adopted lock, stock, and barrel.

---

*ASDIC stood for Antisubmarine Detection Investigation Committee. The lower-case acronym came to be used for the British version of underwater sound gear.

Q: In that area, I should think that a free interchange of knowledge would have been feasible with the Royal Navy.

Admiral Waters: Well, there wasn't too much of it then.

Q: We were not about to be enemies, were we?

Admiral Waters: Well, we had been in the past. I suppose people looked at their history books too much.

Of course, our biggest breakthrough, we thought, was the invention of radar. When World War II came off, we had it, the British had it, and the Germans had it. Different navies made different applications of it. We had applied it mainly to fire control of surface guns. Fortunately for them and also for the rest of the Free World, the British had applied it to aircraft detection, which was really one of the factors in saving them in the battle for Britain. The Germans hadn't developed it along those lines as much as the Allied side had. Of course, the Japanese didn't have it, and that was a great boon to us in the early part of the war. When we did those night battles, we could cut them to pieces before they could see us.

Q: But once the war broke out, there was a free interchange of information with the British, wasn't there?

Admiral Waters: Yes, except there were a couple of peculiar quirks to that. In the fall of 1940, I was sent over to England as an observer. Actually, I was sent over as an assistant naval attaché. I had diplomatic status. There were probably 25 naval officers attached to the embassy at that time to gain experience in various phases of warfare. I was sent over primarily to cover the advent of the magnetic-acoustic mine that the Germans had just sprung as Hitler's secret weapon.*

But by that time, of course, we had concluded the agreement for 50 destroyers and leasing--the 99-year leases for the bases--and so it was pretty much of a free exchange except for one or two things.** The one thing that stuck in their craw was the Norden bombsight.*** They wouldn't give the British the Norden bombsight. Somebody high up in government decided we shouldn't give the British the Norden bombsight, because it was such a great bombsight. They thought so highly of it.

---

*Adolf Hitler was Chancellor of Germany from 1933 to 1945.
**In 1940, the United States traded 50 old four-stack destroyers to Great Britain to facilitate its antisubmarine campaign against Germany. In return, the United States was granted leases on British possessions in the Western Hemisphere to be used as naval bases.
***The Norden bombsight was a precision optical device developed in the early 1930s by Carl L. Norden, a civilian consultant employed by the Navy, together with Lieutenant Frederick L. Entwistle. Its gyrostabilized automatic pilot kept the bomber straight and level during bomb runs. It was used in both Navy and Army bombers in the 1930s and 1940s.

O. D. Waters, Jr. #1 - 42

Q: To pinpoint the . . .

Admiral Waters: Yes, this was the bombsight developed by the Navy for accurate, pinpoint bombing. It wasn't nearly as great as everybody thought at the time, but it was probably much ahead of anything that anybody else had.

But, anyway, when I got over there, we were sitting around talking about things and trying to get the lay of the land and what have you. Gus Wellings was one of the officers assigned as an observer on board British destroyers.* Now, all the Wellings brothers were Gus. This was the second one. He became an admiral. Gus, the older one, who was the real Gus, was also an admiral.** Then there was one in my class who retired as a captain.*** In accordance with the old Navy practice, they were all called Gus because the oldest one was named Gus.

This fellow Wellings had a very fine sense of humor, and he said, "Now, when you get around with the British Navy, there are a few things that you want to watch out

---

*Lieutenant Commander Joseph H. Wellings, USN. His papers concerning his duty with the Royal Navy were published as a monograph, On His Majesty's Service, John B. Hattendorf, editor (Newport: Naval War College Press, 1983).
**Augustus J. Wellings was graduated in the Naval Academy class of 1920 and retired as a rear admiral in 1954.
***Albert A. Wellings was graduated in the Naval Academy class of 1932. He reached the rank of captain on active duty and then received a tombstone promotion to rear admiral upon retirement in 1956.

about. One of them is the Norden bombsight. This is pretty much stuck in their craw. As a matter of fact, I don't see why we don't give them the damn thing, but they'll bring it up. There are various ways you can handle this. I've developed a way that seems to work pretty well--at least temporarily--because it shocks them a little bit."

So we said, "What is it, Gus? What do you do?"

He said, "Well, you'll be sitting around the wardroom after dinner, and somebody will bring up the question of, 'Why in the hell don't you give us the Norden bombsight?' I always say, 'Well, you know, I really think it's because we're pretty sure or at least we think you already have it.' And then they'll say, 'What do you mean?'"

Gus would say, "'Well, about two years ago, one of them was stolen from the Philadelphia Navy Yard, and we were always pretty damn sure the British stole it.'" He said, "That shuts them up for a couple of days on that thing."

Q: I know in 1940 they were awfully free in supplying information on ordnance, because I was in naval intelligence here on the British desk, and the reports that came in were voluminous.

Admiral Waters: Yes, I think that was just somebody's poor judgment or administrative error on that thing, not to give them that. We gave them everything else. We gave them destroyers.

Q: Albeit old ones.

Admiral Waters: That was another thing. We gave them those 50 destroyers, and they had the Mark VIII torpedo in them--the Mark 8, Mod 3. Well, we knew very well that the only variation of that torpedo that we'd ever been able to make work was when you finally got down to the Mark VIII-3D. A, B, and C wouldn't work. So what did we do but give them these 50 destroyers with Mark VIII-3A torpedoes in them, just because they were sitting on the shelf someplace and they sent them along?

One Saturday I was back up in London with the excuse of making my reports but mainly to collect my pay. The senior technical officer there was Commander P. F. Lee, later on Admiral P. F. Lee; he's an ED.* We had a crisis, because the British had attempted to fire these torpedoes, and the only thing they did was circle around and come back and almost hit the firing ship. They wanted to know what to do. So Commander Lee called all of us who were in the technical part of the Navy embassy office together, and he said, "All right, I need a torpedo

---

*Commander Paul F. Lee, USN, reached the rank of rear admiral. ED--engineering duty.

expert." Of course, being seasoned naval officers, nobody spoke up. Nobody was crazy enough to volunteer. So he said, "Okay, you guys." And he went around, and he said, "Have you ever been a torpedo officer?"

"No, sir."

"Have you ever been a torpedo officer?"

"No, sir."

He got to me, and I said, "Yes, sir."

He said, "You're my torpedo expert. You go over to the Admiralty and you see Captain Jackson over there and find out what the hell this problem is all about, and then come back and we'll see what we can do for them."

So I went over, and this Captain Jackson was sort of a vaudeville type impression of an Englishman, the Colonel Blimp type.* Big, rosy, rotund guy; he had a monocle on and he hemmed, hawed, and sputtered. He was very difficult to understand. He told me what the whole thing was. I said, "Are these the Mark VIII-3As?" Well, I knew enough about them. I had never fired an VIII-3D, because they were the kind that were in the old four-pipers. I had never fooled around with anything that antique, but I knew you had to have the VIII-3D for them to work.

I came back to the embassy and saw Commander Lee and told him what we had done to these poor people. I said, "I

---

*Colonel Blimp was a character created in 1937 by British cartoonist David Low. The name indicates a pompous person who holds out-of-date, ultra-conservative views.

think the least we can do is to get all of the drawings over here for how you modify these things to be VIII-3Ds and the spare parts or whatever you need and enough good Navy torpedomen to help them put it together." So that's what they did, and that solved the big torpedo crisis.

Q: At that point, there certainly wasn't uniformity in thinking. I mean, the President of our country was very much aware of the fact that we were in this together and pushed this deal, but the Navy wasn't that aware.

What did your duties involve you with in connection with observing these German mines and so forth?

Admiral Waters: When I finished my tour in the Downes, I had requested and was selected to go to PG school in ordnance engineering.* There were various sorts of subdivisions of the ordnance engineers. In each class you usually had one torpedoman, one mineman, a few in fire control, and so forth. Then the rest were what they called general. Well, I was general. I was supposed to know it all. In the summer of 1940, when these German mines made their appearance--well, they made their appearance the winter before, but they started using them much more. The acoustic one came along about that time. This first one

---

*The Navy's Postgraduate School was then on the grounds of the Naval Academy in Annapolis, Maryland.

was magnetic.

The only person we had in the technical office to look after this was a naval constructor who was very busy on covering the damage to British ships from bombs and gunfire and so forth, and he couldn't cover it all. So he sent an appeal for two mine experts to be sent over, plus a civilian scientist. We were just finishing our course; actually, we weren't quite through with it. They cut off the third year, but we had finished all the academic part of it. We were just going around to the various installations in a makee-learn status. So I was just about to start a month's leave the first part of October.

I had spent the summer at the powder factory and the proving ground at Dahlgren, and I had taken a one-month course along with other members of the class at the Chemical Warfare School with the Army up at Edgewood Arsenal. I had come back and just started 30 days' leave when I got a call from the gun factory, where my orders were kept, that my leave had been canceled and I was to report in to the Director of Naval Intelligence.

I said, "Well, I'm not surprised my leave being canceled," because the war was hotting up.* We'd been told that we probably wouldn't get to finish our third year, that they needed us to go back to work. So I said,

---
*By the summer of 1940, Germany had captured France and the low countries and was threatening to invade Great Britain.

"There must be some mistake. I'm ordnance. I must be reporting in to the Chief of the Bureau of Ordnance."

They said, "No, the Director of Naval Intelligence." So I went down and reported in.

Q: Who was that at that time?

Admiral Waters: I don't know who it was, because I just went into the administrative office, and I told them what my name was. I was Lieutenant Waters and was supposed to report in there. They said, "Oh, yes, you're the one that's going to London, aren't you?"

I said, "Am I?"

They said, "Yes. Start filling out these forms for your passport."

So Moe Archer and I went over.* As I say, at that time there were few enough of us. We were really technical observers, but we had the status of assistant attachés, which was very nice. It was very helpful to have a diplomatic passport. We got over there and were told what the problem was, and they decided to attach us to HMS Vernon, which is sort of the main British establishment for mines and torpedoes.**

---
*Lieutenant Stephen M. Archer, USN.
**Moored in Portsmouth, England, the ship was used as the Royal Navy's school for torpedo, mine, and electrical instruction. In November 1939, staff devised a ship-protection system that used degaussing and exploding mines with a sweep towed by minesweepers.

Q: That was at Dartmouth, wasn't it?

Admiral Waters: No, that's at Portsmouth. You know the system. All of their shore stations are called HMS Something.

Q: It took me a while to figure that out.

Admiral Waters: It was because they couldn't have a shore establishment. That was against the British laws. And they still do this. They had a little spit kit there--a little teeny thing, a sort of mine testing boat or something--that was HMS Vernon. But, anyway, that was the center of all the activity, and we then reported in down there to Commander Thistleton-Smith, who later on retired as a vice admiral.* He was what they called Commander M, "M" standing for mining. They had a Commander M and they had a Commander MS, minesweeping; then they had a Commander T for torpedoes, and so forth. M had all of the mine business, including this newly organized thing of mine recovery. They had intelligence that the Germans were going to plant this thing, some sort of a secret weapon, but they didn't know what it was. They didn't know whether it was acoustic or magnetic.

---

*Lieutenant Commander Geoffrey Thistleton-Smith, RN.

O. D. Waters, Jr. #1 - 50

Q: In the channel?

Admiral Waters: Yes. Actually, in the winter before I got there, the first one had been mistakenly laid on the tidelands at the mouth of the Thames.* There was a pretty good rise and fall of tide in the mud flats there. This German aviator was apparently trying to lay it in the ship channel. It was on a parachute. Anyway, he didn't do a very accurate job of laying it, so it was exposed at low tide. Everybody from the Prime Minister on down said, "Go get it."

It was quite a feat to get it, because they didn't know what they were dealing with. Commander Ouvry did the first thing to help.** A brave guy, he took it apart successfully and got it defanged. They trundled it up to Portsmouth, thinking that it was acoustic from the way it looked, the diaphragms and things. When they got it, they found out it was magnetic, and then they started all of the magnetic minesweeping effort and the degaussing of ships and so forth.

Then, later on, before I got there, they did come in with an acoustic one, so they had to go into hammer boxes

---
*The complete magnetic mine was recovered on 23 November 1939 in the mud flats off Shoeburyness.
**Lieutenant Commander John G. D. Ouvry, RN, successfully stripped the German magnetic mine recovered on 23 November 1939 in the mud flats off Shoeburyness.

O. D. Waters, Jr. #1 - 51

and all that sort of thing. But it was quite obvious that with this kind of sophisticated technical warfare, the only way to really be able to cope with it was to have these mine-recovery teams trained to bring them back alive so you could analyze and figure out a countermeasure. And that's what they were involved in.

We went down to Portsmouth and started working with them. They taught us all they knew about these things, and we saw the actual mines. Then Moe Archer and I started taking turns going on trips to help them recover these mines. We got there in October, and by the end of the winter, we had written all our reports and had pretty well covered the thing.

The naval attaché wrote back to the Chief of Naval Operations and said what an important thing this was and that the U.S. Navy should now start organizing it. There were two people in the U.S. Navy who knew anything about it, and their names were Waters and Archer. So we were stuck. I came back in April '41.

Q: Who was the naval attaché at that point?

Admiral Waters: The naval attaché when I first went there was Alan G. Kirk.* He was relieved by Uncle Charlie

---

*Captain Alan G. Kirk, USN, was U.S. naval attaché in Britain from June 1939 to March 1941. In 1942, he returned to England as chief of staff to the U.S. naval commander in Europe and in 1944 commanded Task Force 122 for the Allied invasion of Normandy.

Lockwood during the six or eight months I was over there.* It was a great experience. Then, of course, we got back here. I came back first; Archer stayed a little longer.

Q: I think that's a good break, where you've been to England. Maybe next time I'll ask you some questions about that experience.

---

*Captain Charles A. Lockwood, Jr., USN, was naval attaché in 1941-42. He was later Commander Submarine Force Pacific Fleet, 1943-45.

O. D. Waters, Jr. #2 - 53

Interview Number 2 with
Rear Admiral Odale D. Waters, Jr., U.S. Navy (Retired)

Place: Admiral Waters's home in Alexandria, Virginia

Date: Wednesday, 7 August 1971

Interviewer: John T. Mason, Jr.

Q: Well, it's certainly good to see you again, Admiral. As I wrote you, last time you concluded by talking about your brief period in London prior to our entry into World War II. Do you want to say something more about that?

Admiral Waters: Well, I think I had come up to the point where Lieutenant Moe Archer and I had been covering the mine recovery work with the British. It had been concluded by the naval attaché that the U.S. Navy had best do something about this, and they pointed the finger at the two of us, the two young lieutenants, to do something about it.

Q: As the two experts in the U.S. Navy on this subject.

Admiral Waters: Yes. So I was ordered back in April of that year, 1941, and managed to catch a ride back in a big British convoy coming across to Halifax. I eventually got back to Washington and reported in. I was told to sit down and start planning something to make the U.S. Navy capable of recovering and dissecting enemy mines.

So I came up with a plan which involved, first of all, a school for training personnel to do this work and then a requirement for the manufacture and production and buying of the special tools that were required. I also established a requirement to do the research and development, which I felt we were much better at than the British. The British were living a hand-to-mouth existence and didn't have time to really check things out.

Q: That was more of a luxury.

Admiral Waters: Yes. So this plan was approved. And in the meantime, Archer got relieved and got back. We started our first class down in the old Naval Gun Factory in Washington in June of '41. The reason we put it down there was so that it would be close to the deep-sea diving school. We felt that everyone in the business had to be capable of diving, because you couldn't tell whether these things were going to be dropped underwater or on land by mistake. So we got going in sort of makeshift quarters.

I think the first place we lived was in one room of the old fire control school that Sam Moncure was running in those days.* We later moved over to the old Naval Reserve armory, and our central office for the place was in

---
*Lieutenant Samuel P. Moncure, USN. Moncure and Waters were Naval Academy classmates.

a little brick building sort of enclosed by the old frame armory that had been a stable at the time of the Civil War. Eventually we got a building across the river in Anacostia, in a complex they built there. We turned out our first class some 16 weeks after we started.

Q: That's the length of time you determined upon, 16 weeks?

Admiral Waters: Yes, and this was a mixed class of officers and enlisted men.

Q: Now, were they volunteers?

Admiral Waters: They all had to be volunteers. We were allowed two more regular Navy officers. That was another classmate, J. P. Roach, and another officer who was two or three years junior to us, Doyen Klein.* All the rest were enlisted men or reserve officers newly brought in, and they all had to be volunteers. In addition, we did have a small group of regular Coast Guard officers and enlisted men that the Coast Guard sent over to be trained and to work with the Navy.

---

*Lieutenant John P. Roach, USN; Lieutenant (junior grade) Doyen Klein, USN.

O. D. Waters, Jr. #2 - 56

Q: And, of course, none of these men had had any experience in this field.

Admiral Waters: Not in the recovery business, but for our first classes, and particularly our enlisted men, we took the pick of the volunteers from the Mine Warfare School down at Yorktown. That's also where our first officers came from. Later on, we took them from lots of different places as the country was mobilized, and we started having all of these indoctrination centers. They came from more or less all over.

But the first groups we got were awfully good people, especially the enlisted men. They were old-time Navy petty officers, first class and chiefs, gunner's mates, electrician's mates who were in the mine warfare business. We brought them up and taught them the recovery thing. They took very aptly to this, because they knew a great deal about it to begin with.

Q: I suppose the Bureau of Ordnance was very much interested in this whole effort.

Admiral Waters: In those days we were directly under the Bureau of Ordnance. We were set up by the Bureau of Ordnance, and L. W. McKeehan was the man that was sort of

O. D. Waters, Jr. #2 - 57

our father up in the bureau.* He was a reserve who served both in World War I and World War II. I think he's a retired professor of physics at Yale now.

Q: Oh, really?

Admiral Waters: By the time that Pearl Harbor came along that fall, we had gotten far enough along so that we had what we felt were the strategically important points covered by trained units, we called them: a group of, say, two officers, two enlisted men. We had such units at Panama, Pearl Harbor, and Manila. We felt that those were the important places for us to cover, because, of course, the British had the other side pretty well covered. So those people were actually there when Pearl Harbor occurred. We lost the whole unit from Manila, because they took part in the defense of Corregidor and were captured. At least one of them didn't survive, but I think one of the officers got out. I know that the senior officer there, who was a Coast Guard officer named Crotty, perished in the Bataan death march.**

Q: When you came back from London, did you have any ideas

---

*Commander Louis W. McKeehan, USNR, who entered the Naval Academy with the class of 1907 but did not graduate.
**Lieutenant Thomas J. E. Crotty, USCG, was one of many who starved to death on Bataan when forced by the Japanese in early April 1942 to march 60 miles to prison camp.

about new types of mines which we didn't then have? I mean, was this an area that you also were interested in?

Admiral Waters: Well, yes. It wasn't my particular interest, but we did bring, or have sent back, some of these recovered German mines. And, as a matter of fact, the U.S. Navy made some carbon copies of those things right to begin with, until they had time to develop their own improved version. But we actually turned out some almost carbon copies of the German magnetic mines to begin with, so we'd have them in our inventory.

At the same time, we worked on developing new techniques and new tools. You had to have so many nonmagnetic tools, and nonmagnetic metals at that time were in very short supply, particularly in Britain. We were able to use things that were more or less exotic in those days, things like beryllium copper, an alloy that's nonmagnetic and was rather scarce and expensive but quite strong enough to do a lot of jobs for us.

We experimented with X-ray machines in trying to develop portable X-ray machines that would work on land and underwater too. We developed several different methods for burning mines that we didn't want to recover but had to get rid of in some way.

Q: Had to destroy.

Admiral Waters: To satisfy the need for doing this development work and also to serve as a place where we could train the people at the school in the use of demolitions, burning mines, counter mining them, and that sort of thing, we got a piece of land that the Navy owned down at the powder factory at Indian Head, Maryland. It was called Stump Neck, a little isolated peninsula sticking out into the Potomac River. It was a place where, as we said, we could go down in the woods and blow ourselves up in peace and quiet. From the early beginning of that place as sort of a practical area for working with explosives, it has grown up now to be the site of a lot of the work of the present-day explosive ordnance disposal school, which has superseded this original work.

Q: In the training of these men, you had to use a live mine, didn't you?

Admiral Waters: Well, no, not a live mine. A lot of times we used mines with what we called squids on them, so that if a man made a mistake he'd get a little pop to make it dramatic.

Q: Just to warn you. But not the real thing?

Admiral Waters: Oh, no. We didn't have enough people to use that.

Q: I wondered. I was about to ask if you'd had casualties as a result of this.

Admiral Waters: No, not in the school. We did have casualties, really a relatively small number, I think--not nearly so many as were experienced in bomb disposal. Particularly in the British bomb disposal they were having to train people so fast that they gave them practically no training and put them out to dispose of these things.

We had time to take more time and to train the people into understanding what they were doing so that they did do a better job of it. Of course, at that particular point in time, the various branches of the Navy were going around to indoctrination centers and looking for volunteers: for instance, the submariners, the amphibious force, the aviators, and so forth. We also went around to try to get people to volunteer to come to our school. It was rather an unusual process picking the people, because we had learned in our experience in England that what we were looking for were intelligent people who were somewhat apt in a technical sense and had some capability technically and could use their hands and handle tools. They had to be smart enough to understand the circuits and what they were dealing with.

Q: And great powers of observation.

Admiral Waters: Yes. But the thing that we stayed studiously away from were the would-be heroes. We had found from the experience in England that a man who isn't really smart enough to understand how dangerous this work was, and who was really sort of stupidly brave and was willing to risk his life and do all these things just for the sheer glory of it, was the person to stay well away from. When you've got a person like that, he was not only likely to blow himself up but several of his teammates too.

Q: Yes.

Admiral Waters: So that was the sort of philosophy we had in looking for people. And I think it turned out pretty well.

Q: Well, did this require personal interviews with all these individuals?

Admiral Waters: Yes. We usually went at some time in the course of an indoctrination group going through, say, the Prairie State up in New York.

Q: The old *Illinois*, wasn't it?*

Admiral Waters: Yes, the old *Illinois*. That was one of the schools for indoctrinating people into the Navy. Someone would go up from our place and give a general briefing on what this was all about and try to glamorize it a bit to attract them to it. After the pitch, you would go down to the mess deck and sit at the table, and the boys who felt they might like to volunteer would line up, and you would interview each one individually. You'd try to find out why they wanted to do this sort of thing and what their interest was.

Q: And really see how sharp they were.

Admiral Waters: Yes.

Q: What percentage did you reject? I mean, is there a percentage?

Admiral Waters: Gee, I've forgotten, but we had a fairly high rejection rate on them. I would imagine it was somewhere around 15% or so. I think it was better than 10%.

---

*The former *Illinois* (BB-7), which had been converted to a barracks ship in the 1920s, was renamed the *Prairie State* (IX-15) on 23 January 1941 so her name could be assigned to a projected new battleship.

Then, of course, the diving requirement always cut us down a bit, too, because the people, when they were accepted, of course, had to be physically qualified for deep-sea diving, and this takes a little bit more than just a plain run-of-the-mine physical exam. Then we found that with every new class, there didn't seem to be anything in the physical tests they got--in those days, certainly--to indicate whether they were psychologically fit for diving.

Q: A very important factor.

Admiral Waters: And every now and then, there would be a man who on the first day of instruction in diving, when he was in the shallow-water tank with a deep-sea rig on, when they would close the face plate, closing him up in his diving helmet, would say, "Let me out; I can't stand this."

Q: Claustrophobia.

Admiral Waters: Claustrophobia.

Q: You didn't have then a psychiatrist on your staff, or you weren't able to subject them to a Rorschach?*

---

*Swiss psychiatrist Hermann Rorschach developed a personality and intelligence test in the 1920s wherein a subject's interpretation of inkblot designs reveals intellectual and emotional factors.

Admiral Waters: No, no, we didn't have that sort of luxury at that time. I was officer in charge of the works--the units in the field and the school--but it was a funny setup. It was really sort of a triumvirate, because the three top people in it were classmates. I happened to be senior by about five minutes, according to the Naval Academy handing out of diplomas. Then there was my classmate Moe Archer and our other classmate J. P. Roach, known as Beetle Roach, who was a submariner. Three of us were so close together that we really sort of ran the thing as a team. I always used to say that the only time I ever knew I was the boss was when we got into trouble and somebody had to go stand on the carpet; then it was my turn.

Q: How many students in your regime did you turn out?

Admiral Waters: Gee, I hadn't thought of that number. We had, I'd say, a couple of hundred when I was there. We started in June of '41, and I stayed on until January of '43, so I was there about a year and a half. Of course, I was getting concerned about getting back to sea. I had been to postgraduate school, then over to London, and then in this job. I felt that with the war going on out there, that's where I ought to be.

Q: For many reasons you were impelled to do that. During that time with the mine school, you must have trained, basically, most of the men that were required during the whole war, didn't you?

Admiral Waters: More or less, yes. Some more classes came out afterwards--I suppose about half again as many, or maybe about the same number. But then a lot of those people were used as the nucleus for the underwater demolition teams which came along a bit later. You remember when we started the idea of underwater demolition teams with the amphibious landings, mostly in the Pacific.

Q: And this is a requirement that was not anticipated at the time you began.

Admiral Waters: No, so that the nucleus of people who made up the underwater demolition teams was taken from the mine disposal and bomb disposal school graduates, the volunteers. So that they sort of permeated a lot of other parts of the Navy.

The bomb disposal school is sort of a sidelight of this story. Our experience in England convinced us that during wartime, particularly, it's not possible to train people who can dispose of both mines and bombs. The problem is just too complex to train someone, particularly a reserve officer, in a hurry to do all of those things. So on their very strong advice, we kept bomb disposal and mine disposal separate. However, after we got our mine disposal school going, there was heavy pressure put on us in the Navy for the mine disposal people to undertake bombs also. We would have probably lost that battle except for Lieutenant Draper Kauffman.* He had graduated from the Naval Academy in '33 and had gotten out and was in Germany when the war broke out in '39. He was captured as an ambulance driver, I believe, in France and was set loose as a noncombatant. Then he went over to England, joined the Royal Navy Volunteer Reserve, and was in bomb disposal in England.

Q: At one time he was in the French Foreign Legion too.

Admiral Waters: Anyway, Draper managed to get leave and came over to this country about that time. I think it was just before Pearl Harbor. He was able to shift from the RNVR into the U.S. Naval Reserve, and he showed up with all this background. It was proposed that he come and join us at the mine school, and we said no. But this solved our problem very neatly about bomb disposal, because that's

---

*Lieutenant Draper L. Kauffman, RNVR, was later commissioned in the U.S. Navy and retired in 1973 as a rear admiral. His oral history is in the Naval Institute collection.

what Draper had been in. We agreed that we would gladly give him all sorts of help and advice on how to start a new school, which is a tough job in itself. And that's what happened. He started the bomb disposal school, and they stayed separate all during the war. The two were brought together as explosive ordnance disposal after the war. That is all right in peacetime, but I think it's a hard thing to cover all of those things in a wartime situation.

Q: Well, and the circumstances are often quite different, aren't they? The mines are underwater.

Admiral Waters: Oh, yes.

Q: But the bombs are sometimes embedded in the earth, aren't they?

Admiral Waters: Yes, and whereas our people spent about half of their time going through the diving school, so as to be able to handle things underwater, by the same token the bomb disposal people had to have a place where they could dig big holes in the ground so they would know how to get down to unexploded, buried bombs. They had to learn how to shore up these excavations and keep them from caving in.

Q: Now, who was in charge of the diving school--salvage people?

Admiral Waters: No, that has traditionally been under the command of a line submarine officer. At that time it was Lowell Stone, class of '29.*

But we started off sending our first class through the diving school, and all of us on the faculty went through the diving school with the first class, just so we could be qualified the same way that our students were. We managed to train up enough people so that eventually, even though we used the diving school's facilities, we had enough of our own people so that we didn't really draw on their faculty very much. We sort of did it ourselves. We managed to steal one of their master divers from them and put him in mine disposal. That's what got us off.

Q: Did you run into any administrative bugs in the development of this school? Everybody at that point was wanting this capability, so it must have been quite a scramble.

Admiral Waters: It was a scramble, and there were some

---

*Lieutenant Commander Lowell T. Stone, USN, was officer in charge of the deep-sea diving school at the Washington Navy Yard.

difficult times, particularly in selling people on what you were doing. They'd say, "What is this outfit you've got?"

And you'd say, "This is a mine recovery school."

And they'd say, "What in the hell is that?" So it would take you another half hour to sort of bring them up to date on what you were trying to do. Money wasn't any problem in those days, of course. There was plenty of money available. BuOrd would give us all that we could use, but it was sort of difficult getting the old Navy to accept this brand-new idea which was foreign to everybody.* It took a bit of doing.

Q: Was it so foreign? Had it not been done in World War I?

Admiral Waters: There had been something like that but nothing on an organized scale. I guess there were always gunner's mates and mine men who had taken things apart when they had to be done, but never had it been done on that scale before and never as an organized specialty.

Of course, when Pearl Harbor struck, our situation was no different from anybody else's. There was a tremendous amount of confusion as to what do we do next, but there was an immediate call for everybody we could send in mine disposal and bomb disposal out to Pearl Harbor, because

---
*BuOrd--Bureau of Ordnance.

there were wild stories of unexploded mines and all sorts of things. Actually, there were no unexploded mines at Pearl Harbor; they didn't use mines there. There were unexploded bombs. Our Moe Archer happened to be on a trip on the West Coast at the time of Pearl Harbor, along with a couple of our better men. We shot him on out there, and we reinforced him a little bit in a few days.

Some midget submarines were in the harbor at Pearl Harbor, and I guess they were stranded and the people in them were killed. There was one of these midget submarines with a torpedo still in it, and Moe and his group dragged a pair up on the beach and got the torpedoes out and dragged the torpedoes up on the old submarine base baseball diamond and managed to rig a sort of a remote-control system using good old Navy lines and tackle and so forth. They got themselves behind the dugout, I think, as a bomb proof, and managed to pull the fuzes out of these things and disarm them. They had never seen a Japanese torpedo before. They did a very nice job.

Q: Was the Japanese midget submarine somewhat similar to the Italian type that had appeared in the Mediterranean?

Admiral Waters: Yes, they were similar. The ordnance in the Japanese torpedo conformed very closely to the general Japanese philosophy. They didn't go in so much for safety;

they just wanted to make sure it went off, and it packed an awful big bang. But what we had known previously and learned previously about Japanese munitions paid off in being able to take the things apart without blowing them up.

Things quieted down after that, and we started turning people out. From then on, though, we were kept busy here in Washington, mainly with false alarms of mines on the beach, although there were some actual cases. If you remember, there were submarines actually in sight of the East Coast and the ship sinkings up and down the East Coast within sight of the people. Everyone was a bit wrought up, and we got all kinds of calls about mines washing up on the beach.

Actually, the Germans didn't use very many mines over here. Those that they did use were very effective, but they had such a field day with their torpedoes that they really could accomplish more using torpedoes than mines, although you can argue that point. For example, in '42 they closed the port of Norfolk for about 48 hours with just a string of, I think, half a dozen mines. They closed the port of New York, I think, about two to three times. Whenever they wanted to go to the trouble of bringing mines over in submarines and landing them, they could do it.

I think it was in the summer of '42, the early summer, that they mined the entrances to Norfolk, and I was called

O. D. Waters, Jr. #2 - 72

down there. We lost several ships in a convoy coming in, and the minesweepers were out sweeping. One of them had snagged a mechanical sweep in something and turned it over to a Coast Guard cutter that was standing there holding the end of the line. They thought perhaps they had an unexploded mine on the end of it, so I arrived with a unit.

We managed to pass the steel minesweeping cable ashore down at Virginia Beach. We hitched it up to a big six-by-six Army truck there. We started pulling on it; the line got taut but nothing happened. We budged it a little bit, and then we stood the truck right up on its rear wheels, pulling so hard, and nothing happened. We finally got a big Army tank that we borrowed and put that on the end of the line and got down behind the dunes as this thing broke water. It was a great big old-fashioned wrought-iron anchor that had been lost by some ship out there and had probably been there for 100 years or so--still in very good condition.

Q: From the Spanish Main.

Admiral Waters: Yes, but we had trouble pulling it out of the water. This anchor was digging in all the time.

There was another incident about that time when we were called down to Jacksonville at the mouth of the St. John's River, which was an assembly point for the coastal convoys.* A German submarine had been in there and had laid a stick of mines. According to our intelligence--the way we found out about that--we didn't lose any ships. The minesweepers that had been sweeping monotonously back and forth across there for about three or four months all of a sudden had mines go off underneath the tails of their magnetic sweeps. This almost shocked them to death. They swept, I think, four mines. The intelligence indicated that a normal German submarine of that time carried a stick of six, so there were two unexposed mines according to the best calculations.

We were sent down to try to get them back alive. We had a device that worked on a new principle of electric field--sort of a hydrofoil that you towed from a boat. It was all breadboard, and it was a good idea, but the thing wasn't well enough made to stand up in the sea. As usual, the shorts. When the thing was working, you weren't sure it was working well. We steamed around there. We had a diving team and this indicator device to try to locate the mines on the bottom. We'd get a strike, as we called it, an indicator from the pointer on this thing. Then we'd mark it with a buoy and put a diving party down, and usually it would be an old tin can or something like that.

We worked down there for about a week, not getting anywhere, and one day the weather got so bad that we

---
*The St. Johns River flows into the Atlantic northeast of Jacksonville, Florida.

couldn't go out. So we didn't have anything to do, and I decided to go and talk to the shrimp fishermen. There were shrimp fishermen there at the mouth of St. Johns, and they were always getting in our way. There would always be a shrimp trawler right where you wanted to run your pattern with the indicator device. I went and asked the shrimp fishermen if they had seined up anything unusual in their nets, and they said, "Sure, you mean those bits of metal we've been getting?"

I went back and looked at them, and they had enough pieces there to make a whole mine. Of course, these were the pieces of the mine cases that had been exploded by our sweepers. Just looking by at them and looking at the markings on them, we determined that these were nothing new, that they were the same old type. I believe they were what they called S-type German magnetic submarine-laid mines. We decided that it really wasn't worth expending any more effort on them. We used this good intelligence we got from the shrimp fishermen and came home.

Q: Did these shrimp fishermen working around there realize their peril?

Admiral Waters: No.

Q: What about the Japanese in the Pacific? Did they do

any mining of Australian ports when they were down in that area?

Admiral Waters: They didn't do much in the way of mining, except they used some of the older moored contact mines with the chemical horns on, the ones that you have to actually hit to set off. But they didn't go in in any strength at all. I imagine they had maybe some experimental types of influence mines, but they stuck mostly to the older things.

Q: And that pertained to the islands that we took and began to use as bases. Did they do anything about that?

Admiral Waters: There was some small amount of it, but nothing very worrisome. The innovations they had, of course, were in things like the suicide torpedo boats. These were just one-way boats with suicide pilots in them.

Q: I was thinking of that in terms of the requirements placed upon your school. I wonder if the need for teams of men in the Pacific grew.

Admiral Waters: Yes, what we did was we had them spread out in the forward areas, where they could be shifted around and, of course, we designed our equipment and our tools so they could be airlifted and carried by a truck and Jeeps. We also had units in the larger ships, particularly in the aircraft carriers. This applied more to bomb disposal people than mine disposal, but in case of unexploded bombs on aircraft carriers, they could be defused.

Actually, at Pearl Harbor, another thing that was done sometime after the attack out there involved one of our very outstanding men. He was a regular Navy chief gunner's mate named Bob Eigell, who came with us initially as a first class.* He had been fooling around with an idea for defusing a Japanese bomb. A lot of the Japanese bombs had a big cylindrical type of fuze that stuck out of the nose. If you could just unscrew that, then it made the bomb relatively harmless. So Ike, in his good Navy fashion, designed a big ratchet wrench that you would put on this thing.** It had one line leading to a fairlead in one direction and another line leading to a fairlead in another direction. You would take these two lines off and get behind something. You'd pull one, and it would pull the wrench over; then you'd pull the other one, and it would ratchet it back so you could get another purchase and eventually unwind the thing. This thing worked; it was sort of crude but it worked.

---
*Chief Gunner's Mate Robert W. Eigell, USN. Eigell was later commissioned and retired as a commander.
**This tool became widely useful in the bomb-disposal program and came to be known as the Eigell wrench.

They were raising the ships that were sunk at Pearl Harbor, particularly the battleships. When they got down to either the main or second deck of the <u>West Virginia</u>, they found an unexploded Japanese bomb--I believe it was a 500-pounder--in the middle of all the debris. So they immediately evacuated ship, and the work stopped. Of course, that work was very high priority then, getting the ships into shape to bring them back to the coast and eventually making them into shore bombardment ships, where they were so successful.

Eigell just happened to be out there on the spot, and he had his wrench with him. He had been assigned out there by us, so he just stepped aboard and rigged up his wrench and actually took his fairleads around behind the barbette on the <u>West Virginia</u>. He unscrewed the fuze and told them it was all right. It was safe to take the carcass of the bomb and take it in a boat and dispose of it. He really saved the day, saved them a tremendous amount of time. I don't know how long it would have taken them to have done it by any other means.

Q: Did you have any provision for feedback from the various teams you sent out, feedback of the new knowledge, technique? How did that get back to you?

Admiral Waters: Yes, that was very important. We insisted on that. We insisted on newsletters periodically, and then if anything occurred in between, they were required to report. Everyone was pretty good about that. It was a rather small, close-knit group, and you always pored over the new reports that people had coming in.

Q: That certainly added to the value of your teaching.

Admiral Waters: It did. Then we would keep changing the course all the time. People were always thinking of new and better ways of doing things, little tools. For example, the German mines were usually equipped with a bomb fuze so that they could be dropped as bombs. They were used a great deal in the early bombings of London, because they came down on parachutes and didn't dig into the ground. When they hit, this bomb fuze took over; it would tick for something like 17 seconds, and then the thing would go off. Well, that meant that you had around 1,500 pounds of high explosives right on the surface. The shock wave and everything was horizontal, being vented into the air rather than coming out of a crater that the bomb has dug in the ground. This had a very destructive effect, particularly on the old London masonry, knocking down a whole block at a time.

The reason that you would get these things unexploded

was that a lot of times the fuze would jam. The fuze was made so that if you were using this thing as a mine and it hit the surface of the water, hitting anything would start the fuze to tick. That's why they had the clockwork mechanism ticking for 17 seconds. If in that 17 seconds it sank down so that it was under 15 feet of water or more, a little hydrostatic plunger would stop the clock and take the bomb fuze out of the circuit. Then it would become a mine.

The inertial thing in this bomb fuze would sometimes jam; that's why you got a chance to recover one. The essential thing to do in recovering one was to get that bomb fuze gagged in some way so it couldn't start ticking on you again. Now, the British, of course, started from scratch and, having nothing to work with, found this out. They first started using just a matchstick, shove a matchstick down this little hole to hold the hydrostatic valve down. Then, of course, the next thing that occurred to anybody--and it was the logical thing to use--was a woman's bobby pin.

Q: It's more durable than a matchstick.

Admiral Waters: It wouldn't snap off. But then there was a little cover on the thing called a three-penny bit, because it was just about the same size as a three-penny bit, which they don't have anymore, unfortunately. They made a thing with a little handle on it, an accurately machined little plug that would go in, so you put that down and fit it snugly in place. You really had it secure. That was, I think, eventually the best thing that was used on German bomb fuzes.

But people were always improving on things like that.

Q: And your pipeline to the British experience has continued.

Admiral Waters: Yes. We sort of grew into a custom of picking two of our better people in each class and sending them over to England to work with the British. The British, in turn, didn't send as many over here, but they did sort of cross-pollinate our people with theirs. We always sent a couple, particularly the ones that we thought were our prize students, because they would get to actually work with the British teams and get experience. That led to our first casualty, actually. We had one of our new ensigns blown up in those days.

Q: What about a pipeline to our other Allies, the Russians?

Admiral Waters: No, there was actually no association with

them. I don't think they had to worry about it that much.

Q: Well, you had a very important tour of duty there at that school. How did you get away from it?

Admiral Waters: Well, I did what so many people do. I trained my own relief. By the time I got away, Roach had been selected and gone back. He was exec of a submarine in the Pacific by that time. Archer had gone up, as this business had grown, and was dignified with a special desk at OpNav at that time.* We didn't have any daddy in OpNav when we started, but we grew into it, and Archer took over that job. I was left with the school and with the people I trained. One of the graduates of the first class was a Coast Guard officer named Fred Nichols, a very good man and very good at the business.** So it was arranged that in January of 1943 he relieved me as the officer in charge of the Navy's Mine Disposal School.

Q: I might ask--did Admiral King evince any great interest in this school?***

Admiral Waters: No, I don't think so. He knew it was

---
*OpNav--the large, extended staff of the Chief of Naval Operations.
**Lieutenant Commander Fred F. Nichols, USCG.
***Admiral Ernest J. King, USN, served as Chief of Naval Operations from 18 March 1942 to 15 December 1945.

there, because at that time, you know, he lived down on a yacht in the Navy yard, but he had a lot more important things to worry about than us.

One of the interesting little things that we did was to start some of the commercial concerns fooling around with what we called an independent diving suit that we were required to use. The only thing available to use was the old Navy deep-sea diving rig, which is big and cumbersome. We wanted to try to give our divers a little more freedom of movement and have a self-contained suit with a rebreathing apparatus of some kind on it. We got a lot of people interested in this, and I think it gave a start to what eventually turned out to be the scuba diving effort.* We didn't end up with a scuba outfit that early in the game, but we were pushing a little bit towards getting something like that.

Q: What companies particularly got interested?

Admiral Waters: Gee, I've forgotten the name of the company. All I remember is a guy named Brown up in Milwaukee.** He developed this completely independent suit with its own tanks of gas and a rebreathing, recirculating device. One of our people went up to see him

---
*Scuba--self-contained underwater breathing apparatus.
**Jack Brown units (a type of self-contained underwater breathing apparatus) were used by underwater demolition teams during World War II.

demonstrate this. He put it on, and he jumped with no line on him from a pier 20 feet into the water, which I always thought showed he was a little bit more stupid than he was bright. I've forgotten the names of the outfits then, but I always thought it was interesting that we were pushing towards something that eventually got to be a pretty big enterprise.

Q: Well, when you were sprung from the school, you went to a cruiser, didn't you?

Admiral Waters: Yes, I went over to the Bureau of Personnel and did my very best to get back in destroyers. I was told that I wasn't welcome in destroyers, that I had been trained as a gunnery expert, and I had to go back to bigger ships. So I got a long lecture on how valuable this gunnery training was, and then I was assigned as gunnery officer of the cruiser Memphis, the CL-13 that had fire control equipment that was so old and so fundamental that I didn't know anything about it.* We hadn't studied it at PG school. I had to learn it all over again. But it was a very interesting cruise.

---

*USS Memphis (CL-13) was commissioned 4 February 1925. She had a standard displacement of 7,050 tons, was 556 feet long, and 55 feet in the beam. She had a top speed of 35 knots and a main battery of twelve 6-inch guns, seven 3-inch guns, and six 21-inch torpedo tubes.

Q: Where was this?

Admiral Waters: It was in the South Atlantic. There were five old four-pipe cruisers down in the South Atlantic with the mission of blockading the narrows between Brazil and Ascension Island. The British took the part from Ascension Island to Dakar, on the African Coast. We were to keep the German blockade runners from coming through those narrows with cargoes of rubber and electronics equipment from Japan. It was a very monotonous kind of duty and not very glorious as far as the warfare went. There was plenty of danger from submarines down there, but the job was largely just patrolling.

These ships were pretty well suited for this job, because they carried the little OS2U aircraft.* This extended their visual range a great deal. We were able to cover a lot of territory that way. Actually, I think that during the time that the Germans were trying to run that blockade, I don't know whether any of them got through successfully or not, but very, very few. If we couldn't get them in the narrows, then somebody else got them. Usually air got them as they were going into the Bay of Biscay, which was usually their end port.

---

*The OS2U was a Vought-Sikorsky Kingfisher two-seat floatplane that had a wing span of 36 feet, length of 34 feet, and top speed of 164 miles per hour. It was used mostly for antisubmarine patrols and gunfire spotting.

Q: Had you received any warning about the approach?

Admiral Waters: Oh, yes, there was intelligence. Sometimes it was good, sometimes not so good. But we kept people on patrol all the time. It was usually a case of about two to three weeks out and three days in and then back on the line again. We operated either out of Recife or Bahia, Brazil, under Admiral Jonas Ingram.* We were part of the Fourth Fleet.

One day when the Memphis was in and some of the other ships were out, they had the famous triple play. They got three blockade runners in one day. We weren't in on it.

Q: That was unfortunate that when you had a chance to make a kill you weren't there. What about the German raiders?

Admiral Waters: Well, they never came down there. We did have, particularly in the early part of 1943, a lot of German submarines down there. We did an awful lot in ASW.** But this was mostly done by shore-based planes from the coast of Brazil and the islands. This was the main part of the ASW war. We had a squadron of blimps, and they did a lot in convoying. Of course, we convoyed all

---
*Vice Admiral Jonas H. Ingram, USN, Commander South Atlantic Force.
**ASW--antisubmarine warfare.

the way down to Rio.

Q: Is that what the German subs were after--the convoys to Rio?

Admiral Waters: Yes. And then across the Atlantic to Africa. Of course, we had a fighter field in Ascension Island, and that was the way we got fighter aircraft. We flew them down to the coast of Brazil, and they took off from Natal, which is right at the hump, and flew the hop over to Ascension Island, and then from there to Africa. That's the way they got the fighter planes over for the North African campaign.

Q: That was a considerable problem for us, wasn't it?

Admiral Waters: Yes, it was. Tremendous problem. And, of course, those places, particularly places like Ascension Island, had to be stocked with supplies of gasoline and oil and that sort of thing. The Germans were after them. Those were pretty big convoys. So it was a pretty interesting time.

I think the most interesting thing to me was that I got to know Admiral Jonas Ingram in that tour of duty. Have you had any interviews about Admiral Ingram?

Q: He's been mentioned occasionally, but not a great deal. Tell me about him.

Admiral Waters: Very unusual and colorful man. Well, in the first place, as far as our class at the Naval Academy was concerned, I don't think we had a very high regard for Admiral Ingram. Because as a commander, he was the director of athletics at the Naval Academy, and he was always making rather flamboyant speeches about the football team.* The one thing he was famous for with the people at the Naval Academy at that time was he'd get up before a big football game at the pep rally and give his right arm to win the game the next day but always hold up his left.

After I got down there with him, I really changed my opinion of him. He was a great man in many ways. He was sort of rough, but he was a great leader. He understood mass psychology; actually, at that time, the ambassador to Brazil was wasted. Jonas Ingram was the U.S. ambassador to Brazil. He was highly regarded by all of the Brazilians, mainly because he would promise them things and make good on his promises. But he was a very colorful man, particularly in the way he talked. He could make up new epithets with every paragraph. Some of the things he did I'll never forget.

Those blockade runners, you know, would always destroy

---
*Commander Ingram was Naval Academy athletic director from 1926 to 1930.

themselves. They would always have explosive charges planted. They would set the time fuzes on them and take to the boats. Before you could get there to recover these very valuable cargoes of rubber, why, up they would go. But the Germans pulled one trick on Jonas that didn't work very well and didn't set very well. That was to put a booby trap on the gangway when they abandoned ship. One of the destroyers had caught this ship, and it had sent a boarding party to go aboard and try to cut off the scuttling charges before they went. But the Germans set a booby trap right at the top of the gangway that went off and killed half a dozen men, and it was a pretty dirty trick.

Shortly thereafter, we caught another blockade runner, and it scuttled itself. They took to the boats, and it scuttled itself about 300 miles from the coast. Admiral Ingram said, "Let them row." I'm sure it was a week or maybe more to shore for these boatloads of survivors from this German ship that had scuttled themselves. They rowed and maybe sailed a little bit and maybe drifted a little bit towards the coast of Brazil. He kept planes over them to keep track of them all the time, just to make sure they didn't get away anywhere. They were very glad to see the coast of Brazil when they got there.

Q: Very sorry their comrades had sprung that booby trap on

the other one.

Admiral Waters: Admiral Ingram was a very flamboyant man. I would compare him in many ways with Admiral Halsey; he was the same type of individual.

Q: The type who could make the headlines.

Admiral Waters: A lot of magnetism, a lot of personal leadership. The enlisted men all loved him. As I say, the Brazilians loved him. I think he was always trying to get out to the Pacific, and President Roosevelt wouldn't let him leave Brazil. He said, "Jonas, you behave yourself and keep on doing that good job down there, and we'll reward you." Well, they eventually did. They gave him a fourth star and the Atlantic Fleet.

But I got to know him because after I had been on the Memphis for a year, I had everything all lined up. The captain and the exec had been relieved and had gone to Washington, where they were pleading my cause and I got orders to go as gunnery officer of the new battle cruiser Guam. I was sort of ahead of my time in getting a job like that by about three or four years, but the orders came down, and I was relieved. Just before I was going to go to the airport to catch a Navy plane to go north, I got word from headquarters, "Tell Waters to report to Fourth Fleet headquarters. Admiral Ingram wants to see him." I was not to carry out my orders yet.

I reported in, and he said, "You're going to be on my staff and stay here." Of course, I was crushed. Actually, he had let Captain Converse go to take a squadron of destroyers.* The admiral picked me to be his fleet gunnery officer because the Memphis was his flagship. I was just a junior commander then, so I stepped into a captain's job. But it wasn't much of a job; there wasn't much to do. I was very unhappy. Every time I would complain, old Jonas would say, "Now, you just take it easy, young fellow. We'll take care of you later on." That was in about March, and I stayed on that staff until the fall. Then my father was taken seriously ill, and I was allowed to come home. He had a terminal case of cancer. He died while I was home. At the same time, Admiral Ingram was in Washington, and I knew this, so I went down to the Navy Department to try to catch a ride with him to go back to my job the day after my father's funeral.

I bumped into the admiral in Admiral King's office, and he was very surprised to see me. He said, "What are you doing up here?" I told him about my father. Well, he was a very sentimental man, and he put his arm around me and said how sorry he was. He said, "I'll tell you what.

---
*Captain Adelbert F. Converse, USN, became Commander Destroyer Squadron Ten.

Come over here, I want to tell you something." So we walked outside and he said, "They're giving me another star. I'm getting the Atlantic Fleet. I'll be moving right on up here. You know, I always like to bring one member of my old staff along with me to show these new fellows how to do things and how I like them done. How would you like to come on up with me?"

I said, "I think that would be great, Admiral. I know my mother would appreciate it."

He said, "There's no reason for you to go back to Brazil. You just stay right here with your mother. I know you'll be a help to her, and so forth."

So I said, "What do I do about this?"

We were walking back in and the aides were sitting there and he said, "Well, if you need some kind of a piece of paper, get one of those jokers to write you up something. But if anybody wants to know what you're doing around here, you are under orders of the prospective Commander in Chief of the Atlantic Fleet, to report to him when he shows up in Washington."

I said, "Aye, aye, sir," and that's how it was. Two weeks later, he showed up, and I was there to meet him, and I went on the staff with him. I was then put in operations, the Atlantic Fleet staff, for about another six months.*

---

*Admiral Ingram took command of the Atlantic Fleet on 15 November 1944.

At that time there wasn't any talk in the Bureau of Personnel about not getting back in destroyers because I was a big-ship gunner for two reasons. Number one, Admiral Ingram told them to get me a destroyer. I think that was the most important one. The other was that times were really tough in destroyers. This was about Okinawa time, when they were getting shot up so badly with the radar picket ships. They were looking for people to command them then.

Q: Well, tell me about that period on his staff there, Admiral.

Admiral Waters: Well, that was very interesting and a most unusual part of the Navy. The flagship, you know, was USS Vixen.* She was a converted yacht that had belonged to the Forstmann of Forstmann woolens. A beautiful thing, built in Kiel, she was all mahogany paneled, and actually it was a very good idea. Of course, it started off she was Ernie King's flagship when he was CinCLantFlt at the beginning of the war.** It was a great way to run a war because there wasn't room enough to have a great big staff.

---

*USS Vixen (PG-53) was originally the steel-hulled yacht Orion built in 1929. The Navy purchased her from woolen manufacturer Julius Forstmann 13 November 1940. Converted to a gunboat, she was commissioned 25 February 1941 and decommissioned 24 May 1946.
**CinCLantFlt--Commander in Chief Atlantic Fleet.

O. D. Waters, Jr. #2 - 93

You know, you couldn't keep adding on appendages here and there. We divorced all of the routine things like supply. Those things were important but weren't necessary immediately to the operation of the fleet.

Q: Was Ingram one of these men who wanted a small staff?

Admiral Waters: Yes. He worked very well with a small staff. Of course, he relieved Royal Ingersoll, who believed the same way.* No matter what the admiral felt, the quarters in the Vixen were pretty crowded. When I went aboard, I moved into a four-man stateroom with three captains. I didn't like that very much, and I managed to get myself moved out. I moved into a smaller stateroom with two other commanders, one of whom was junior to me, so I didn't have to get up first to use the washbasin.

The ship was fitted out, of course, with all kinds of special communication equipment, particularly to couple into land lines for teletypes and that sort of thing, so we could get very rapid communications. We had the regular berths that were fixed up for the Vixen, one in Norfolk, one here in Washington, one in Philadelphia, one in New York, and one in Newport. We would go into this assigned berth and throw the lines over, and at the same time throw

---

*Admiral Royal E. Ingersoll, USN, Commander in Chief Atlantic Fleet, January 1942-November 1944.

the ends of the cables over and plug them in. Then we were in business again with our fancy communication system.

Q: A wonderful system.

Admiral Waters: So the only thing was, when we were going from port to port, somebody had to take the watch for us, but it worked very well. It was a tremendous experience because it was small--very high-powered, lots of captains on that staff. There were four of us in the operations department, which was headed by Captain Connie Converse, who had by then come back, you see. He was the fellow that I relieved.

Q: Yes, down in Brazil.

Admiral Waters: He had had his destroyer squadron and come back. The offices were small; they had just little partitions between them that went three-quarters of the way up. So in operations if we had a problem with an escort getting something tangled in its screw leaving New York with a convoy, you just tilted your chair back and hollered to Hugh Webster around the corner who was the materials man and said, "What dry dock can we put her in and how soon can we get her out?* Can she catch up with the convoy, or do
_____
*Captain Hugh P. Webster, USN, an engineering duty officer.

O. D. Waters, Jr. #2 - 95

we have to scrounge up another ship?"

All of the things like the Service Force and supply and the paymasters, all those sort of big things--of course, in those days there wasn't any public relations. The chaplains and the doctors came under the Service Force command.

It was a very interesting setup. We ran all the convoys out from our side of the "chop" line, where the British took over, and we did it with a very small staff.*

Q: You were concerned about the Icelandic convoys, too, weren't you?

Admiral Waters: Oh, yes. You had the ones that went up to the northwest approaches, and then you had a group of convoys that went over to the southern English ports and then the Gibraltar convoys. Those were the main transatlantic ones we had.

I got into sort of an interesting thing towards the end of my six months there. The intelligence boys came up with the fact that the Germans were known to be experimenting with putting guided missiles on their submarines. The question arose: what would we do if the

---
*"Chop" is a contraction of "change operational control." The Americans ran the convoys up to a certain point in the Atlantic, then turned them over to the British.

Germans suddenly showed up in the Atlantic with missiles and started firing them at our cities? Whose job was it, and how would we handle it? I was the junior guy in operations, and so they gave me the job. Everybody else thought I would do well on this job. It was a lot of fun; it took a lot of work.

All of the plans had names, and this was called plan Tear Drop. Actually, it was really just a sort of an emergency antisubmarine warfare plan, because the big thing that we were able to do was to get together with the Army Air Force. We got up an agreement with them that if these submarines should appear, the Navy would be responsible for them until the missile was launched. Then after the missile was launched, the Air Force would be responsible for shooting it down, which made sense, really. To get people to agree to something like that is sometimes hard, but they did. So from then on, it was just a super ASW plan that we had. We had emergency pools of ships that we could call on in code words so that they would execute the plan in a great hurry in case we needed it.

Jonas Ingram did one of his great publicity appearances on that. He was interviewed by the New York press, and this was after we had gotten the plan and it was approved by Admiral King and it looked like it would work. Jonas was interviewed by the press, and they asked him about the Germans firing missiles at us from submarines. He said, "Boys, any ones that those Germans fire at us I'll catch in my bare hands." He was quoted in the papers on that.

Q: The skipper of a jeep carrier operating in the Atlantic told me that the intelligence on submarines and the location of submarines and the anticipated location of submarines was astoundingly accurate. Now, a lot of that data came from you people, I imagine.

Admiral Waters: No, that came from the big intelligence setup that was actually centered under Admiral King in Washington. Remember, that was called the Tenth Fleet.

Q: The Tenth Fleet, yes.

Admiral Waters: I don't know too much about the Tenth Fleet because I wasn't in it, but I always understood that they were the fellows that sort of spearheaded and coordinated that whole intelligence-gathering bit. It was partly information from agents, shore observers, undercover people watching their base operations in France. And a lot of it, of course, was communications intelligence, picking up transmissions. A great deal of it came that way, because the old methodical Germans insisted on their

O. D. Waters, Jr. #2 - 98

submarines reporting back to them on what they were doing. That gave them away, because you could maybe get a radio direction-finder bearing on a submarine transmission. And you get two or three, and you've got a location. Then they must have had a hell of a fine spy network, because they knew not only where the submarines were coming but a lot of times exactly how many and where they were going to rendezvous.

Q: That was the time of the wolf pack, wasn't it, when we were operating in the Atlantic?*

Admiral Waters: Yes.

Q: Do you have any recollections of the wolf packs or any incidents that stand out?

Admiral Waters: Of course, there was some activity at that time. See, I'm talking about the end of '44 and early '45. By that time, we pretty well had the upper hand on the submarines in the North Atlantic. Everything was going down as far as the Germans were concerned.

Q: Did you reach down into the Caribbean command, in

---

*An organized force of submarines coordinated against a specific target or on a particular mission. This tactic was employed by Germans in the Battle of the Atlantic.

Puerto Rico? Was Hoover there?*

Admiral Waters: Oh, yes. Oh, yes. Of course, by that time that area was all pretty well cleaned up. You remember, in the early days of the war there was an awful lot of activity in the gulf and the Caribbean, and they were pretty much unopposed. But as we grew stronger and got forces to oppose them, they were less likely to go there, because, of course, it was a long ways for them to come. As long as they had good pickings in the North Atlantic, where they didn't have to come very far, they wouldn't come way down there. They came down and got driven out.

I can recall submarine hunts, submarines being spotted along on our side of the ocean, which was somewhat unusual in those days. I remember old Jonas getting very mad one day, because there was a German submarine known to be up around Casco Bay, and they had some special antisubmarine forces. Of course, they had the land-based air, and they had some destroyers.

Q: That's where we exercised some of our new ships.

Admiral Waters: Yes, our destroyers and DEs were out there looking. I remember Jonas getting so mad. They had some

---
*Vice Admiral John H. Hoover, USN, Commander Carribbean Sea Frontier, 1941-43. Dr. Mason had previously done Hoover's oral history as part of the Columbia University program.

O. D. Waters, Jr. #2 - 100

of the operational analysis people who had these mathematical arrangements, the best geometric array to put your ships in to catch a submarine in the various conditions. Jonas would snort about that and say, "Look at those damn fools. They're looking for that damn submarine every place except where it is. Now here's where it is." And, sure enough, somebody went back and looked, and there it was. He was sort of an intuitive fellow.

Q: Yes. Well, is there anything else about that tour with Ingram?

Admiral Waters: No, that was a rather short one, I think, and that about covers it.

Q: Would you say a word about the ability of the Canadian Navy, because they were assisting, weren't they, in these convoys with the corvettes they had?

Admiral Waters: Oh, yes, they were great, they were great. I forget the designations of them, but they were working with us in the northern task force.

Q: Out of Halifax.

Admiral Waters: Yes. They did a tremendous job. I don't

recall anything specific about them, I suppose, because they always did their jobs so well. You just sort of depended on them. Those convoys went pretty well across there. That was the most direct route, and lots of the fast convoys went across the northern great circle route.

Q: You used some jeep carriers, didn't you?*

Admiral Waters: Oh, yes, there were jeep carriers spread across the Atlantic there in various areas to hunt down submarines. The most sought-for jobs of escorting in those days were the Gibraltar convoys, because that was the longest distance. The Gibraltar convoys consisted of barges towed by Army tugs. With shortage of shipping, we put an awful lot of heavy stuff and things like that in regular lighters towed by tugboats. We had a big convoy of them, escorted usually by, say, a division of DEs.

Q: They were vulnerable to the Focke-Wulf.**

Admiral Waters: Oh, yes, they were vulnerable to air; they were vulnerable, and they just were so slow. I think we figured them for a speed of advance of six knots, so once you took off with one like that, you were gone for a long

---
*Jeep carriers was a nickname for the small escort carriers, designated CVE.
**German Focke-Wulf fighter planes were characterized by great speed and maneuverability.

time. That was the most unpopular route for the convoys in those days.

Q: With the exception of Murmansk, I suppose?

Admiral Waters: Well, Murmansk was over by then, the rough part of Murmansk.

Q: Did you have protective cognizance of the Queens and the big transports, fast transports?*

Admiral Waters: Well, we kept them plotted, and if any danger looked like it was coming, then we would react to that particular case. But they went out of convoy, and they were on their own unless something specific happened.

Q: Their protection was their speed.

Admiral Waters: Yes. They just kept plowing.

Q: Tell me more about Admiral Ingram.

Admiral Waters: Well, this is a story that they told about Admiral Ingram. It may not be exactly accurate, but there

---

*This is a reference to the Queen Mary and Queen Elizabeth, two large British passenger liners converted to troop transports for World War II.

is some evidence that it actually occurred or something like it occurred. It was when Admiral Ingram had the task force in the Caribbean and was assigned to keep an eye on what the Free French were doing in the island of Martinique. Jonas had been running scouting lines around the island for quite a long time and got a little bored. So he sent a message up to Admiral King, who was CominCh, and said, "I am making a sweep to the north."* Shortly thereafter, he and his force dropped anchor at Miami for a little liberty. The story goes that Admiral King sent him a message to the effect, "What the hell are you doing in Miami? You were supposed to be watching Martinique."

Jonas got under way and sent a message back, "I am making a sweep to the south." That's really supposed to have happened. He and King were very good friends.

Q: I gather that they were.

Admiral Waters: Of course, most of the Jonas Ingram stories involve a little blasphemy or four-letter words.

Q: We can put that on tape; there's no rule against it, you know.

Admiral Waters: He always used to impress me because he

---

*CominCh--Commander in Chief U.S. Fleet.

was such a gifted cusser. He never repeated himself, and he had so many very unusual expressions. I'll never forget one time when the chief of staff, Commodore Braine, was away.* I was the chief of staff's assistant, so I was acting. We had a Brazilian rear admiral who was a task force commander out of Recife. By that time they were taking part in escorting the convoys. This fellow was quite a talker, and he came to call on Admiral Ingram one day. We had our headquarters in an office building we had taken over in Recife. He came up on the elevator, and I greeted the Brazilian admiral and took him into Admiral Ingram's office.

Admiral Ingram invited me to stay, so we sat there and this Brazilian admiral was a tremendous talker. He had a cup of coffee, and he talked and talked and talked until finally he got tired of talking. So Admiral Ingram and I escorted him together back to the elevator and put him on and bid him good-bye. Then we turned and were walking back to the office. He always called the chief of staff "Chief" and me "Little Chief." Ingram said to me, "Little Chief, what did you think of that son of a bitch?"

I said, "Well, sir, he sure could talk, couldn't he, Admiral?"

He said, "Talk? Son, if bullshit was music, that son of a bitch would be a brass band."

---

*Commodore Clinton E. Braine, Jr., USN.

O. D. Waters, Jr. #3 - 105

Interview Number 3 with
Rear Admiral Odale D. Waters, Jr., U.S. Navy (Retired)

Place: Admiral Waters's home in Alexandria, Virginia

Date: Thursday, 27 May 1971

Interviewer: John T. Mason, Jr.

Q: Good to see you this morning, Admiral. In the last chapter of your recollections, you dealt with your service on the staff of Admiral Ingram. In June of 1945 you were given command of destroyer number 724, the USS Laffey.* You want to resume your story at this point.

Admiral Waters: Yes. I had been trying to get to sea and get a command, and Admiral Ingram had kept putting me off by promising that he'd take care of me, and so in about April of that year, which was '45, he came through on his promise. I was ordered to the Pacific destroyer skippers' pool, to go out to Pearl Harbor and catch a ship. Of course, destroyer skippers were very much in demand at that time, because we were losing a lot of destroyers with the Okinawa campaign. So I started off, including going through a couple of schools on the East Coast. Before I started for the West Coast, I was called by the Bureau of

---

*USS Laffey (DD-724) was commissioned 8 February 1944. She had a standard displacement of 2,200 tons, was 376 feet long, and 41 feet in the beam. She had a top speed of 34 knots. Her weapons included six 5-inch guns, four 40-mm., 11 20-mm., and six 21-inch torpedo tubes.

O. D. Waters, Jr. #3 - 106

Personnel and told that my orders were being changed. When I got to San Francisco, instead of going on to Pearl, I'd go up to Seattle and take command of the Laffey, DD-724.

Q: En route, you said, you went to a couple of schools. What schools?

Admiral Waters: Well, on the East Coast I went for two weeks, I think it was, to the fleet sonar school in Key West. I had my choice; I could have gone to either Key West or San Diego. I chose to take that one on the East Coast.

Q: Did you find there were some new developments that you hadn't been cognizant of?

Admiral Waters: Oh, yes. There were new developments since I had been in destroyers. Things had been improved greatly, particularly in sonar. Also, the school was very good in teaching you, through the use of trainers and simulation, the latest tactics in antisubmarine warfare from a destroyer standpoint.

Q: I guess they had acquired a lot of new knowledge in that area, hadn't they?

Admiral Waters: Yes. For instance, the school covered the techniques and the methods of using voice radio most effectively. Those were all taught in actual problems, where you went through the drill. So this was very useful.

Then, as I say, I came back to Washington and was told that I was taking command of the Laffey, which had been very badly battle damaged at Okinawa. So I went on to San Francisco. I went to the damage control school there, down to San Diego to the CIC school, and then up to Seattle.*

Q: Tell me a little about the damage control school. What did you focus on?

Admiral Waters: Damage control was a combination of controlling damage in a ship that was hit in battle. There was heavy emphasis on fire fighting--control of the spreading of fires in a ship that's been struck, and a brief review of ship stability and maintaining watertight integrity, shoring bulkheads. It covered all of the really practical things you are faced with if you try to save a damaged ship.

Q: Very valuable information too. So many ships were lost because the rules weren't applied, I understand.

---
*CIC--combat information center.

Admiral Waters: Yes. And, of course, it was most important at that time, because when I reported in to Seattle, I took over a ship that was only about one-third left. It had a sort of a miraculous survival of this battle on one of the radar picket stations off of Okinawa.*

Q: She must have had an excellent damage control officer aboard.

Admiral Waters: They had very excellent damage control, and they were lucky too. You had to have a combination of both.

Q: Oh, yes.

Admiral Waters: They were jumped by 20-some kamikazes and had hits from eight of them. Fortunately, none was in an engineering space except in the engineering aft. The engineering aft was flooded, and they lost control of the rudder for a while. But they still had their full power, so they were steaming in a tight circle at 35 knots. Number three mount was completely blown off the ship. Everything from the after stack aft was sort of cleaned

---

*For a detailed account of the Laffey's kamikaze ordeal, see Rear Admiral F. Julian Becton, USN (Ret.), and Joseph Morschauser III, The Ship That Would Not Die (Englewood Cliffs, New Jersey: Prentice-Hall, 1980).

off, the 40-millimeter mounts. They had one bad hit forward, right under the bridge, that killed a lot of people. There were 33 killed outright and 70-some wounded. There were lots of Navy Crosses given to that ship. They brought her in. She was commanded at that time by a commander, later admiral, Julian Becton.* It was quite a ship.

When I took over in Seattle, as I say, there wasn't much ship left. We were working very hard to get her back in commission. About every week, we'd get a dispatch from Admiral Nimitz's staff who wanted to know our progress, because we were counted on to be in the final landing on the mainland of Japan.

Q: Yes, Olympic.**

Admiral Waters: Yes. We would be in the forces that landed on the main island of Honshu, so they were very much interested in getting us back into service. As the summer wore on, we were making good headway getting her back together, but the atom bomb was dropped in August.*** I

---
*Commander F. Julian Becton, USN, later rear admiral. He has been interviewed for a Naval Institute oral history.
**Code name for the Allied invasion of Kyushu, scheduled for 1 November 1945. The first phase was Operation Downfall, an overall assault on Japanese home islands. It was to be followed by Coronet, an invasion of Honshu.
***In the first combat use of atomic bombs, U.S. B-29 bombers hit Hiroshima, on the island of Honshu, on 6 August 1945 and Nagasaki, on Kyushu, on 9 August.

was standing on the bridge of the <u>Laffey</u>, and the whistle started blowing. The yard workmen just dropped everything, and everybody went off to celebrate; the war was over.*

Q: Were you disappointed that you didn't get in on the finish?

Admiral Waters: Well, it's hard to say you were disappointed. You couldn't be disappointed about missing all that obvious danger and rough fighting you were going into. But there was sort of a feeling of letdown, of having pushed so hard to get this ship back in shape and ready to go into the combat zone. Then it just all of a sudden seemed to evaporate, although it didn't really. We went ahead and finished her up.

Q: Did you have a very tight time schedule?

Admiral Waters: Yes, we had a very tight time schedule. As soon as we got her ready for sea and passed our post-repair trials, we were supposed to provision her and get our ammunition back aboard. You do this in that area by going up around Puget Sound, the various depots and storage facilities. You get your depth charges one place and your

---

*Hostilities ceased in the Western Pacific on 15 August 1945, which was 14 August in the United States.

torpedoes another and your gun ammunition another. We got our stores at Pier 91 in Seattle, and that took a couple of days to do.

Q: It must have been quite an experience, a learning experience, rebuilding a ship.

Admiral Waters: Yes. Of course, it was my first command, too, and I was very proud of her but a little bit nervous about handling her. In those times, it was considered a big destroyer. She was kind of small by present-day standards, but she was quite a ship.

One amusing thing occurred when we went on our two-day trip of loading up. The last place we came into was back to Seattle, Pier 91. I had managed to rent a house in southwest Seattle on Duwamish Head, the southern headland of the Seattle Harbor. Our two oldest girls were very small when we were living there. I had a pair of binoculars at home, and my wife could look out over the whole harbor from where we were living.

As I came in with the ship from my two-day trip, she and the two children were watching for Daddy's ship. We came into Pier 91, and I had to go into a rather narrow slip, ahead of a CVE, which took up most of the room. On the other side of the channel, on the charts, was a big mud bank. As so often happens in Seattle, the current was running pretty strong and right across the mouth of where the slip I was trying to make. I started in and didn't like the looks of things, so I backed down hard to make another try and got her all lined up. That time I slid it in just right and had practically a no-bell landing ahead of the CVE and was very proud of myself.* I went over to the pier to the pay telephone to call my wife to tell her I was home and to come get me. She said, "Yes, I know. I saw you come in. Why didn't you make it on the first pass?"

Q: Your critic.

Admiral Waters: Well, as I say, we got her put back together. No one had changed our orders. We were still on a tight time schedule to get to Pearl Harbor.

Q: Did she have any very new equipment?

Admiral Waters: A very minor amount. As a matter of fact, there was so much urgency about getting her back into the combat zone that we actually cut corners on the repairs. We just did what we had to, and we actually took some shortcuts that were contrary to good accepted engineering

---

*Each order to the engines is accompanied by a bell. The most desirable landings alongside piers are those that require the fewest engine changes and the fewest bells.

practice, which later plagued me a bit.

One of the things that was done that caused trouble later on involved the two steering cables. You see, a cable runs down each side of a destroyer from the bridge to steering aft to control the rudder. You have two in case one goes out. You always have a redundancy. These are required to be continuous cables; they're not to be cut at any place. Well, half of these two cables was burned up back in steering aft, where they had the fire in the engine room. So to save time and because of the shortage of material, they cut the cables about midway in the ship and put junction boxes in and very carefully spliced all of the parts of the cables together for the steering control. I had nothing but trouble with that from then on.

We got so we were awfully good at shifting steering control aft. When we'd lost steering control on the bridge, it just got to be sort of a routine thing. We even lost steering control going alongside another ship to fuel or something. By that time it had gotten to be sort of second nature, and we did all right. But one time it happened on a replenishment, and we were out at sea--this was later on--and we had some time on our hands. I had two good electrical men on board, one a chief fire controlman and one a chief electrician's mate. So I called them up on the bridge at 8:00 o'clock in the morning and said, "Now, we're going to steer from steering aft all day, and I'll cut out the steering system. I want one of you to start aft and one of you start here on the bridge. You work down both cables, one working towards the other until you meet. Let me know everything you find wrong."

So they did. It took them about eight hours, and they found innumerable little things, but nothing that you could really put your finger on that was causing the trouble. But they corrected all the little things, and we had no more trouble with the steering system.

Q: I suppose in that hurry-up process, there were many things on board ship that wouldn't meet the standards of the damage control school that you'd been to.

Admiral Waters: Yes, it took a long time to get that ship in shape. There were loose wires in the fire control wiring trunk. One of them fell out into my cabin one night, and this was a loose wire that had just been cut off and another one run through. But the old wire hadn't been pulled out; they were in too big a hurry. When this wire fell out, sparks started dancing around the steel deck; it was still live. We had things like that.

One of the most gruesome things, I suppose, was just before we left the yard and we were having a real good, final cleanup of the ship. Up in the wardroom country we cleaned out a hidden-away part of the overhead, and we took out a shoe with a foot still in it. That was a place where one of the big explosions was during the battle.

Q: In retrospect, is it a wise thing to rush the repairs of a ship in that fashion, intending that she should go out to battle?

Admiral Waters: No, it isn't, but I think that overall, under those circumstances, we could have done it all right. It would have been all right. We had our problems, and we had to work hard. But you must remember that at that time, you had some awfully good men in your crew. And you had, really, too many people in the crew.

Q: What was the complement?

Admiral Waters: We had slightly over 300 officers and men. Nowadays, you run a destroyer of that size with less than 200. So we had excess people, and we had an awful lot of good people, combat-trained people.

Q: Were many of them from the former crew of the Laffey?

Admiral Waters: Yes, yes, a large number of them were.

Q: Did they have psychological problems?

Admiral Waters: Yes, that was one of my great problems in Seattle. See, the captain left, the exec left. We had a big change in officers and some change in the crew, but they tried to keep the crew together. We got a new doctor, for instance. He was a very fine doctor but a young fellow just out of his internship.

Everything was fine until the leave party started coming back. We divided the ship up into, I guess, two or three groups, and then they would go home for a month's leave. Well, they had been big heroes. They had done a very heroic job, and many of them were decorated. The war was still going on in the Pacific, but their families quite rightly felt that young Joe had done his part.

So when they started arriving back from leave, that was when we got the people going to the doctor with combat fatigue. And the young doctor was very sympathetic to these men. Before I knew it, I had a large number of my crew undergoing psychiatric observation in the hospital over in Bremerton.*

I called the young doctor in and said, "I realize this is your business, but part of it is mine. I have to worry about keeping my crew intact, and so from here on, before you send a man for psychiatric treatment, please discuss the case with me." I could see that this didn't sit very

---
*The naval hospital was at the Puget Sound Navy Yard, Bremerton, Washington.

well with a young, inspired medico, because here was a layman interfering with his special field of competence. But everything turned out all right a couple of days later, because his chief hospital corpsman, who was sort of the backbone of the small medical department in the ship, wrote himself up a piece of paper and got himself sent to the hospital for psychiatric treatment. So the doctor agreed that this was being overdone a little bit.

Q: And being sent to Bremerton to the hospital automatically canceled them out of the . . .

Admiral Waters: Well, you see, then they were under a psychiatrist whose main job was to worry about them. So he would always take the safe course and recommend, "This man has had a lot of stress under combat." Well, he had; everybody on the ship had had it. "He seems to have suffered some ill effects, so to be on the safe side, it is recommended that he be shifted from the Laffey and be ordered to duty for at least six months stateside before returning to the combat zone." You can see how a fine, well-trained unit could disintegrate in no time under those circumstances. Some of them were funny, the things that they would pull to try to get over there.

Q: That must have been a considerable challenge to you as a young officer with your first command, being confronted with an unusual problem of that kind.

Admiral Waters: I lost one man, although not because of that. He was captain of the number three 5-inch gun mount that was completely wiped out by a direct hit from a kamikaze, just completely blew it over the side. I've forgotten this fellow's name, but it was a Polish name, so everybody called him Ski.* He was a great big, bulking, huge man and an excellent gunner. When the mount was blown over the side, he was found slightly dazed, having been blown through a sight port, which was much smaller than he was. How he got through it, nobody knows to this day except that he still had on his telephones, and his cord went in what was left of this gun mount, went inside through the sight port. So somehow or another, he had gotten out through there. But he was a tough one and a very good one.

I lost him; he was really grief-stricken. He went over to the dentist, and they found he had terrible teeth, so they transferred him off of the ship to take care of his teeth. He was a perfect physical specimen who got left behind because they had to work on his teeth.

---

*As reported in The Ship That Would Not Die, the captain of the Laffey's mount 53 was Gunner's Mate Second Class Lawrence H. Delewski, who was awarded a Bronze Star medal.

Q: Well, in spite of all those vicissitudes, you finally got under way.

Admiral Waters: When we left Seattle to go to San Diego, we left from Pier 91. As soon as we left the piers and swung out into the main channel, the fog settled in--the good old Puget Sound fog. We never saw the shoreline again until after we passed Cape Flattery in the entrance to the straits. Yet we steamed right along with this combat-trained crew in the fog, plotting every ship and with no problem at all. It was a beautiful thing to see because it was so good. We got on down to San Diego, and the pressure was still on us to complete our training in record time and go on out to Pearl. That was where I stumped my toe and had sort of the nadir of my naval career.

Q: What percentage of your men were new?

Admiral Waters: Oh, I would say 20%. It was rather low.

But we got into San Diego in the afternoon and gave liberty. Of course, a lot of these people were from San Diego, and that contributed a little bit to my problem. The next morning we got under way just about sunup, around 6:00 o'clock, and headed for the ASW area to work with one of our own submarines. You had to go out about 70 miles or so there to get to water deep enough to really conduct ASW exercises with a submarine.

So we started down the channel, and it was one of those typical San Diego days, where it had been foggy during the night, but at sunup it was clearing up. There was fog around the hills and the headlands and questionable visibility out ahead of you, but you could see around you all right. I had a representative of the training command on board, so I said, "What do ships usually do in getting out to this training area? Do you want us to barrel out there at high speed or what? Do you go at a reasonable cruising speed?"

He said, "Well, it depends on the skipper, really. Some of them get up to 28 knots, and they charge out there; some of them even put on four boilers, others take it easy. It's up to you."

So I said, "I'll compromise since the visibility is a little spotty in here, and when I get around the sea buoy, I'll go up to about 22. How does that strike you?"

He said, "Fine."

We were still sort of testing out our engines, and I didn't want to put any undue strain on things. So we went down the first part of the channel all right, where the speed limit, I think, is ten knots. Then it goes up to 15, and then it's unrestricted as you get out towards the sea buoy. We made our turn towards the sea buoy, and I went up to 18 knots. As I was looking ahead, I couldn't pick out the sea buoy. The sun was behind us, and I found out later on there was fog out there, patches of fog, but you couldn't really tell from the lighting conditions whether it was fog or not. It wasn't very late in the day anyway.

So I asked combat to check the channel ahead to see if it was clear and to see if they could pick up the sea buoy. And I got no answer. I asked them a second time and the officer of the deck, I guess, asked them the second time. And we got a confused answer from them. And, finally, on the third time, by that time I was getting ready to slow down, because I still couldn't see the sea buoy, and I knew there was some bad visibility there. And just at that time, combat came in and said, "Target's dead ahead about 500 yards."

At that time I saw the top mast of this ship sticking up through the fog, and I backed emergency full and started swinging right as fast as I could. I was over on my side of the channel, and this thing was right ahead of me. It turned out that it was a PC boat, the PC-815, and she had picked up a submarine out at sea and was escorting her into harbor.* At that time every submarine coming in had a surface escort.

---

*The PC-815 sank on 11 September 1945 as a result of the collision with the Laffey in San Diego Harbor. Her ammunition and depth charges were later detonated, and she was stricken from the Navy register on 11 October 1945.

O. D. Waters, Jr. #3 - 122

Q: For identification.

Admiral Waters: Yes. The submarine was on the surface astern of her, but they were right around this sea buoy. Apparently, for about a three-mile radius there was a patch of very dense fog, and they were in this fog and were not sounding fog signals. They were also on the wrong side of the channel; they were on the left side of the channel rather than the right, so they were right dead ahead of me. Fortunately, the submarine was well astern of the PC boat. The PC boat, I suppose, saw me at about the same time I saw him. But he had only one engine working, which, unfortunately, was his starboard engine. Those PCs were diesels, you know. He backed down on that one engine, and, of course, that swung his stern to the left, which was right over ahead of me. I think if he hadn't backed down, we'd have missed him all right, because he backed down and threw his stern over so that I struck him a glancing blow right amidships, right in the fuel tank.

It was a very terrifying thing, because my bow knifed into this fuel tank and the thing went up in flames. Huge flames shot up and smoke all over the place. Meanwhile, I was backing and backed clear, and the crew did a tremendous job of rescuing people. There was one man in the PC boat who was apparently asleep in the bunkroom, very close to where the collision occurred. He must have been crushed by the blow and didn't get out. There were a couple of other men in the same compartment who were injured who we picked out of the water and got back in. They were sort of touch and go for a while, but we saved them.

Between the *Laffey* and the submarine, which came steaming up, we got everybody out of the water, but the ship went down in about 15 minutes. You can't close up ships that small very much, so she just went down like a rock. So we were fortunate that we didn't lose any more people.

My ship actually caught fire. She was holed slightly, right in the forward peak tank, in the collision. The fire from the PC went into the hole there and set the boatswain's stores on fire. But this was sort of duck soup to a crew who had gone through what they had. They put it out in no time. But it was a horrifying thing to have this happen.

Of course, as soon as we got everybody out of the water and made a good count, I notified the hospital. We steamed back up the channel and were met by a hospital boat. Actually, my young doctor had been treating these two or three badly injured people on the wardroom table.

Q: Did they have fire burns?

O. D. Waters, Jr. #3 - 124

Admiral Waters: No, they were cut up and scratched and knocked about the head. One of them who was the most badly injured went over the side with a plasma bottle dripping stuff into him. But, as I say, they got him back to the hospital and saved all of them.

But then we had a court of inquiry on this, which was a terrible experience, because it went on for 21 straight days, including Saturdays, Sundays, and holidays.

Q: Why so long? The evidence?

Admiral Waters: It was just one of those things. We got a court that was composed of some people who were very detail conscious. We went over and over and over things. All sorts of things were in the record; much of it, in my opinion, was extraneous.

Q: And you were on the griddle for 21 days?

Admiral Waters: Yes. The first thing that happened was the court of inquiry opened, and they put me on the stand and said, "Who was conning the USS Laffey at 6:45 on the morning of September so-and-so in 1945?" I said I was, and they said, "The court is cleared." I walked out and came in, and I was the defendant from then on. I wasn't a non-defendant for more than about five minutes in the eyes of the court. It was a funny thing; we had a Marine—I've even forgotten his name—who was the judge advocate. I think he was a Marine Reserve and prided himself on being an admiralty lawyer. That was one of the reasons that the thing was so long and involved and drawn out. He was a great "if the court please" man, you know, and made little speeches.

Q: What is the normal length of such a thing?

Admiral Waters: Oh, I would say it could be done in a week, certainly. But, anyway, that's how long it took. The rather ironical thing about it was that a year later when the papers stopped going around, there was an opinion from the Judge Advocate General concerning all of us who were made either defendants or interested parties. For instance, I was made a defendant immediately and then continued to testify. The record of the court did not show that I did this at my own request, that I consented to do it. Therefore, my rights had been violated, and the same was true of everybody else who was either a defendant or an interested party. So none of the court of inquiry's voluminous record could be used in a court-martial, so a court-martial for anybody was out of the question.

Q: Was there any question of it anyway?

Admiral Waters: Well, it could have been. As a matter of fact, I believe the first recommendation of the board was for a court-martial, but the reviewing authority cut it down to a letter of reprimand. I was reprimanded, the commanding officer of the PC was reprimanded, and a couple of people on there. I was reprimanded, as was my officer of the deck and my CIC officer. I was reprimanded for making too much speed when in or near a fog, and the officer of the deck was reprimanded for not sounding the signals. We weren't in fog, and we couldn't see it, so we weren't sounding signals. But the PC and the submarine, of course, were both at fault, because they were in the fog, and they weren't making signals either.

Q: That was indeed a grueling experience. How much weight did you lose?

Admiral Waters: I don't know. I think that's when my hypertension started. But another thing that was a little bit on the ironic side as we got through this. We finished our refresher training, and then we charged out to Pearl and went in there sort of breathlessly, because they were still sending messages wanting to know where the _Laffey_ was. I reported over to ComCruDesPac at Middle Loch in

Pearl.* John Sylvester, a captain then, was the operations officer; later on, you know, he was Vice Admiral Sylvester. I went in and said, "Well, Captain, here I am."

He said, "Great, what do you want to do?" Nobody really had anything for us to do, and so we were joined up with a group of six or seven lost souls who had strayed away from their squadrons. We became sort of a training detachment at Pearl Harbor to help train aircraft carriers, to plane guard them when they were having flight operations, to be targets for submarines to fire torpedoes at.

Q: Just marking time, really.

Admiral Waters: Mark time. It kept us very busy, because they had a lot of training to do, and they very jealously kept ahold of us and wouldn't let us go. See, all the rest of my squadron was still out in WestPac, and it wasn't long, though, before they came back.** They didn't come through Pearl; they went directly to the coast. The war was over, and here they were on the coast, being heroes and having fun. Pearl Harbor was a very unattractive place to be at that particular time. It wasn't anything like the present travel folders.

---
*ComCruDesPac--Commander Cruiser-Destroyer Force, Pacific Fleet.
**WestPac--Western Pacific.

Q: It must have been a little chaotic too.

Admiral Waters: Well, it was chaotic, and there were many too many people there. It was overcrowded. Of course, most of the people were not in a very good mood, because they were people who had served in the armed forces, especially in the Navy, and they had their points, and now they wanted to get out.* It was just a question of holding them there for transportation or processing and so forth. But nobody liked that; they all wanted to get home.

Actually, in the six months that I spent around there, I managed to get a cruise or so away from Pearl, like a weekend in Hilo, just to give my crew a change of pace. We played a lot of softball, and that was it. And, of course, all of the ships were going downhill in a hurry, because they were losing all of the good people. The people who had the most points, of course, were naturally your best people, the people who'd been around the longest, who'd gotten the awards and decorations, and they just went. The ships got down to the point where--in the wardroom, for instance, instead of having a man as the chief steward who had been a cook at Antoine's, which is what I had when I

---

*For the demobilization of the U.S. armed forces after World War II, the services had a point system to determine individual priorities for leaving the service. Points were awarded for length of service, overseas service, battle stars, decorations, and dependent children. Those with the highest number of points were the earliest discharged.

first joined the ship--we ended up with a third class steward's mate and almost starved to death. You had your choice of starving to death or dying of indigestion, you know, because he didn't know how to cook.

Q: This sudden demobilization process is a very demoralizing thing. Is there any way that this can be retarded?

Admiral Waters: I don't know, Jack. It's a political thing, you see. The war was over and we had won, the boys wanted to get home, and Congress was going to bring them home. There wasn't much you could do about it. What happened to us was that while we were at Pearl, my squadron was designated as the operating squadron for the Bikini operation, Operation Crossroads. I got to Pearl in the fall of '45, and Operation Crossroads started in April of '46.*

Q: Yes.

Admiral Waters: So the ships that were designated to be in the Operation Crossroads had priority on personnel and equipment and everything else. Our problem was that there

---

*Operation Crossroads involved the testing by U.S. forces of two atomic weapons, detonated at Bikini Atoll in the Marshall Islands on 1 July and 25 July 1946.

were no personnel left in Pearl to get. We weren't just on the way home, and I was trying to get us sent back to the West Coast, where, incidentally, my family was waiting in San Diego. I would go in about once a week with a big story to John Sylvester, and he'd say, "Well, you didn't cry quite enough, Muddy. Come back next week, and I'll see you again. You didn't move me, and besides that, we've got a lot of work for you to do yet."

Q: I would think a project like that, if it were understood, would be an inducement for recruiting men.

Admiral Waters: Yes, it was. It was. For example, a reserve, either officer or an enlisted man, would be allowed to extend for just one year or maybe just a fraction of a year--I've forgotten the exact details. But if he wanted to go to Operation Crossroads to see an atomic bomb go off, he could sign up for it and go just for that particular event.* We had quite a few that did that.

Q: And those in targets, too, I think.

Admiral Waters: Oh, yes. My argument was that here I had priority to get people, but there were no people to get in Pearl, and, therefore, I should be sent back to the coast.

---
*The tests, conducted under the direction of Commander Joint Task Force One, Vice Admiral William H. P. Blandy, were designed to determine, primarily, the vulnerability of a carrier task force to an atomic weapon attack.

Q: Where the pool was larger.

Admiral Waters: Where the pool was larger to draw from. John Sylvester knew all this. He was just biding his time, and he let me go, and I was back on the West Coast about a month before we took off again to come to Bikini. I got people, but it was a strange assortment. It was all chiefs and no Indians, because, of course, the main people staying in the Navy at that time were career people. All of the non-rated people were mostly reserves who were getting out.

For example, it was very difficult to keep your engine rooms running with the type of experience you had. I had eight chief machinist's mates assigned to my two engine rooms. The normal complement in wartime was one chief for each. I got them all together and said, "Who are the two senior guys?" They finally decided who were the two seniors. Then I said, "Well, you have the forward room and you have the aft engine room. The rest of you might just as well forget those caps and buttons, because you're going to be throttlemen and work for your living again." They took it very well, and, as a matter of fact, it worked.

Q: And they were very knowledgeable.

Admiral Waters: Oh, yes. We did a miraculous thing. I had never seen it done before. We started off for Pearl Harbor coming back, and we were to pick up Admiral

Fahrion's flagship and go on out to Bikini with him.* We just had, I think, 24 hours in Pearl Harbor. So on the way out, I had developed a hot bearing on a cruising turbine. We tried various things, flushing it, and it didn't work; it kept heating up. So I got permission in the formation to drop back and lock the shaft and catch up again on one shaft. We held our place in formation on one shaft.

These eight machinist's mates took that bearing out under way in a destroyer, which is a very, very difficult job to do. We put the spare in, and they did such a good job that it was no problem and it worked. So by the time we got to Pearl, we were operational, but we had used our spare bearing and we were going out all summer in Bikini, where there wasn't much help. So we radioed ahead to the Navy yard at Pearl. When we got there, we sent over the bad bearing they had taken out, and the yard people repoured it and remachined it in the hours we had. So we went out with a spare, but it was a great example of the knowledge of these eight chiefs, being able to do a job like that under way.

Q: It must have been kind of exhilarating for them too.

Admiral Waters: Yes, it was. They felt like they were earning their pay. They were a little disgruntled having

---
*Rear Admiral Frank G. Fahrion, USN.

eight chiefs getting in each other's way.

The Bikini operation was very good, a most exciting thing. Of course, the eight destroyers were assigned just as workhorses. We did all sorts of things, including looking for downed aviators and Air Force planes that went in between Eniwetok and Kwajalein, and that sort of thing. I took Admiral Blandy, who was the task force commander, out to inspect the reef and to look at a position for the Charlie part of the test--there was A, B, and C--which never came off. That was to be a deep-water, non-moored test, and they were thinking about having it in the lee of the atoll on the other side with ships tethered to the atoll to drop the bomb underneath. But that was called off.

That was my first brush with oceanography. The working destroyers were fitted with special additions to the amidships winch and about a mile or so of piano wire and some strange things called nansen bottles--that I got to be shipmates with for the first time--for sampling the water at various depths. When we weren't doing anything else, we went out and made oceanographic stations. We'd make these nansen casts at the spots we were told to make them; we carried a couple of scientists on board.

Q: You did have scientists?

Admiral Waters: Yes. And we took plankton samples and that sort of thing. We also had monitoring scientists with Geiger counters; there was a crew of them. Well, you couldn't exactly call them scientists. They were a strange sort of collection of people. Many of them got their jobs from political connections.

Q: Adventurers.

Admiral Waters: Well, they wanted to see the thing. There were a bunch of nice guys, but they came from such a broad spectrum. Usually the senior one was a public health service doctor who knew what he was doing, and then you might have a man who ran a book shop in Azusa, California, and knew the local Congressman, and he was taught how to look at a Geiger counter. That was your crew of monitoring people. The main reason this operating squadron of destroyers were there during the first test was to be in what was called the radiological downwind patrol. When the bomb went off, we were, oh, some 12 or 15 miles outside of the atoll and on either side of the downwind sector so that once the mushroom cloud started blowing downwind, we had tracks under this downwind sector, where we would crisscross back and forth under it, taking Geiger counter readings of the fallout. And there actually wasn't any.

Q: This was a great surprise, wasn't it?

Admiral Waters: Yes, that there was as little as there was. It was practically indiscernible. We had a lot of funny things happen. Of course, no one really knew what was going to happen when you blew up an atom bomb. It had only been done twice before and then in anger. This was supposed to be a controlled experiment with a target array of ships inside of the Bikini Atoll.

Q: Speculation was that it might set off a chain reaction and blow up the universe.

Admiral Waters: The most interesting thing to observe was the growth in the size of the safety supplement to the operation order. Like all naval operations, we had an operation order, and it covered various things. The appendix having to do with safety started off with a little appendage to the operation order, maybe a quarter of an inch thick. Each day a different scientist would think of some new thing to worry about, and there would be an addition to this safety appendix. It was bigger than the operation order by the time the thing came off.

Q: Why?

O. D. Waters, Jr. #3 - 136

Admiral Waters: Because there was this degree of uncertainty. Nobody knew what was going to happen. For example, about a month before the thing, all of us who were going to be around the thing were issued a special kind of dark glasses, but we were warned that they might not be good enough and all that. These were the rather strange orders we got. Every ship, before the live bomb run was made, was supposed to go to general quarters and set maximum watertight integrity. You had to have all engines on the line, ready to go fast in any direction. Then you had to assemble your crew topside. This is very hard to do in a ship that's ready to make full power and is also completely battened down for battle, to get the crew out and then button up again. But we more or less did it. We were to keep track of the relative bearing of where the bomb was going to be, and we'd have the crew face away from that direction, shut their eyes, and cradle their eyes in their elbows just to give them additional protection with their arm across the face. No one was to look in the direction of the blast with the dark glasses. Well, we carried out all of these orders.

I had one young ensign who had signed up, as I had told you before, especially for this. He came to me and said, "Captain, I signed up just to come out here and see this thing, and I don't want to hide my eyes. I'd like to see it. May I have your permission to use the dark glasses?"

So I said, "Okay, go ahead. If you want to do it, fine." So he was on the wing of the bridge, and, of course, it was a very dramatic thing, because you had a loudspeaker system all around the ship tuned in to the bombardier's frequency in the dropping aircraft. He would say, "Ten minutes to go, live bomb run."

Q: A countdown.

Admiral Waters: Yes, a countdown thing. And they picked a guy who sort of had an undertaker's voice anyway.

Q: The voice of doom.

Admiral Waters: The voice of doom, yes. So it would say, "One minute to go, live bomb run." And then, "Bombs away!" and then nothing happened. Everyone was getting a little restless, and finally this guy out there, whose name was Koreopolis or something, said, "There she goes!"

I said, "I didn't hear anything."

He said, "There she is, Captain." So I looked at it, and there was a mushroom cloud coming up over the horizon, and about that time there was a little "poom" from the slight concussion you could feel, and that was it.* This

---

*See "Crossroads at Bikini" by Captain Thomas M. Daly, U.S. Navy, July 1986 Proceedings, pages 64-73, and "As I Recall . . . Crossroads: A Tin Can Perspective" by Rear Admiral Odale D. Waters, Jr., pages 72-74 of that same issue.

was very disappointing to everybody. It was a terrific anticlimax with all the preparation that was made. It was this little "poom" at the end. But we immediately got under way at high speed to charge over and get under the mushroom cloud and go back and forth with the other destroyers. We all had designated tracks to make.

On the bridges of those ships, you know, there are fuse boxes to control the various radars and things like that, the electrical circuits. They are little square things, and they are handy things to set things on, like a cup of coffee. The head monitor had set his Geiger counter on one of these things. Well, the fuse boxes heat up and get a little warm, and just as we were starting under the atom cloud, the head monitor said, "Captain! Captain! Do something! Go to general quarters! Do something! We're getting fallout!" His Geiger counter pointer had gone off the scale, but then somebody realized that all he'd done was heat the thing up. So we didn't pay any attention to him anymore. But, actually, we got no evidence of any discernible fallout.

So we all eventually came back into port, and there was some fun and interest going over and looking at how some of the ships in the target array were knocked around. Then, of course, we started getting ready for the next test, which was about a month later. That was the spectacular one, the one underwater in the middle of the lagoon. We were a lot closer to that one; that was the Baker Test. We were only about eight miles away, as I remember, and could actually see this huge plume of water come up and ships in the middle of it, throwing them all around. It was an awe-inspiring thing. Then we had a real job to do there, because as soon as they had boats that could go in and measure the radioactivity in the water, and as soon as it was anywhere at all near reasonable for us to go into the lagoon, the squadron of destroyers went in. We went in and anchored ourselves in a line fairly close to the center of the target array and started taking Geiger counter readings of the water.

Q: What was this reasonable time?

Admiral Waters: Oh, I think it was within about a couple of hours afterwards.

Q: It was deemed safe enough to go.

Admiral Waters: Yes, because they had drone boats in there and drone helicopters, and they decided it was going about the way they expected, so we went in. What we did was to take this data on the radioactivity in the water, and then this was radioed back to the flagship. They kept a plot,

O. D. Waters, Jr. #3 - 140

and they could see which way the currents were going. So they brought the laboratory ships and the ships that were necessary to do this part of the experiment in, and the support ships and the flagship, and anchored them in behind us. Bikini Lagoon is a pretty large lagoon, and they anchored in behind us. Then when our data indicated that some of this water was going over and getting around the big ships, they would shift them over to a different anchorage clear of the contaminated water. Then we would shift and interpose ourselves in between them and where the greatest hot spots were. Of course, in doing all this, we got our destroyers quite highly contaminated. We did this for, oh, several days.

Q: What precautions did the crew take against this contamination? Were you in special suits?

Admiral Waters: Oh, no, we weren't in special suits, but it was very calm in there, and the contamination was in the water.

Q: Not on deck?

Admiral Waters: The water wasn't splashed up on deck or anything. But it was funny. There again, people started worrying in degrees and in increasing amounts about this.

They apparently hadn't thought too much about what would happen to the destroyers. Nobody had given it too much consideration. Of course, we didn't worry about it if nobody else worried about it.

Q: It's something you can't see.

Admiral Waters: Yes. We were due to come back about the middle of August, I think. We had a commitment to go into the Navy yard. This whole squadron of ships had been built early in the war and had never had a really good Navy yard overhaul. Even my battle damage repair, they skipped a lot of things that should have been fixed for maintenance purposes. So this Navy yard overhaul was very important. They gave us a sort of a safety inspection and monitored us a little bit and thought, "Well, yes, you do have a little contamination, a few hot spots here and there."

Then we got under way and left with Butch Parker as commodore of the squadron.* By the time we got back to the West Coast, everyone was quite concerned about us. They had looked at the data and had seen that there were hot spots, particularly in our fire and flushing system of saltwater lines, where the contamination in the water had been filtered out into the barnacles. The growth inside of the lines had just stayed there and concentrated there.

---
*Captain Edward N. Parker, USN, Commander Destroyer Squadron Seven. The oral history of Parker, who retired as a vice admiral, is in the Naval Institute collection.

When we went into Hunters Point for our overhaul, the Laffey was supposed to be the first ship into dry dock.* By that time they decided they didn't want to put us in the regular graving dock, because we might contaminate that and they couldn't ever use it again. So they had a floating dry dock brought down from Mare Island, and we went into that.** The Laffey got about halfway out of the water in the floating dry dock in a sort of condition of just about stable equilibrium, but it was not as good as having the dry dock all the way pumped out and the ship firmly on the blocks.

This was a Friday afternoon, and we were ordered to stop everything right there and hold the ship until Monday morning when an admiral, who was an expert on the thing, could get there from Washington. You could see the degree of uncertainty.

Q: And experimentation.

Admiral Waters: Yes. Actually, we did have some contamination, but it could be cleaned out.

Q: How long does it take for that contamination to disappear?

---
*Hunters Point was a naval shipyard at San Francisco.
**Mare Island Naval Shipyard, Vallejo, California.

O. D. Waters, Jr. #3 - 143

Admiral Waters: It took several days. There was contamination in the barnacles and the growth on the bottom. They had to use special techniques to get that off and to clean out the condensers and the fire and flushing system of the ship. They used special chemicals and things. It took a little longer, but it worked all right, and we got it done. I'll never forget, though, right in the first day or so, we had a whole bevy of experts from the radiological laboratory conferring down on the quarterdeck and talking to each other. They were comparing samples, when I walked up to them and said, "Well, gentlemen, I see you're concerned about our radioactivity contamination of the ship. But, you know, we've made some tests of our own, and if you'll just wait a little while, I think we can give you a good answer."

They said, "What do you mean?"

I said, "Well, it's very simple. You know when we came back to the coast, we had been away for four months. We're home-ported in San Diego, and we were there for two nights. Two-thirds of the crew went ashore. Most of them were married, and I'm sure they conducted some tests of their own. If you'll just wait for nine months, I'll give you the radioactivity effect on the crew."

Q: Were you out there in advance? Did you have any part

in the evacuation of the natives from the island and the preparations for the bomb tests?

Admiral Waters: No. Somebody else did that. That was one of the few jobs that the destroyers didn't get. We did things like bringing VIPs up from Eniwetok or Kwajalein, the ones that didn't want to fly, and bringing special bits of equipment, stuff that had to be very carefully handled for the experiments. And, as I say, we did the oceanographic stations and such things as just usual police work like harbor entrance control ship for a day.

Q: Were you tied in with Fitzhugh Lee's operation?* He was the PR man for the whole project, wasn't he?

Admiral Waters: I believe he was, yes. I used to see him.

Q: If you were conveying VIPs and that kind of thing, you must have been in touch with him.

Admiral Waters: Yes.

Q: Well, the members of your crew who signed on for this particular operation, like this ensign--when it was over,

---

*Captain Fitzhugh Lee, USN. The oral history of Lee, who retired as a vice admiral, is in the Naval Institute collection.

did they seem satisfied that they'd seen something of significance?

Admiral Waters: Yes, they enjoyed it very much, particularly since the Baker Test was a lot more dramatic than the Able Test. I think they were quite happy about what they had seen.

Q: Why did they not go on and do the third one?

Admiral Waters: Well, I think it was a question of how much information they would really get from it in addition to what they had from the static test in the lagoon. Also, I think it was because it turned out to be a very much more difficult thing to do than at first was thought. It's pretty hard to do a test in deep water, where you can't moor the target ships in an array. See, the idea they had was you have the trade winds that blow steadily and more or less in one direction across the atoll there. On the leeward side, one idea was to put a deadman into the coral reef and have big mooring arrangements so that you could tether a long line of ships out.* Hopefully, they would stream out in the direction that the wind was blowing. I think they made a few tries at this, and the drag of the

---

*In nautical parlance, a "deadman" is a timber or some other object buried in ice or the ground to secure guys, tackles, or ship's lines.

cables and things like that were pretty hard to figure and it didn't work.

So the expense of it and the usefulness of the data, if the ships weren't in a known array or a known position, I think probably were controlling reasons for canceling it. That and the fact that the information gotten from the first test or the second test, and in combination with the first test from the air burst, probably gave them enough data to work on and to extrapolate and get the deep-water effect.

Q: Well, that was a fascinating experience. Was there any effort at security control with this whole operation, or was it very largely public property?

Admiral Waters: Well, yes, there was security control, but at the same time, it was of great world interest and thoroughly covered by the press. There were an awful lot of people from the press and radio out there. Of course, certain parts of it were controlled, such as the actual technicalities of the bomb and how it worked and the results of the underwater burst. All of that was highly classified, but it was pretty easy to protect. Of course, an effort was made--using the destroyers again--to make sure that the whole area around was clear of shipping. Of course, shipping was warned that this was going to take

O. D. Waters, Jr. #3 - 147

place, but we did patrols--mostly air--and this was for their own safety. Nobody really knew what was going to happen.

Q: Any foreign naval vessels about? Were they permitted?

Admiral Waters: No, I don't recall. The only foreign naval vessels were ones that were in the target array. You know, we had a captured Japanese battleship in the target array, and we had the famous Prinz Eugen, the beautiful German cruiser that was in the array.*

Q: Were there many foreign observers?

Admiral Waters: Yes, yes.

Q: Did you have any of those on your destroyer?

Admiral Waters: No. Fortunately, I wasn't saddled with those. I think that was probably Fitzhugh Lee's job.

Q: He had many headaches as a result too.

Admiral Waters: I think they had special ships for them. Of course, there were lots of ships involved in this thing,

---

*The Prinz Eugen was the German heavy cruiser that accompanied the ill-fated Bismarck in her attempt to break out into the Atlantic in May 1941.

all kinds of peculiar ships. One ship was a floating menagerie of animals, such as monkeys, used to test the radioactive effect. They were tethered around in various places on the ships.

Q: After that strenuous episode, very shortly thereafter, you got some shore duty, did you not?

Admiral Waters: Yes, I was relieved of command of the Laffey in October of that year, '46, and came back to Washington permanently for the first time since I had left in '43. I was ordered to the Naval Ordnance Laboratory as the senior technical liaison officer. At that time, the new Naval Ordnance Laboratory was being built at White Oak, Maryland, near Washington. The old laboratory was still operating in the gun factory in the Washington Navy Yard. That was where I first went to work for Captain Freddie Withington, who was commander of the Naval Ordnance Laboratory.*

Q: I am going to interview him.

Admiral Waters: Are you? The technical director was Dr. Ralph Bennett, who had been a captain in the Naval Reserve

---

*Captain Frederick S. Withington, USN. The oral history of Withington, who retired as a rear admiral, is in the Naval Institute collection.

during the war. By the time I got there, he had reverted to civilian clothes. He was also the technical director of the new laboratory. I was in that job from the fall of '46 until January of '50.

Q: What were your particular duties?

Admiral Waters: It was a full three years. It was rather unusual and a very pleasant experience for me. We tried a new philosophy, a new technique for a Navy technical laboratory. There had been a lot of criticism of the way the Navy had run development laboratories, because in the past they had put people in uniform in all of the directing jobs, from the commanding officer on down. The department heads were all uniformed officers, and this made it difficult to attract really good scientists who, in the first place, didn't like to take their orders from a military man who didn't know as much about their subjects as they did.

Secondly, under the Civil Service system, if the civilian was not the boss, you couldn't pay him as much. So we decided in the new Naval Ordnance Laboratory that the commander would be a naval officer. It turned out we had an admiral when we went to the new laboratory, and the sort of purely military housekeeping jobs--such as communications, security, and various administrative details—would be attended to by people in uniform. But the whole scientific job and work would be under the technical director of the laboratory who was Dr. Bennett, a civilian.

Q: There could be more continuity, too, couldn't there?

Admiral Waters: There would be more continuity and, besides, in matters of the actual end product of the laboratory, he was really considered to be sort of coequal with the commanding officer. Actually, a person can never be really coequal with the commanding officer, but he was responsible to the commanding officer for the technical output of the laboratory. All of the department heads—the head of research, the head of engineering, the head of the wind tunnel—were civilians who reported to the commanding officer, but through the technical director to the commanding officer. This created a requirement for some blue-suit input. It was recognized that you couldn't completely divorce this from the Navy if we were to produce products and things and weapons that the Navy needed.

Q: Sure. Some operational knowledge had to be incorporated.

Admiral Waters: Yes. So the office that I headed was set up, the technical liaison office, to provide this. But it was an unusual job, because, you see, we had no part in the administration of the actual development work. This was run by civilians, and we were just there as sort of advisers to them. It made it interesting, because first of all, you had to get the confidence of the scientists and engineers that you were working with. You had to convince them that you knew what you were talking about so that they would come to you with their problems. This was a lot of fun, and I think we worked it out pretty well. I think it's a good system, and it's still working there.

Q: It depends very heavily on the individuals, doesn't it?

Admiral Waters: Yes. You can't have a real militarist in the job who just has to give orders to people. In the job I had, there was nobody to give orders to except my secretary. But I found myself in a lot of interesting situations and made some very warm friendships amongst the people that were there then.

I think that the system has proved its worth, because the kind of people it attracted went on to head various other laboratories, either Navy or civilian or other federal government.

O. D. Waters, Jr. #3 - 152

Q: And this came at a particularly difficult time, didn't it, when scientists were in large measure deserting the military and going back into civilian laboratories?

Admiral Waters: That's right. That's right. So we really had to do something to attract some good ones, and I think we got some good ones this way. We had several who went on to other places. Dr. Bennett, incidentally, had a policy of never trying to hang on to somebody if he had a better job someplace else. He said we'd miss him at first, but it would do the laboratory good in the long run to have produced the man who is now running another laboratory.

Just as one example, one of the younger scientists who was there with me and was quite friendly was Dr. Paul Frye, who is now the director of Woods Hole.* This was a useful and close relationship to me in my five years as oceanographer.

Q: I'm sure.

Admiral Waters: We did get some peculiar requests from people. I think we did a lot of good convincing them that some of the things they wanted to do at sea in ships you could do in a bathtub or test tank, but you couldn't do them in the actual real world.

---
*Woods Hole Oceanographic Institution, located in Woods Hole, Massachusetts, was founded in 1930. It specializes in biology, chemistry, geology, geophysics, physical oceanography, and oceanographic engineering.

Q: This is a little bit the counterpart of the job that Admiral Willis Lee had in OpDevFor for a while before his death, when he brought the know-how of the operational man to the laboratory.*

Admiral Waters: Yes. That was really slightly different, in that you were conducting a very intensive and rapid development program into how to meet a specific problem. As you recall, the main reason for creating OpDevFor in the first place was to find an answer to the kamikaze. So what they did was to bring the operational people under Admiral Lee, who knew firsthand about the kamikaze and the problem it presented. He formed them up to work with qualified scientists to provide a solution for the thing.

Q: Admiral, tell me about some of those interesting situations you got into in this job.

Admiral Waters: There were some that were interesting. They were rather amusing, and there was no solution to them. For example, we had a man working on a mechanism to do with firing a mine. He had one of our experimental ships, which was really a minelayer. He had it in the

---

*In 1945 Vice Admiral Willis A. Lee, Jr., USN, was Commander Task Force 69, which was the forerunner of the Operational Development Force (OpDevFor).

Potomac River, and he wanted to test this device that he had on board, but the ship was not to move and couldn't be anchored and couldn't use its engines. These were the orders he gave to the skipper of the ship, which obviously put the skipper of the ship in a pretty impossible situation. It took a little explaining to convince the scientist that you couldn't have all of these three conditions obtaining at one time.

We had a group of anywhere from three to four officers there at a time. A lot of times they were augmented in the summer by officers going to postgraduate school in the various ordnance engineering branches. One of my student officers one summer was Admiral Osborn, who is now, you know, a very famous young nuclear type admiral.* Jim Osborn was there with me one summer. Anyway, we had these people, and we kept track of what each was doing. It was a small enough group that we sort of stuck our noses into each other's business so if one person was away, the other one could take over.

Having been in the mine business a great part of my career, and because NOL was the sort of center of mine design, that was my main project. Harry Hull had torpedoes and so forth.** In addition, you got thrown other jobs to

---
*Rear Admiral James B. Osborn, USN. While in the rank of commander in 1959, Osborn was first commanding officer of the blue crew of the USS George Washington (SSBN-598), the Navy's first ballistic missile submarine.
**Commander Harry Hull, USN, a Naval Academy classmate of Waters.

do, and I found myself in a very interesting one concerning the design of the fuze for a new atomic bomb, which was being in those early days undertaken out at Sandia Base in Albuquerque. I became the sort of project officer for it. Because of the security requirements, this required somebody in uniform. I had one of the early Q clearances, which was a very, very high security clearance at the time and required extra background investigation.

We had a group of very excellent people in fuze work there; they worked on the fuze for one of the new atomic bombs. This was a lot of fun because it was sort of cloak and dagger, and you had special cards to get into special places in Albuquerque, and I enjoyed that very much. I was trying to think of other examples.

One of the interesting things that we did while I was there was the development of the fuze for the ASP. You may recall Weapon A--Weapon Able--which was the first rocket-propelled antisubmarine weapon that was developed in high priority there. In '47, '48, or '49 they were working on it. We took a firing device that had been developed for a depth charge. Right at the end of World War II it was developed by Bell Laboratories. It was a magnetic device that would fire when the weapon got close to the target. The depth charge didn't necessarily have to hit the submarine. It would fire within a certain range of the submarine when it was affected by the submarine's magnetic field.

It was a very, very good firing device. Then the next step was to put this into something that could be fired out ahead to give the destroyer a greater range on the submarine. So they went to the rocket-propelled Weapon A or ASP. We were given the job of providing an influence fuze for it, a fuze that would go off in the vicinity of the target but not necessarily have to strike it. So we set about adapting the magnetic device that had been developed for the depth charge by Bell Laboratories and making it work in something that hit the water a great deal harder. It had to survive a much higher impact to forces and stresses.

This used a principle which was new at this time called a total field magnetometer. In other words, you used all three axes of the magnetic field, and so it was independent of tumbling or motion or anything like that. We tested this in a device down at Hiwassee Dam down in North Carolina, which is part of the TVA dam system down there.* The reason we went there was we had about a 250-dam with water behind it. You could fire a device into that depth of water and by simply putting a net on the bottom, recover the device afterwards. You could also put wires on it and bring back telemetered information as it went down through the water.

_____
*TVA--Tennessee Valley Authority.

Well, our first attempts with the influence fuze for Weapon A were absolute failures down there, and nobody could figure out why. So we then went over across the river from the old gun factory in Washington and set up an arm driven by an old turret-training mechanism. With that we could put this device in a holder on the end of the arm and whirl it around and around very fast. You could put it right in the plane of the earth's magnetic field, so that the field would have no effect on the device. Then you could measure what other things were affected and bring these measurements out on slip-rings from this whirling arm.

By bringing it up to very high speed and then stopping it suddenly, you controlled the rate at which you stopped it so that you could control the deceleration. It doesn't make any difference whether it's deceleration or acceleration. With acceleration, you get the same forces applied. So with this device, we measured the thing and we put the device in it and subjected it to these tests. We found out we were getting vibration--I forget whether it was a very high frequency or low frequency--out of this mechanism, which was causing it not to work.

Q: It was causing its own problem.

Admiral Waters: Yes, it was causing its own problems, and

this was a very simple thing to fix. So we got the fuze going before they really got our rocket to work very well. We were proud of ourselves. We had trouble with the rocket.

Q: That was an ingenious scheme for solving it.

Admiral Waters: Yes, it was the damndest thing you've ever seen. It was a great, long rotating timber arm with a weight on one end to counterbalance it and sort of a little capsule to put the device in. Then there were wires that ran down the arm to the center to slip-rings to come out to instruments. The thing was all very carefully canted so that it rotated right in the earth's magnetic field at that point over in Anacostia. Of course, we had protective mounts of earth that you hid down behind and a little bit of concrete poured around, because you couldn't tell when that thing was going to fly apart. The reason it was done there was that right across the river at the gun factory was land that we owned, and also we had this hydraulic turret-training device to furnish the power to whirl this thing around and stop it very suddenly, or less suddenly, as you wanted to control it.

Q: Was there any feed-in from the British at this point in time?

Admiral Waters: Yes, we still had very close relationships with the British, and actually at the Naval Ordnance Laboratory we had one of their senior scientists assigned there and we kept people over in Lee Park, I think it was called, the Admiralty Mine Development Laboratory. They had a Dr. Shaw over with us, and he liked it so much at the Naval Ordnance Laboratory that he retired and stayed on in this country and acted as a consultant for NOL. He's dead now, but he was getting along at that time. He had been all through the war.

Q: Did you have any association with work going on at Taylor Model Basin?*

Admiral Waters: No, not so much because it was a pretty good way to divide off the hydrodynamics of ship design from the work in weapons. Of course, there were certain things that had to be tested. A new torpedo shape, for instance, had to be tested at David Taylor. But as far as the main part of their work, которая was concerned with the hull designs of ships and that sort of thing, we didn't get into. That was their business, and it was easy to keep them divided.

NOL was very strong on work in explosives and in

---

*The David Taylor Model Basin in Carederock, Maryland, is used for testing model hull designs in a towing tank.

O. D. Waters, Jr. #3 - 160

research work in developing new explosives. Some of the new plastic explosives were developed there, and actually the present technical director at NOL, Greg Hartman, was the chief of the Explosives Research Division when I was there as a commander.

Of course, one of the most spectacular things at the new Naval Ordnance Laboratory at White Oak was the ballistic wind tunnel that was set up there. You may recall that the Germans were able to make the advances they did in jet aircraft and their missiles and the V bombs and that sort of thing.*

Q: At Peenemunde.

Admiral Waters: Yes, and one of the reasons for it was their wind tunnel arrangement. Instead of forcing the wind through with fans, they built a huge steel sphere and evacuated it to as close to a vacuum as they could get it. Then, by opening a valve, they would let the rushing air stream in through a working throat, a nozzle, where they did the experiments. Of course, unless you could pump real fast, it wouldn't last very long, but you could get a very, very high velocity of air flow in that way.

Right after the war ended in Europe, the group that

---

*During World War II the Germans used unmanned V-1 and V-2 rockets to cross the English Channel and deliver explosives on targets in England.

went over from this country managed to get one of these devices intact--the whole thing, the sphere and everything. It was sent back to this country and it was decided to install it at the new Naval Ordnance Laboratory in White Oak. After they got it back with these pieces all marked, it had to be put back together. It was found that it was cheaper to start from scratch in this country and to use our own techniques, using that principle.

Q: Using the idea of it.

Admiral Waters: But not using their actual equipment. We didn't have the techniques to do it; we didn't use those techniques the same way they did. So that was the beginning of the ballistic wind tunnel, using that principle. It's still quite an extensive facility there.

Q: Was it also adopted by the Bureau of Standards? They've long had a wind tunnel of sorts.

Admiral Waters: I don't know whether they used one of this type or not. Several others--the Air Force, I'm sure, and NASA--now have wind tunnels of this type.* But this was the first one. And, of course, it's obvious that if you can install more powerful pumps, you can not only pump the

---
*NASA--National Aeronautics and Space Administration.

vacuum down, but you can hold it at a certain level so that you can continuously have air flowing into this big place. That was what they did. At first it was a very small size throat cross-section because of the power involved in pumping the thing down. As you got more power applied to it, you could get it bigger and bigger, and therefore have the larger scale models.

Q: Was there anything learned from the mines the Japanese had developed that was useful to us in this postwar period?

Admiral Waters: Not very much as far as the Japanese were concerned. There was a great deal learned from the Germans, particularly, and the British, of course.

Q: We knew that all the time, though, didn't we?

Admiral Waters: Yes. And a great deal from the Germans. The Japanese had relatively simple mines, but the best lesson we learned from the Japanese was not to complicate things and fix them so they'd go off when you wanted them to. The Japanese certainly did that; they must have blown up a lot of their own people in the process of manufacturing and storing and handling, because they had very few safety precautions. But their mines were very effective once they got them where they wanted to use them. They had plenty of explosive in them and a very reliable detonating system.

One interesting thing during that period was that we had probably assembled at the Naval Ordnance Laboratory more scientists and engineers who knew about the mine business than at any other time in history. Because a lot of them during the war had worn uniforms and had gone out as special advisers to various commanders in the field in the Pacific to take care of the mines and the mine campaign. I'm thinking especially of Operation Starvation that was run in the Western Pacific by the Air Force and was so successful.* A lot of people believe that because this mining campaign against the Japanese, using NOL-manufactured mines laid from aircraft, was so successful that the dropping of the atom bomb was unnecessary. That's a moot point that's still being argued. But it was there that Curtis LeMay made a great contribution to his fame, because he was in command of a large part of that Operation Starvation.**

But, anyway, as I started to say, we had this assembling of people. We got them all together and sat down and said, "Well, now, knowing all that everyone here

---
*Mines were sown in Japanese waters by Army Air Forces B-29 bombers.
**Major General Curtis E. LeMay, USA, commanded the XXI Bomber Command with headquarters on Guam. He was later Chief of Staff of the Air Force.

in this group knows about mining and the mine campaign and our experience in World War II, how should we now design mines for the United States Navy? What changes should we make? What should we try to do?" We came up with what I always thought was a very fine paper. I was very proud to have been a member of this group, because at that time--that was about 1949, as I remember it, when we finished up on that work--we recommended what we called a long-term mine development program. This was supposed to take about ten years.

The principal philosophy everyone there agreed on was that in World War II there had been some entirely new devices used, such as acoustic mines and magnetic mines, pressure mines, and combinations of mines, which had never been actually used successfully in combat before. These caused a tremendous reaction in trying to counter them, out of all proportion to what it cost to use them. We felt that we had looked into all other characteristics that we could think of that could be used to trigger a mine, and that there wasn't much possibility of anything new. We didn't want to completely rule it out; we recommended that various things be investigated.

But we felt that the way to go in the future was to take what we now had and refine it in development and to develop mines that would be modular mines. That is, there would be a fixed piece of ammunition, and the device that would cause it to explode would be, say, three little black boxes of the kinds that you could put in there in the field. This would be easy to do, just to plug in and plug out, that kind of arrangement. You could mix up the mine so that, say, it required an acoustic look from the ship first and then a magnetic look and then an acoustic look. You could keep varying this thing statistically so that you would always be a lap or so ahead of the mine countermeasures man.

That was what we decided to do at that time, and then, of course, we came upon the hard times of '49 and '50 of cutting back and things got slowed down.* Then when things started up again, we were in the Korean War, and there were things that were much more important than developing mines, because we really didn't need to use mines out there. So the whole thing got stretched out and only about five or six years ago--maybe seven or eight--the first of the new family of mines came on the scene. They are the mines that are now relatively new, and this is 20-some years later. So it took about twice as long as we expected, but not because we couldn't have done it.

Q: Admiral, when we went off tape, I was asking how many sessions you had as a composite group before you were able to develop the paper and the long-range plan for the mines.

---
*Louis A. Johnson, Secretary of Defense, 1949-50, instituted a vigorous cost-cutting program during his tenure.

Admiral Waters: I've forgotten exactly. It wasn't one of these long things that meets a year or so and comes up with a piece of paper that everyone has forgotten. I think it extended over a couple or three months with meetings once or twice a week or sometimes more often. But it was a rather intensive sort of brainstorming discussion. We came up with what was called the long-range mine plan, and we had a secondary short-range plan of what to do in the interim. But it was very valid because it has been followed religiously for over 20 years now since it was first started. I still think it was the right idea. I still think it is just as valid today as it was then.

Q: You said that in the Korean conflict, mines were not required, yet the Koreans used them, did they not?

Admiral Waters: The Koreans and the Chinese. They were mostly Chinese supplied, and were tremendously effective against us.

Q: Were they of Chinese design, or were they Russian?

Admiral Waters: There were some that could be traced back to the Russians, but they were mostly plain old circa

O. D. Waters, Jr. #3 - 167

1900-type mines, going back to the Russo-Chinese War, moored mines with chemical horns on them that you actually had to hit. But they had lots of them and they were very reliable and they worked. You know, they used them most effectively at Wonsan Harbor, and they actually held up a landing there for about a week.* We lost minesweepers trying to sweep them, because the density of them was so great. They were just laid in a random pattern--not in fields--and lots of them. We just couldn't get them out of there and couldn't get them swept well enough to risk bringing the ships in. The Marines were very much embarrassed at Wonsan, because this was the Marines we were landing there to take it while the Army moved up overland, and the Army got there first.** I don't know whether it's true or not, but the story is that Bob Hope was holding an entertainment on the beach when the Marines landed.***

A little bit later in the Korean War I was sent out by the Operational Development Force. I sent back something that is always quoted, attributed to various people. It comes back to haunt me, but I put in a report that I thought it was worth noting that the Communists in the Korean War were using a weapon that had been developed

---
*Minesweepers operated in the port of Wonsan, North Korea, from 10 October through 25 October 1950 to clear lanes in preparation for a landing.
**The First Marine Division landed unopposed at Wonsan on 26 October 1950.
***Bob Hope is a comedian who has made dozens of overseas trips during his career to entertain U.S. servicemen.

before the turn of the 20th century. As laying craft, they used junks and sampans that had been designed before the birth of Christ and were able to stop the 20th century's most powerful Navy cold in its tracks for two weeks. And it was true. It happened. We just weren't able to cope with that high a concentration of mines.

Q: You said they had so many of them. They weren't leftovers, then. They must have been manufacturing them.

Admiral Waters: They were furnished, I suppose, from the Russians. It's hard to tell exactly where they came from, but they were either Russian or Chinese Communists. And they could have been old. They could have been around in a magazine for a long time. Those things age pretty well.

Q: Why were we not able to use mines in that conflict? There was a certain amount of coast-wise shipping, was there not, in sampans?

Admiral Waters: Yes, but it's very hard to mine against sampans because their draft is so shallow. Of course, we wanted to use the waters ourselves, and you don't want to foul up your own nest. If you put them down, you have to worry about where they are. As sure as you put a mine field down, somebody is going to make a mistake and go into it. Because the sampans and junks are such shallow-draft things, it's pretty hard to mine against them. Actually, at that same time, we did work on the development of an anti-junk mine, which turned out to be pretty good and is available if you want to mine against junks.

O. D. Waters, Jr. #4 - 170

Interview Number 4 with
Rear Admiral Odale D. Waters, Jr., U.S. Navy (Retired)

Place: Admiral Waters's home in Alexandria, Virginia

Date: Friday, 4 June 1971

Interviewer: John T. Mason, Jr.

Q: It's good to see you again today, Admiral. Last time you concluded with your period of service at the Naval Ordnance Laboratory. In January of 1950 you began a course of study at the Armed Forces Staff College in Norfolk. Would you tell me in thumbnail fashion something about this college. I mean, what is the intention? What does a graduate achieve?

Admiral Waters: Well, I went down there in January of '50 and started into the seventh class that had been held at the Armed Forces Staff College, in February. The school was set up as a sort of a combined school for all services, to train them in operating together in combined and joint staffs. We had Army, Navy, Air Force, and Marine students, mostly in the rank of commander, lieutenant colonel, some captains, and a few colonels.

They had two classes a year; the course was for about six months. It was a very interesting course, particularly from the standpoint of meeting and getting to know your contemporaries in the other services. I think this was really one of the great benefits of the course. That I knew a lot of these people served me in later years when I bumped into them in professional contacts.

Q: I suppose it's anticipated that the men who go there will go on into positions of influence and power in their respective services.

Admiral Waters: Yes. And they always tried to maintain a level of equality with the other colleges: the Naval War College, the National War College, and the other service colleges. This was mostly talk. It was pretty hard to do, because, in the first place, it was only a half-a-year course, and the others were for a full year.

Q: Yes.

Admiral Waters: They tried to maintain that stature, and they did, in effect, because they had some pretty good people running the place. When I was there, I was particularly fortunate, because Vice Admiral Jimmy Hall of the Navy was the commandant.* The commandant shifted between the Army, Navy, and the Air Force. It was a tremendous experience to go to a school run by Admiral Hall, because he probably had more combat experience as a

---
*Vice Admiral John L. Hall, USN.

flag officer, actual combat experience, than anyone else in our country during World War II. You know, he commanded landings both in the European theater and in the Pacific theater.

Q: Which was rather unusual.

Admiral Waters: Yes. So he was really a fighting admiral. And since the combined operations that we studied gravitated towards amphibious operations, he was the ideal sort of person to have in command of the school.

Q: Did service personnel comprise the teaching staff? Did you have outside people?

Admiral Waters: No, they had service personnel on the teaching staff. We had a few civilians, but they were mostly Army, Navy, Air Force, or Marine officers.

Q: Because the studies were largely technical?

Admiral Waters: Yes. And we divided up into groups and studied various fictitious campaigns. We would shift around, and each one would have different jobs and plan the campaigns and sort of war-game them.

O. D. Waters, Jr. #4 - 173

Q: Was there an emphasis on amphibious operations?

Admiral Waters: Yes, amphibious and airborne, because this brought in all the different services. One of the interesting things at the course--it started off with a few weeks of orientation in which we were divided into groups equally balanced among the services. Right at the beginning the course was designed to give each student an understanding of not only his own service, but the other services that he was dealing with. For example, the Navy students within the group spent a week orienting the other service people as to the functions and missions of the Navy and how it carried them out.

Q: That sounds very practical because there are so many false assumptions.

Admiral Waters: The unusual thing in my particular group was that we had a commander aviator whose experience had been entirely in patrol plane operations, and he had never served in a carrier. And our Air Force officer had been a naval aviator and had gone into the Flying Tigers in World War II.* When he had an opportunity to transfer back

---

*The nickname for the American Volunteer Group (later the 14th Air Force), so-called because the volunteers painted shark's teeth on the noses of their planes. Trained by retired U.S. Army officer Claire L. Chennault, they entered combat against the Japanese on 20 December 1941.

into the U.S. forces, he chose the Air Force. The funny thing was, though, that we had an Air Force lieutenant colonel who did most of the briefings on carrier operations because he was better founded in it than our naval officer.

Q: What were some of the immediate benefits that you reaped from this course of study?

Admiral Waters: Well, of course, I think you always get a tremendous benefit just by being sent to a service school, where there is a list of required reading and a list of optional reading. You have time to read all of the books that are particularly oriented towards professional subjects--biographies and things like that--that you always intend to read but never seem to have enough time for. That was one of the great benefits. Aside from the things you learn from the subject matter of the course, I think there was another tremendous benefit that's really hard to evaluate--knowing your contemporaries in the other services. I had several occasions after that when I had to officially call on these men. I remember one time I had to call on an Army general in a U.S. command in Paris. I went in to see the general, and it turned out his chief of staff was a former classmate of mine at Norfolk. This made the meeting that much easier.

Q: The door swung open.

Admiral Waters: The door swung more widely open.

Q: I don't imagine you had much difficulty in applying yourself to books and to focusing in that direction at the school.

Admiral Waters: No, it was really a pleasant interlude; I enjoyed it.

Q: Did some men find this difficult, men whose careers had been entirely action careers?

Admiral Waters: Not so much, because there really wasn't that much stress on the actual study. You were required to do the reading, but there really were no examinations as such and no marks. You really performed by working on the joint staffs together on staff problems. The work was divided up so that you could see who the individuals were who really were good and knew what they were doing, as distinguished from the average student. But there was no distinction made in a marking system of any kind.

Q: In the six-month term, how many men were involved in a class?

Admiral Waters: I've forgotten now, but it seems to me it was somewhere around in the neighborhood of 200, I would say.

Q: How did you get the appointment? Was it something you applied for?

Admiral Waters: You applied for it in your officer's data card. You could say you were interested in going to any of the colleges, but actually you are screened for any of the service college training. My name came up on the list, and I went.

Q: Well, that was an interesting interlude. You went on from there as ordnance and gunnery officer in the staff of the Commander of Operational Development Force.

Admiral Waters: Yes, I barely had to move more than a few hundred yards, because the headquarters of what was then called the Operational Development Force was also in Norfolk. It's now the Operational Test and Evaluation Force.*

---

*The command was renamed in May 1959.

Q: But that doesn't indicate any change in directions.

Admiral Waters: It's really a more exact title now, because the word "development" was often confused with research and development, with developing technical things and equipment. Whereas the "development" in the title applied to tactics, really, for the use of new weapons. That's why it was called Operational Development Force. It really was a test and evaluation force back then also. The main work was to give an operational test to new weapons as they were brought out by the technical establishment.

Q: So they truly applied for the operating fleet.

Admiral Waters: In these operational evaluations we were saying that a certain weapon or weapon system had been evaluated and was accepted for service use. Also, because of the facilities we had and the way we worked, the staff did technical evaluations for the people developing weapons as they came along. Before they were ready for operational development, we did engineering evaluation of them too.

Q: Sort of anticipating.

Admiral Waters: In other words, helping the development

O. D. Waters, Jr. #4 - 178

agency, whether it be a Navy laboratory or an industrial contractor, to test his hardware when he had a piece ready to go. It was a very interesting tour of duty.

Q: What were some of the things you were working with at that point?

Admiral Waters: Well, I was called the ordnance and gunnery officer, and at that time I had all of the fire control systems, guns, and weapons--anything that makes a bang, including mine warfare and missiles. At the time that I was there, the Terrier missile was just being developed, and I set up in my department a missile division which came under me.* After I left, this had gotten so big that the missile division was split off from the ordnance and gunnery department. A separate missile division was established just to evaluate missiles of all kinds.

We had the old battleship Wyoming first and then after her the Mississippi as a sort of a test platform.** We had several destroyers that were specially configured to test weapons, equipments, and systems of all kinds.

I think the most interesting job I had while I was there, which I got shortly after I arrived, was the job of

---
*The Terrier was a surface-to-air missile that had a long service life in the fleet.
**The USS Mississippi (AG-128) successfully test-fired a Terrier missile on 28 January 1953 off Cape Cod, Massachusetts. She was orginally a battleship, later converted for use as an ordnance test ship.

trying to find out how one would stop a huge fleet of Chinese junks if they should try to invade Nationalist China from the mainland. The reason for this was that at that time we had some pretty good intelligence reports that the Red Chinese were gathering a large force of junks on the mainland, and that there was the likelihood that they might try to attempt an invasion and take over Chiang Kai-shek's forces on Formosa.* So the problem given us on a very high priority was to determine how one would stop this sort of thing--given the weapons and ships and forces in the then-existing Seventh Fleet. It was a very interesting job.

It was high priority, so I got all of the resources that I needed without too much trouble. I also got a tremendous amount of free advice, most of it bad, because it's an interesting problem, and it's one that everyone has a bright idea about. There were many suggestions. This suggestion was made many times, for example, that if you have a fleet of junks, each one filled with Chinese soldiers and maybe mortars, and a couple of thousand of them descend on you, why not spread oil on the water and set it on fire and burn up the whole fleet? Well, lots of people thought of that one, and it doesn't work. We even

---

*Chiang Kai-shek was President of Nationalist China from 1950 until his death in 1975. The government began existence on the island of Formosa, now Taiwan, following expulsion from the mainland in 1949 by the Communists.

tried it, because we had to show people that it wouldn't work. In the first place, it's hard to get an oil film on the water to burn. If you get it thick enough, it won't cover much area.

Q: It has to be pretty placid water, too, doesn't it?

Admiral Waters: Yes, it has to be very smooth. But if you finally do get a patch of oil to burn on the water and run a junk through it, you'll find that a junk is usually a fairly old vessel and has been around a long time.

Q: It's made of teak wood, isn't it?

Admiral Waters: Yes, teak wood. They absorb a lot of water. They have a lot of absorbed moisture in the wood, and they just steam merrily through any burning oil and hardly even get singed. So that one was, of course, crossed off, but it was a sort of a fun project.

Q: And this was before the Formosa Doctrine was promulgated in the Senate?*

---

*Following the outbreak of the Korean War in 1950, the U.S. Seventh Fleet was interposed between Formosa and the mainland to protect it from Communist attack. The formal agreement, concluded in 1955, committed American money and military to protect Formosa and the Pescadores.

Admiral Waters: Yes.

Q: We weren't committed at that point. Did you derive any lessons from the retreat from Dunkirk?*

Admiral Waters: No, that wasn't the same kind of a problem. There, you were trying to get a lot of people off the beach to save them from being captured by the Germans. They just did it by hauling people out in all kinds of peculiar craft. A tremendous amount of good seamanship got most of those people off.

Q: That was innovative, and it was organized presumably.

Admiral Waters: Well, at Dunkirk the mission was to rescue people off of a beach. Here it was a mission of trying to stop people who were trying to come from the mainland to attack you. You could approach it either by trying to destroy the craft they were in, the junks and sampans, or you could do it by destroying the people in the boats, killing enough of them or wounding enough of them to put them out of commission so they wouldn't be a fighting force. We used a combination of these techniques with the weapons that we had as an answer to the question.

---

*In May 1940, with the fall of France imminent, the British Expeditionary Force was evacuated from Dunkirk, France, and returned to England so its soldiers wouldn't be captured.

O. D. Waters, Jr. #4 - 182

The rather funny epilogue to this is that the answer we gave was a pretty straightforward one about how to use the various ammunition most effectively and that none of these kooky ideas would work. One of the ideas was to blow the junks out of the water with 5-inch ammunition of the proper type so that it would go off when it hit a junk and not just put a hole through it and explode on the other side. The other was to use ammunition set to cause fragments and create casualties in the exposed people on deck.

One of my big problems in running the project in Norfolk was that you needed a junk to work with, and it's rather difficult finding a junk around the Virginia seaboard anyplace.

Q: In a museum somewhere.

Admiral Waters: The closest approximation to a junk we could find was a small craft called an APc that had been used fairly extensively in World War II. It was a small wooden cargo carrier with diesel engines and roughly approximated the size of a big junk and about the weight. They were all laid up. We got one out of mothballs and got permission to destroy it. In order to do this--I'll never forget--we had to have President Truman's signature on a piece of paper, but we finally got through that part of the

O. D. Waters, Jr. #4 - 183

procedure, and we actually tested out our procedures on this wooden craft.*

That was the basis for our final report. Well, apparently there were some people in the Navy Department who thought that perhaps this thing wasn't close enough to a junk, and maybe we didn't know what we were talking about.

About a year later I was sent over to Korea by ComOpDevFor. He usually kept one of his department heads over in Korea, just to keep tabs on what was going on and what was really needed to be pushed back at OpDevFor to assist them in fighting the Korean War. By that time the Korean War had reached the point where we had captured quite a few Chinese junks over in Korea. I got over there just in time to witness a test that was done by the forces over there using these actual captured junks.

Q: And the techniques that you people had developed in Norfolk.

Admiral Waters: Yes. Well, they tried those out. They repeated a lot of new ideas and some of the same wacky ideas. Just as we had, they found out that these things didn't work. This was under Admiral Bat Cruise, who was given an LSD full of junks and all the planes and ships and

---
*Harry S Truman was President of the United States from 1945 to 1953.

different gun types and things that he needed.* It was done off of Tokyo in, I think, Sagami Wan. I went out on the ship with him and observed these tests, and they came to exactly the same conclusions that we had. So our amateur junk experiment back in Norfolk the year before was proven to be correct.

Q: And you personally were fairly optimistic about the techniques you developed there?

Admiral Waters: Yes. Well, we felt we had done a rather thorough job, and I was perfectly willing to change my mind if somebody could think of a better way of doing it. It was still open. But it turned out that you really had to fire slowly and hit them, and that you couldn't depend really even on missiles from aircraft hitting them. Aircraft were very effective using their machine guns, such as 20-millimeter, and this was a real good way to handle them. But a junk's too small a target for an aircraft firing a missile at them. It's too easy for a missile to not quite get there. Even a near miss on a junk doesn't do much good. The junk is such a well-built, sturdy, wooden craft, and it has so much buoyancy, that a missile going off right alongside it in the water just makes it move over

---

*Rear Admiral Edgar A. Cruise, USN. LSD--dock landing ship.

a few feet, and it keeps on going.

Q: In such a contemplated invasion with lots and lots of junks, I mean, how far distant from each other would they have been employed?

Admiral Waters: That was one of the first things that came to mind. But remember, the problem we were given was how to control these things with the weapons then available in the Seventh Fleet. There wasn't any mine designed to be effective against a small wooden craft like a junk. What we did do at that time was to recommend very strongly that such a development be made, and this was backed up by the people in Korea, particularly Rear Admiral Arleigh Burke, who was then over there.* Such a mine was developed.

Q: Did you anticipate using the Taiwanese Navy in offsetting this operation?

Admiral Waters: No. At that particular point in time they weren't very effective. They weren't enough to count on. They didn't have very much.

---

*Rear Admiral Arleigh A. Burke, USN (Ret.). At the outbreak of the Korean War, he was ordered to the post of Deputy Chief of Staff to Commander Naval Forces Far East. His oral history is in the Naval Institute's collection. Burke became Chief of Naval Operations in 1955.

O. D. Waters, Jr. #4 - 186

Q: Well, that was an interesting project. What else did you do?

Admiral Waters: Well, the general things. We tested all sorts of peculiar devices to try to sweep pressure mines and most anything that came along--new fire control systems, new guns. As I said, the most interesting thing we did during my time was to form the new missile division and to take the old battleship Mississippi and turn her into a missile-firing ship. She was our first missile-firing ship.

Q: At that point in time, the beginning of the decade of the Fifties, were there a great many things coming off the drawing boards?

Admiral Waters: Of course, there was a slowdown in '49, you know, when we cut back. We had to cut back in the Navy. That occurred just before I left NOL and went down to the Armed Forces Staff College. It affected me, because just before I went to the staff college, I was slated to go there and then to get command of a division of destroyers from Norfolk. With the cutback in the Navy and the decommissioning of ships, I suddenly found myself too junior to command a division of destroyers, and so they said, "What other job would you like?"

O. D. Waters, Jr. #4 - 187

I said, "Well, since I'm going to be in Norfolk, I would like one in Norfolk." That's how I ended up in the Operational Development Force, rather than an actual operating job at sea.

Q: So it was almost an accident. And I was thinking in my own mind how qualified you were for this particular job with your immediate past experiences. They showed great wisdom in putting you in that.

Admiral Waters: Well, it was a good job and, actually, there was certainly quite a bit of screening for it. I had preferred, as most people do, I think, the job of being a division commander. That's a great job. When I first talked to the detail people, it was available. Then it was cut off. When I had been in OpDevFor about two or three months and was just getting my feet on the ground, I got a call from the detail officer saying, "You can now have your destroyer division. Which ocean do you want to go to?" Of course, the Korean War had been started, and all of the armed forces were being built back up. The whole trend had been reversed. I think I was right in the middle of that junk business then, and I didn't quite have the nerve to go up and tell Admiral Curts that I had been on his staff for two months and wanted to leave, so I missed having my division.*

---
*Rear Admiral Maurice E. Curts, USN, Commander Operational Development Force, October 1948 to October 1950.

Q: Is that the same Curts that was with Nimitz?

Admiral Waters: Admiral Germany Curts. Germany was his nickname, and he was a great man. We had him first, and then he was succeeded by Admiral Entwistle, called Louie by his contemporaries, Louie Entwistle.*

Q: Now, is there something else?

Admiral Waters: I think that's about all we can milk out of that.

Q: This was a successful application of the whole idea of OpDevFor, was it not? It continued to justify its being.

Admiral Waters: Oh, yes, it has. It was a great staff to work on, because we had a philosophy which I'm sure was right--that the staff should not be any larger than was absolutely necessary, but it should be of very high quality. That is, high quality in that the people concerned with doing these tests and evaluations should be as expert in their field as you could get ahold of, because it didn't do you any good to test equipment if the people testing it didn't know what they were doing. So for the people assigned to the staff, we were a great source of

---

*Rear Admiral Frederick I. Entwistle, USN, Commander Operational Development Force, October 1950-February 1954.

trouble to the Bureau of Personnel. We were very choosy about the people they sent us.

Q: Well, you were a kind of rare breed, were you not?

Admiral Waters: We said, "Look, we're experts, and if you don't send us experts, don't send anybody, because it'll just be a waste of time." This policy prevailed all the time I was there. The chief of staff usually worked very hard at this, backed up by the department heads. But I can recall that when I was there as the gunnery officer, I had seven very brilliant ordnance PGs working for me.* It was a nice spot to be in; I had tremendous talent. Three that I can think of right offhand have been flag officers following me. Ray Peet is now the commander of the First Fleet; he's a three-star admiral.** Scotty Goodfellow has the PG school.*** And Ben Pickett has just retired.**** There are probably some more in that group, but I can't recall offhand.

Q: Well, you were rare in that you were in possession of real technical knowledge, but you also had command experience at sea, did you not?

---

*PGs--postgraduates.
**Vice Admiral Raymond E. Peet, USN. Following his later retirement as a vice admiral, Peet contributed his oral history to the Naval Institute.
***Rear Admiral Alexander Scott Goodfellow, USN.
****Rear Admiral Ben B. Pickett, USN (Ret.).

Admiral Waters: Oh, yes. Yes. That was very much a requirement, because we were the people that determined whether these things were acceptable at sea. So you had to have people with sea experience. Of course, I've just been talking about one department, the ordnance and gunnery department. There, of course, were others. We had an air department, for example, which was a very big thing. While I was there, the comparable department head, the air officer, was John Hyland, who has just retired as a four-star admiral.* Another very important part of OpDevFor was the antisubmarine department, where we had actually a test facility, which still exists down in Key West.

Q: That was a very fortunate time, too, from the point of view of OpDevFor, was it not? A war was still going on, and you could test some of your things in actual combat.

Admiral Waters: You couldn't do a real operational test there, because you had to have controlled conditions for that, but it certainly helped you to find out whether your findings were really valid or not. It gave you more confidence if you said something was good and it went to Korea and was used and was good. It just backed up your own confidence and the capability of your team to do these things.

---
*Admiral John J. Hyland, USN (Ret.), whose two-volume oral history is in the Naval Institute's collection. Hyland discusses his OpDevFor tour in his oral history.

After the Korean War got going, Admiral Entwistle started a policy that I mentioned before of keeping one of the department heads over there all the time. We sort of relieved each other, like a two- or three-month period of temporary duty. As I remember it, John Hyland, the air officer, went first, and when he came back, I went over.

I had a great time. It was an unusual assignment. I checked into Tokyo with Admiral Turner Joy and told him what I was up to.* He gave me sort of a carte blanche to look at anything I wanted to that was going on in Japan and Korea. He sent me down to Sasebo with a message to Admiral Smith down there that he wanted him to see that I got wherever I wanted to go.** The only proviso that Admiral Joy had was, "After you go around and see things and write your report for your admiral, bring it in here and show it to me. I'd like to see it." Which I did.

At that time, Admiral Burke was sort of an assistant to Admiral Joy. If you remember, at that particular point he was a rather junior rear admiral, and I think his official business was being commander of a cruiser division. But they had grabbed him off of his flagship and stuck him in the headquarters in Tokyo, and he was really sort of helping Admiral Joy mastermind the Korean War.

From talking to the operational commanders, I had some quite detailed discussions in my report on what I thought

---
*Vice Admiral C. Turner Joy, USN, Commander U.S. Naval Forces Far East.
**Rear Admiral Allan E. Smith, USN.

were things that needed to be pushed back home to help them. One of the things I recall was that anti-junk mine you were talking about. He strongly backed me on that.

Another interesting thing comes to mind that we discussed: the fact that this particular war was an unusual one, so we needed something smaller than destroyers to work inshore--the old gunboat idea. It appeared at that time that if we were lucky, we would be faced with nothing greater than this sort of a small or a limited war. This, of course, proved to be the case in Vietnam later. That being the case, it was a good idea for the U.S. Navy to start looking into building inshore types of vessels, gunboat-type ships. There was a strong need for them in fighting insurrections and that sort of thing wherever it might happen in a war that the Navy got involved in. So that recommendation was made. Of course, it took a little time, but we ended up with a great big gunboat Navy in Vietnam.

Q: There was the obvious application, so then we got busy.

Admiral Waters: In Korea, it was a little bit different in that we were having to use rather large, expensive destroyers on what were then called fly-catcher duties. They were controlling the traffic up and down the coast at night when the enemy were resupplying themselves at sea.

The craft you were controlling were, of course, junks--ships of that size, a light draft. It was rather dangerous for destroyers to go into those shallow waters and try to control them. Obviously, what you needed was something smaller.

Q: At the same time, didn't the destroyers prove their worth in terms of shore bombardment, bombardment of the railroad lines that were near to the shore and that kind of thing?

Admiral Waters: Oh, yes, yes, very much so.

Q: Perhaps a smaller craft would not have been capable of that.

Admiral Waters: No, no, no. Smaller craft couldn't do it. Our idea was that the destroyers were very valuable at that sort of thing, and they should stay outside in the deeper water, where their guns could be used effectively on the shore bombardment. One final thing on that temporary tour over there in Korea was that I thought it was rather interesting that I arrived back in Tokyo on my return on the day that President Truman fired General MacArthur, which was quite a day to be in Tokyo.* Everything was

---
*General of the Army Douglas MacArthur was Commander in Chief United Nations Command. President Truman relieved MacArthur from the post in April 1951 for perceived insubordination and differences over Korean War strategy.

sort of in a state of shock there.

Q: He had achieved a sort of semi-divine state as far as the Japanese were concerned.

Admiral Waters: Yes. The city was quiet, and nobody was saying very much. It surprised me that having arrived on that particular day and reporting in at the naval headquarters to see Admiral Joy, I had no expectation that I would get to see Admiral Joy that day, but I did. He invited me in, and I had a long talk with him, not only about my report, but, of course, he was very full of the whole thing.

Q: What was his reaction?

Admiral Waters: His reaction was one of very great loyalty to MacArthur and a feeling that regardless of what MacArthur had done, that MacArthur had done his job. He was loyal to him and felt that it was a mistake to bring politics into military matters. Of course, that's a very argumentative question. I've read a great deal on it, but I think it's typical of a fine man like Admiral Joy that he would be loyal to his commander under the circumstances.

Q: Did that seem to be the prevailing point of view among

military people out there?

Admiral Waters: It seemed to be amongst them there in the headquarters. Of course, subsequently there have been many accounts of it written and many sides. You can get an entirely different idea of the whole thing from reading Dean Acheson's memoirs, who was decidedly in the other camp and a great backer of Truman.*

Q: Yes, it depends on where you sat at the time.

Admiral Waters: Yes, on your point of view.

Q: Tell me, was there ever a study made of the effectiveness of OpDevFor in time of war, contrasted with times of peace? Are developments brought to the state where they are put in use more swiftly during the time of war than they are in time of peace? Is it a more leisurely pace or what?

Admiral Waters: It's pretty hard to give you a really definitive answer to that. My feeling, based on experience over both kinds of periods, is that aside from the money being available in war to start more things, there are also some things that slow you down such as having to fight the

---
*Dean G. Acheson was Secretary of State under Truman from 1949 to 1953.

war and the country's industry being involved in so many things. I imagine it really doesn't make much difference in the time that it takes. Usually, it takes about the same length of time, no matter whether you're fighting or not, to develop something in a research and development stage.

Of course, if you really put top priority and all resources and people on anything, you can do it fast at any time, such as the Manhattan project in World War II and the Polaris project in more or less peacetime.* Both of those things were pursued with the very highest priority and really no restraints on money, men, or materials. And you can do them fast; it costs you a great deal to do it. OpDevFor in time of war--because there's more money being put in and more different things are being worked on--it gets an awful lot busier. It has more projects to do than during the sort of doldrum times. It certainly has been an effective organization, because it's been in existence since right at the end of World War II. I've never even heard of any attempt to do away with that kind of an idea.

Q: Did your particular job with them in Norfolk involve you with manufacturing? Did you have to consult with

---

*The Manhattan Project developed the atomic bomb between 1942 and 1945. Research on the submarine-launched Ploaris ballistic missile began in 1956, and by 1959 the program had moved to the commissioning of the first submarine.

people who might be called upon to turn out these things? Did you have to visit factories?

Admiral Waters: No, there wasn't very much of that because that was the responsibility at that time of the material bureaus, now the Naval Material Command. It's their responsibility to interface with the manufacturers. We would see them, of course, because they would be present at a lot of tests. They were interested in the things we were making and how they fared.

Q: But I would think the anticipation of manufacturing some bit of ordnance might involve adjustments in it during the test period.

Admiral Waters: Oh, yes. We got out formal official reports on all the projects. Of course, those went back to the Navy Department in Washington and then were made available to the manufacturers. But as far as our going to some factory to say, "You shouldn't make that this way, you should make it another way."--that wasn't our business. We just said it was wrong for the following reasons and then left it to the material bureau, which had the responsibility for producing it and also the money to produce it with. We didn't have that. We left it up to them as to how they were going to make the fix.

My tour at OpDevFor ended rather suddenly with the opportunity to get command of a deep-draft ship. But just before that, Admiral Entwistle, in connection with the then-Commander in Chief of the Atlantic Fleet, Admiral Fechteler--between the two of them they conceived the idea of doing something about the conditions under which our people lived aboard ship.* Admiral Fechteler then went on and became CNO and, of course, gave this idea strong backing. And so the habitability project was placed with OpDevFor. The idea was that a lot of things were being done for the machines, but nobody had given any thought to the man who had to make the machines run. Some of the living conditions aboard ship were deteriorating very fast, so we should look into ways and means of making ships better and more comfortable places for people to live. We had lots of horrible examples.

I was put in charge of the planning phases of this project. When we started off, we found cases where, for instance, you would have air-conditioning put into the plotting room, where the fire control equipment was, because any dampness would cause a malfunction in the electronics. Whereas if you had to put in an extra motor generator to run some piece of equipment, that was quite likely to be stuck under a man's bunk, and he would be

---

*Admiral William M. Fechteler, USN, was Commander in Chief Atlantic Fleet from February 1950 until August 1951, when he became Chief of Naval Operations.

required to sleep with his bunk on top of a rotating machine giving off fumes and noise and heat. There were many things like that that needed to be changed, and we conducted this program for over a year. We finally came up with a long list of recommendations of things to be done to various classes of ships to improve the habitability of them.

As I say, I was in charge of the planning for that. I could see it was going to be such a big project and also a favorite one of the admiral, that if I didn't get out of it, I might as well not think of running the gunnery department. So I talked him into setting up a separate task force to run this, and he got another captain in to do it. I turned over the actual conduct of the habitability program to a classmate of mine, Walter D. Coleman.*

About that time, I had an opportunity to go to sea, and Admiral Entwistle released me. But a year or so later, my ship was in overhaul, and he got back at me because he got the Bureau of Personnel to order me down to temporary duty to his staff to put the final report together and deliver the briefing on it to the Secretary of the Navy.

Q: Did this habitability project, in effect, usher in a new era in the Navy which we see coming to fruition now?

---
*Commander Walter D. Coleman, USN.

Admiral Waters: Yes, it was the start of giving actual hard thought to the men that had to make the ship run. Before that, there wasn't much thought given to them. There were standards, but they weren't very high. And lots of times they were waived--how much headroom a man had over his head in a bunk and that sort of thing. It was sort of taken for granted that a sailor's lot was a hard one. But this thing really started a new era, because now it has become automatic. The standards have fed into the design of ships, and habitability is a very real consideration. And, of course, it's resulted now in things like modern ships being air-conditioned in the living quarters and these sorts of things.

Q: How do you account for the attention coming at this point?

Admiral Waters: Well, it got to be quite noticeable that we were paying much more attention to the machine than the man. This example I gave you of air-conditioning the spaces where the electronics were and forgetting to air-condition the space where the man had to sleep who ran the electronics.

Q: We now had the means to achieve more comfort.

Admiral Waters: Yes, and also it's all a part of one of the main responsibilities of command, which is the morale of the crew. This contributed greatly to it. It started a lot of things. It started these contests they have every year for the best mess in the Navy, the quality of the food served, having a crew's recreation lounge, where a man could write a letter home instead of sitting on his duffel bag over in the corner with no light to write by. All of these things came in.

Of course, because it got such high backing, it was overplayed at first. When the troops found out about it, if you really wanted to get something done on your ship, you put it in as a habitability item, and it had a pretty good chance of being funded.

Q: How did this new attitude in our Navy compare with the attitudes that prevailed in other navies?

Admiral Waters: Well, I wouldn't say we were the leaders in it, but certainly it spread throughout all navies and particularly the ones that we are closer to, such as the Royal Navy and the Canadian Navy. At about the same time, I think, they started thinking the same way, and they have gone to air-conditioned spaces and more comfortable quarters and that sort of thing.

Q: I suppose one could argue that it's only one phase of a manifestation of many things of this order today.

Well, you did get command of the Glynn.*

Admiral Waters: Yes, I did. Admiral Entwistle sort of got cornered on that one. He wrote a strong letter to the Bureau of Personnel saying that I should have a deep-draft command and a good one. As usual, I think they were trying to give me something that he didn't think quite measured up.

Q: An oiler or something.

Admiral Waters: No, an oiler is a pretty good command. I think this was a small supply ship or something like that. All of a sudden, one of the attack transports became available in a hurry, because they were just about to start on a long summer cruise up in the Arctic to supply the bases that were being built up there at that time, the Air Force radar system. The captain of one of them had a health problem, and they had to relieve him to keep him from having to make this long cruise. They needed somebody in a hurry, so they came back to Admiral Entwistle and said, "You said Waters should have a command. Would you be

---

*USS Glynn (APA-239) was commissioned 17 October 1945. She had a standard displacement of 6,720 tons, was 455 feet long, and 62 feet in the beam. She had a top speed of 17.7 knots, and her principal armament was one 5-inch gun.

willing to release him now if you really mean what you said?" And, of course, he did.

There was a slight gap between me and my OpDevFor relief out there, which they usually didn't accept, but in this case they did. I just sort of packed my bag and jumped aboard this ship and took off for the Arctic. I actually rode as a passenger, getting somewhat familiar with the ship and the operation on the way up, and relieved in a rather desolate place named Cartwright, Labrador. The skipper I relieved managed to catch an Army plane out to Goose Bay and come on down. I thoroughly enjoyed my duty. I had never been in the amphibious force before, and it was an entirely new Navy for me and a lot to learn. In particular there was a lot of basic seamanship about handling boats and getting them into the water and out of the water and back aboard ship when you had to.

Of course, the cruise that summer was a particularly interesting one. I was one element of the task group, which also included an LST and an LSD.* We carried an Army Transportation Corps detachment of people who operated bulldozers and all sorts of heavy equipment for building things. We carried a huge boat group aboard the LSD; the LST carried the heavy equipment. We would go into one of these sites which were along the desolate reaches of the coast of Labrador and make a beachhead. About a week after

---

*LST--tank landing ship; LSD--dock landing ship.

we arrived, Liberty ships would start coming in, and we unloaded them and unloaded the construction equipment on the beach for the Army to take over and build a radar site which the Air Force would operate.

It was quite an involved undertaking. It was a lot of fun, though. We were really on detached duty. My boss had the other element, the same sort of ships, and we sort of leapfrogged each other at about 200-mile intervals up the coast of Labrador, putting in half a dozen of these stations.

Q: They were all radar?

Admiral Waters: They were the DEW Line radar stations for the protection of planes coming across the pole.* You know, those stations have always been operated by the Air Force. The Army engineers constructed them with the help of some contract labor they had.

One thing that made it interesting was that it was really detached duty, because up that high, and particularly in the summertime, communications are very bad. The magnetic conditions were such that from 200 or 300 miles away, my boss had a terrible time giving me orders. We just didn't get many and just sort of went on our own. We'd find that under those peculiar

---
*DEW--Distant Early Warning Line.

electromagnetic conditions that a lot of times the best way to communicate with each other was to deliver a message to the radio station in Balboa in the Canal Zone, which would then relay it back to the other person.

It was a lot of fun. We were up there all summer, and, as I say, it was a desolate part of the world--just a few Eskimos around.

Q: Were they a part of the labor force?

Admiral Waters: No, the Eskimos we had to treat very carefully. They were protected by the Canadian Government, by the Royal Canadian Mounted Police. We had to be careful that their villages were not disturbed and nobody interfered with their hunting and fishing.

The contractors were out of Newfoundland. They were brought up under contract to the Army, as laborers and stevedores and that sort of thing, to build the sites.

Q: Was the habitability idea in operation with them?

Admiral Waters: Well, yes. It hadn't gotten very far, but we managed to stay pretty comfortable up there, although the weather was about the worst you could imagine. In the summertime up there, it varies. There can be sort of slightly freezing rain, and then in the course of six hours it can get up to 80 degrees and go back to freezing again. When it gets hot, it's hot and sultry, and there are clouds of man-eating mosquitoes. Of course, when the ships came in, the idea was to get them unloaded as quickly as possible, get this site set up, and get on to the next one. We wanted to get this whole thing over before the summer ended, before the ice came in.

We went up in June, and we had to have icebreakers take us in through the ice to these harbors.

Q: Canadian icebreakers?

Admiral Waters: No, they were our own U.S. Navy icebreakers, which have since that time been taken over by the Coast Guard. We don't have any more Navy icebreakers. But they were Navy icebreakers and actually going into our first port, Cartwright, we were stuck in the ice one night and stayed there for about five or six hours until the icebreaker could finally get us loose.

Q: And this was in June.

Admiral Waters: Yes. By September, October, new ice starts forming. So it's a rather short season. The navigation was very interesting, because the sites were selected by the Air Force. Some of them were from aerial surveys, which didn't give you much confidence in how deep the water was in getting in close to a little bay or someplace where you were supposed to put up the site.

Q: And completely uncharted, I imagine.

Admiral Waters: Well, I'll never forget one of them. It was Saglek Bay, which was the farthest north we went. The chart I had was based on a Russian survey of 1882, but I had some pretty good resources. I had an underwater demolition team, and I had also a navigation team that I formed out of the navigator and the personnel on the flagship. When we got to a place like that, we would lie off in deep water. Of course, we had lots of boats, so we'd send the boats in, and the navigation team would check the landmarks against the chart and find that some of them were wrong and get that squared away. The underwater demolition team, the swimmers, would go over in this cold water and actually wire-drag the bottom for pinnacles and check the depth of water. After we had been lying to like this for a couple of hours, they would have a walkie-talkie and radio back "all clear" or "watch this landmark or that landmark," and then we'd get under way and go in and anchor.

O. D. Waters, Jr. #4 - 208

Q: Were the swimmers not handicapped by the coldness of the water?

Admiral Waters: Oh, yes.

Q: Could they stay but a very limited length of time?

Admiral Waters: They were limited, but those people are very proud of their capability, you know. I've seen them dive in, swim out, and come up on an ice floe, a bergy bit broken off of an iceberg. Of course, they are limited, even though they had on their protective suits and so forth. The time they could stay in was limited, but it was enough to do their job.

We had two doctors along for the large number of people we were carrying, one Navy doctor and one Army doctor. We went up supplied with all sorts of drugs and things to try out against the colds, especially with the variations in temperature and the weather and the fact that once we started working on a ship, we worked three eight-hour shifts right around the clock to get the work done. So a man could be out in the cold and wet for eight hours at a stretch and then get a little rest, and he was back on the job again. Well, it turned out that the doctors were very sorely disappointed, because even though we had all of these changes in temperature and weather and very hard conditions on the men, the fact that there just weren't any germs up in that part of the world made us have the healthiest crews I've ever seen. Practically nobody got sick the whole time.

Q: From that point of view, a good place to live.

Admiral Waters: At that time, the use of antihistamines was just coming in. Benedryl had been developed, I think, in part by the Navy. The doctors were trying out these different drugs, but they didn't get much opportunity to use them.

Q: That leads me to another question. I mean, this was in essence an amphibious operation, was it not?

Admiral Waters: Yes.

Q: One usually associates the Navy and amphibious training and what have you with warm water. Was this a very unusual expedition, or has it been done many times?

Admiral Waters: Starting about that time--I think the year before was the first start of it--the Navy has done an awful lot of operating up there in supporting those northern bases. Of course, the big air base at Thule,

Greenland, has to be resupplied all during the summer. We've gotten quite a bit of cold-weather experience. It is entirely different from an amphibious operation in the South Pacific, doing it up there with the cold water. As I say, the surveys that we had available before we went into various ports were very, very sketchy, and many of them very inaccurate.

The first place we went into was Cartwright, and the site there was supposed to be gravel beach. It turned out to be a combination of mud and large boulders. In order to get the heavy equipment ashore, we had to use floating causeways to bridge over this rough stuff on the beach that was practically impassable.

The one up at Saglek Bay, the one farthest north, was really the best one of all. It was practically ideal, because it was a gradually shelving, fine gravel beach, and so everything worked just beautifully there. We had a company of DUKWs.* A large part of the cargo, was petroleum products, POL, and a lot of it was in 55-gallon drums.** The DUKW was a tremendous thing on unloading a cargo ship from an anchorage, handling these drums, because you could just stack them right in these DUKWs, roar on up on the beach up the gravel driveway, and off-load them. You would just have a continuous line of DUKWs going in this way and handling these things.

---

*DUKW was the Army designation for an amphibious truck that was designed to operate like a boat while in water and then use wheels to drive on land.
**POL--petroleum-oil-lubricants.

It was a lot of fun; it was an unusual naval experience.

Q: Has the hydrographic office since that time been more alert to the need for charts?

Admiral Waters: Well, they were alert to it. As a matter of fact, in our first port, Cartwright, another ship in there was the USS Tanner, one of the hydrographic survey ships that were doing surveys in the area. But, of course, it's a big coast, and they were doing only the most important ones. Actually, I got a letter of commendation from the hydrographer that summer. We had many reserves in the ship then who had been called in for the Korean War. And my navigator was a bright young reserve who was actually in civilian life a schoolteacher in California. He was very much interested in navigation and a very good navigator. While we were in Saglek Bay, he took the navigation party, which he was in charge of, and did as well as he could on a resurvey of the whole harbor and sent in all the details to the hydrographic office. He did such a good job that we got commended from the hydrographer for sending this information in. On the charts, some of the landmarks weren't named. I remember that one of the things we sent in was a Mount Waters up in northern Labrador. I think it's probably on the chart there now. I doubt if many people will ever see it.

Q: Did the aurora have any effect on navigation as such?*

Admiral Waters: No, it only affected our communications. On our navigation, we relied, when we were piloting, a great deal on radar. But the electromagnetic conditions didn't affect that. The radar was very useful in picking up icebergs and ice floes. With the floating winter ice, depending on which way the wind currents were setting it, you couldn't tell where it was going to be. You might approach some point on the coast where you wanted to go in, and it would be completely ice-free. Or it might just as easily happen that the ice had been driven there and packed in around the entrance, and you couldn't get in without either waiting for the weather to change or for an icebreaker to take you through it if he could. We found in going up and down the coast that radar was very helpful in plotting your course. A lot of times you could look ahead and from the radar, PPI scope, you could tell where an ice field ended, so you could change course far enough in advance so you didn't lose a lot of distance, and get

---

*A luminous phenomenon that consists of streamers or arches of light that appear in the upper atmosphere of a planet's polar regions.

around it.*

Q: So icebergs, as such, were no longer the danger they once were?

Admiral Waters: Not so much, although you still have to be careful, because they don't give back as good a return as a solid piece of land the same size. They don't give you as good a radar return as you would think they would do. But they're big, and they're very solid if you hit them.

Q: There was something we were talking about this morning, the fact that the United States lacks land buffer areas, in contrast to Russia, which has many in Siberia and so forth. Canada has been something of a land buffer area for us and certainly was at that period of time, was it not, when we were setting up these radar stations in her waters?

Admiral Waters: Yes.

Q: Did it constitute any sort of a problem with Canadian authorities?

Admiral Waters: No. All of those agreements had been taken care of. In those isolated outposts the only

---
*PPI--plan position indicator, a type of radar scope that presents a chartlike picture of the land and sea around the antenna.

dealings we really had with the Canadians were with the Royal Canadian Mounted Police. They are sort of few and far between, but they cover an awful lot of territory. On any given site, you could usually depend on the Mounties showing up at some time or other to see how things were going, mainly checking on the Eskimos that they were responsible for protecting. Usually they were making sure that their own subjects, the contractors, weren't molesting them.

Q: The Mounties get around by plane, do they?

Admiral Waters: Plane and boat and snowshoes. But there, covering those large expanses in that territory, it was mostly by plane. Of course, there are lots of fish up there, a lot of good salmon. The Eskimos seine them up.

Q: What about the white bear?

Admiral Waters: No, no bear along in there.

Q: Well, that was fascinating. Did you ever have an urge to have an arctic or antarctic duty after that?

Admiral Waters: Not any particular urge. I wouldn't mind going again. I think it's an interesting place to go. Of course, later on, as oceanographer, I had a great deal of interest in both, because we did work in both the Arctic and the Antarctic. I particularly tried to stress doing more work in the Arctic, which I thought needed to be done, but I never got back there.

Actually, just last summer, I had very detailed plans and arrangements made to go up to the Navy's Arctic Research Laboratory at Point Barrow in Alaska. Just because we had been doing so much work and because I had talked about it so much, I thought it would be good for me to see the operations firsthand. But about that time, a relief was named for me. Although I very much wanted to go, I couldn't see using up the new admiral's travel funds just to gratify my own personal whims since I wasn't going to be oceanographer anymore.

Q: Sort of like a congressional junket.

Admiral Waters: It would have been more of a junket. I would have liked very much to have done it, and we had the arrangements all made. Some of the oil companies operating there near Point Barrow offered to give me rides in their company planes up to see that oil operation on the North Slope, which would have been very interesting.

Q: How many operations of this sort, the one you were on,

have taken place since then? Do you know?

Admiral Waters: Well, that sort of thing went on for roughly the next couple of years, establishing the base and bringing in the construction materials for the Army to build the thing. After that, it sort of dwindled down because it merely got to be a resupply project, and it wasn't nearly as great a magnitude as the initial thing of starting the whole business up. But they still go on, on a reduced scale. Every summer there are resupplies of various stations up all through the Arctic.

Q: Well, obviously the Navy, through these operations, has acquired a great residue of knowledge of Arctic waters and problems. Is this information available to the oil companies now involved in Prudhoe Bay and that sort of thing? Is this passed on?

Admiral Waters: Oh, yes, it's available to them, particularly the oceanographic information that we've obtained through the oceanographic program over the years. As a matter of fact, before the Manhattan project, the idea of a souped-up super icebreaker tanker, which the oil companies did a couple of years ago--before that was ever attempted, the oil companies came to us to get our opinion on whether or not it was feasible.* We went over their plans with them and told them that we thought they could do it. And we actually provided some assistance to them, mainly by training their people and the Coast Guard people who were going to be in on the operation in certain techniques of predicting the drifting of ice and how to detect the thickness and judge conditions for getting through. We actually trained them before they went up.

Q: Now this is entirely a tangent, but did the Manhattan prove or disprove the possibilities of transportation of that sort? Or is there another project to come?

Admiral Waters: Well, they proved that it is possible to construct a huge tanker with proper strengthening so that it can break its way through ice at most any time of the year. They also determined it's very expensive, so I think the situation right now is one of determining where you want to put your money. Do you want to put your money into a pipeline, which has lots of obvious drawbacks that you can read about in the papers almost any day? It could possibly do damage to the environment. Bringing a pipeline all the way from northern Alaska down to southern Alaska, a warmer water port, and over the big mountain ranges will

---

*This is not to be confused with the Manhattan Project that developed the atomic bomb in World War II. This is a reference to the ice-strengthened tanker Manhattan.

involve the dangers of pollution, of a broken line, and that sort of thing, to the wilderness. Of course, that thing is hugely expensive, but so is the idea of the tanker. You have the additional problem with the tanker that if you run into trouble and hole it and have an oil spill, what happens to the oil in the Arctic Ocean? It probably just stays there, sort of semi-frozen into the ice. What does it do to the environment? There are all these things, and these things are still being played off against each other.

Q: This very morning I heard and saw Walter Hickel on television, and he spoke as though it was a foregone conclusion that it would be the pipeline.* He weighed the environment against the needs of men.

Admiral Waters: Well, it appears that way, although the new Secretary of Interior, I think, has put off the decision on it for further study. I think the date for coming up with a ruling on whether the government will or will not give its blessing to the pipeline is September of this year.** Of course, there are advantages to both things and there are disadvantages. But if you could do it

---

*Walter J. Hickel was U.S. Secretary of the Interior from 1969 to 1971.
**The pipeline project was approved, and the pipeline has since been constructed.

by sea, it gives you a great deal more flexibility. If you could do it by sea, you could bring that oil to the East Coast, where it's needed much more badly than on the West Coast, which has the California oil fields to supply the West Coast industry, the West Coast refineries. If you could bring it down around the east side, by Greenland, you would probably balance up the oil supply. Or you could ship it on over to Europe or on the other side, you could take it into Japan, which needs it badly.

Q: I seem to remember that there were some political rumblings beginning to develop in Canada as a result of the Manhattan project, which might grow in proportion.

Admiral Waters: Yes, that's probably one of the other disadvantages to the Manhattan project that I hadn't mentioned. A lot of that route is through Canadian territorial waters, where the Canadians would have jurisdiction. The ball would be in their court if those waters were polluted. They might require huge fees to be paid for the privilege of bringing the oil through their waters, just as a sort of insurance in case you did have a big oil spill and pollution problems.

Another thing that faces the Canadians on that is that if you do go through their territorial waters, it's really up to them to survey them and to properly mark them with navigation aids, which would be a pretty prodigious project and which hasn't been done yet. That's another drawback to it.

Of course, the Canadians tend toward the pipeline. They'd like to have it come down through Canada, though, rather than just across Alaska. You know, the Canadian route has been one of the ones considered because it would help to open up all of that northern Canadian territory.

Q: And there would be a fee, too, I suppose.

Admiral Waters: Yes.

Q: Well, that was an interesting interlude, wasn't it, with the Glynn, because you came down to something extremely fruitful as a service? You came to the staff of the Supreme Allied Commander of the Atlantic, and you were concerned with strategic applications and policy. You'd better give me a definition of that job.

Admiral Waters: Well, the staff of the Supreme Allied Commander Atlantic then had a large segment that was called plans, policy, and operations. It was headed by a U.S. rear admiral. Of course, that was an integrated staff.

O. D. Waters, Jr. #4 - 221

Q: It was a NATO staff.*

Admiral Waters: A NATO staff made up of officers from all of the countries furnishing forces or committed to furnishing forces in time of war to the Supreme Allied Commander Atlantic, who was also the Commander in Chief U.S. Atlantic Fleet.

Q: Who was he at that time?

Admiral Waters: The first SACLant under whom I worked was Admiral McCormick, and he was later relieved by Admiral Wright.** As I started to say, the operational part of the staff, which I was attached to, was called plans, policy, and operations. I was in the plans section of that. It was called strategic applications and policy.

We had the job, really, of establishing policy for the admiral. The section I was in included the senior British Navy captain, the senior French Navy captain on the staff, the senior British RAF group captain, the senior U.S. Army colonel, and me.*** I wasn't senior anything; I just told them I was there to keep them all honest.

---
*NATO--North Atlantic Treaty Organization.
**SACLant--Supreme Allied Commander Atlantic; Admiral Lynde D. McCormick, USN, was appointed the first SACLant in a ceremony on 10 April 1952 in Norfolk; Admiral Jerauld Wright, USN, relieved him in April 1954.
***RAF--Royal Air Force.

Q: Where were you based?

Admiral Waters: In Norfolk. The SACLant staff is still set up the same way. The Commander in Chief Atlantic has his U.S. headquarters right alongside of his NATO headquarters, two separate establishments. The SACLant headquarters is the one with the row of 15 flagpoles, a semicircle of 15 flagpoles, in front. They have to hoist 15 flags in the morning and take 15 down at sunset, representing all of the nations.

Q: Like the United Nations Plaza.

Admiral Waters: Of course, not all of the NATO nations were represented on the SACLant staff. Quite a few of them didn't furnish naval forces to SACLant such as, for example, Greece and Italy. But we did have Norwegians, Danes, Canadians, British, Portuguese, and Dutch. I guess that's about it.

Q: No Belgian?

Admiral Waters: No. The Belgians are committed to SACEur.* They're committed to minesweeping duties in

_____
*SACEur--Supreme Allied Commander Europe.

Europe. They didn't come under SACLant for their sort of blue-water Navy.

As I said, my job was working on strategic war plans and policy matters. We had a lot of things to worry about, especially things like the organization of the command and quite a few political matters. For example, I was the expert on what was called IberLant, the Iberian-Atlantic area. The ocean areas for which Supreme Allied Commander Atlantic were responsible were divided into two big divisions--EastLant and WestLant. EastLant was, of course, the eastern side of the Atlantic; WestLant was the western side. Then south of and adjoining to the eastern Atlantic sort of area was supposed to be the IberLant, which included the waters south of the Bay of Biscay and south of England and bordering on the Iberian Peninsula. Everything had been settled in all of the political discussions between Truman and Winston Churchill, where they sorted out who was going to get command of what and there was lots of horse trading around.* We had a Mediterranean command, and the British got the Eastern Atlantic command. The U.S. got the overall thing--the Supreme Allied Commander Atlantic--because we had the preponderance of forces committed.

The Iberian Atlantic was there on paper, but it had never been established, because the NATO countries, for

---
*Winston Churchill was Prime Minister of Great Britain from 1951 to 1955.

years, couldn't agree as to who should be the commander of that particular section of the world.

Q: Well, Spain wasn't actually a member of NATO.

Admiral Waters: No, but Portugal is, you see, so the headquarters were supposed to be in Lisbon.

Q: Where they are meeting right now.

Admiral Waters: Yes. It went on for a long time. While I was there, we kept having negotiations with the French and the British and the Portuguese. The Portuguese were always willing to have the Iberian Atlantic headquarters in Lisbon, and they didn't really have much concern as to who commanded it. They didn't make a claim to command it themselves, because they didn't have a large enough Navy.

Originally, the U.S. wanted it. Even though the U.S. had control of the whole thing, that was really the only operational command on that side of the water. The British really didn't have a bid to have it, because they had all the rest. They had the whole Eastern Atlantic and the Northern Atlantic command.

The French sided with us at first, and then when we thought that we just about had an agreement with the

British to have a U.S. commander in there, the French jumped the boat and said they wanted to have a Frenchman in there. That threw the whole thing out again, and it went on for quite a few years. It finally was settled about two or three years ago, that it was finally agreed to have a U.S. commander in Lisbon, which is the way it's now set up.

But at that time, keeping the IberLant file was one of my jobs. I went to all of the negotiations on it and briefed anybody at a moment's notice on what was the latest situation regarding it.

Q: You attended the NATO meetings?

Admiral Waters: Oh, yes, particularly since I was in the policy section. Whenever the admiral went over to Paris to meetings, why, I was in the row behind him with the briefcase. When something came up, I shuffled the papers and got the right paper to him. It was a lot of fun and a very interesting experience, particularly with these foreign officers. We had a lot of fun. We worked together pretty well. In spite of representing different nations, we tried to have it be an integrated international staff and take off our national hats as well as we could and be international. Sometimes hard to do.

Q: At that time, were we dealing with the idea of nuclear

strikes against the homeland from carriers? Was that one of the concerns?

Admiral Waters: Oh, yes. And, of course, at that particular time in history, it made it difficult because even though that was our biggest weapon, the security requirements were such that there were some of the people on the staff you couldn't talk to about the details.

Q: How did you deal with that kind of a problem? In case of the outbreak of hostilities, I mean, how were you going to cope with it?

Admiral Waters: The plans were all made, and, of course, there were certain things you couldn't talk about, the technical details of the weapons and how they were used. But most of the people were privy to the information as to what the strike would be and what it would hit and how much it was expected to accomplish. That sort of thing was divulged. You had to.

Q: Was there any feeling among the nationalities who were not party to the knowledge?

Admiral Waters: Well, I suppose there always is some of that, but there wasn't much you could do about it, particularly because you were controlled by a congressional statute on the subject.

Q: Yes. The idea of the Navy, traditionally, has been in time of war to protect shipping, largely. Was this concept lost sight of with you?

Admiral Waters: No, that was a big part of our mission, to protect and control shipping. That was one of the big parts of SACLant's mission.

Of course, at the same time, you have to take cognizance of the other probably just as equally important mission of projecting Allied power overseas. In other words, through carrier task forces, to project your naval power to support the armies and the flanks and to control the seas for the supplies that you'll need to get there. That was, of course, one of our big worries with the masses of Russian submarines--how would you keep the seas clear? How would you get these things over?

Q: How did the Royal Navy fit into this picture and the thought of the carrier task force?

Admiral Waters: Well, of course, at that time they still had some carriers of their own, but we were planning on having integrated task forces. We actually had NATO exercises, where the various nationalities worked together. We, on the staff there, had developed tactical manuals for Allied use that were tried out and used by all the different navies operating together, common signal books and that sort of thing and common tactical doctrine for formations of ships and moving ships around.

The British, of course, were very active, because, as I say, they had the Commander in Chief of the Eastern Atlantic--a British officer located in England for that whole area--to control the shipping there on that side. He was one of the principal commanders under SACLant.

Q: This was just about the time, though, that we began to witness the decline of the Royal Navy, was it not?

Admiral Waters: Yes.

Q: And why? Was it something more than just lack of finances?

Admiral Waters: It was mainly economical; they couldn't afford it, and they were having a hard time and had to cut back on their defense budget.

Q: Well, simultaneously, was there any dilemma for them in terms of the role of the Royal Navy in modern warfare? It was so different from their traditions.

Admiral Waters: Yes, it was. It was pretty hard for them to take. It was while I was on SACLant staff that the Royal Navy came up with the idea of the wet list and the dry list. Are you familiar with that?

Q: Tell me about it.

Admiral Waters: Well, they were cutting down on the Navy, cutting the Navy back. There were fewer ships, and they decided that since the opportunity to serve at sea and to command at sea was getting more and more limited, they divided their Navy into two different kinds of officers. They had a formal name for it, but it became the wet list and the dry list. If you were sort of a fair-haired boy and a good operational type, you made the wet list, which meant that you went on up to command at sea and to glory. If you were on the dry list, you stayed ashore in administrative jobs. The first such list of officers was published while I was at SACLant, and several of the officers that I knew quite well were put on the dry list and immediately went about turning in their suits to get out of the Royal Navy.

Q: This they considered a demotion?

Admiral Waters: They were badly shaken. They were awfully fine officers too. In the case of a couple of them, I just really couldn't understand how it happened to them. They took it very badly; it was a great blow to them.

Q: With a limited number of ships, there was a limited number of commands.

Admiral Waters: Yes. And also, since they were cutting back, they were having to cut back the size of their officer corps, and this was one way of doing it. If a man was put on the dry list, or either list, and he wanted to get out of the Navy, there was an inducement to do it by some kind of a large bonus being paid on his application for retirement. It was known in the Royal Navy as the "golden bowler" program. In other words, you trade your seagoing cap for a bowler hat to wear ashore, but it meant some money to you, so it was known as the "golden bowler" program.

Q: And the French began to more or less pull out of NATO, did they not, I mean, except to maintain a formal tie?

Admiral Waters: Well, after I left, they did pull completely out, you know, except they still associated with

O. D. Waters, Jr. #4 - 231

it, but they pulled their forces out.

Q: Is this what made it possible for the ultimate decision to be made that the U.S. would have the Iberian command?

Admiral Waters: It may have. I didn't follow the politics of that when it actually happened, but we do have a flag officer over there now who is ComIberLant.

Q: Is that Fluckey?*

Admiral Waters: Yes. He's double-hatted as Chief of MAAG Portugal and ComIberLant.**

We had some fine officers on this staff. One of the British officers who was there as a captain with me went up to flag rank. I bumped into him after I made rear admiral. We were out in the Western Pacific together. He was down at Singapore. He was known as FOSIC--that's flag officer second in command. He later made four stars and was CinCEastLant in the NATO hierarchy.

The first Frenchman with me in staff, the senior French officer, was then-Captain Guy de Toulouse-Lautrec, a relative of the old artist. When people asked Guy if he was a direct descendant, he liked to say, "Well, I hope

---
*Rear Admiral Eugene B. Fluckey, USN.
**Chief of Military Assistance Advisory Group Portugal and Commander Iberian Atlantic Command.

not, because the old man was a bachelor." He later became a flag officer in the French Navy and has since retired.

I suppose one of the things that turned out to take more of my time than anything else while I was on the SACLant staff was being chairman of what was called the classified briefing team, which was sort of a dog-and-pony show. We put it on for all kinds of VIPs and visiting firemen whenever the occasion demanded, which was quite frequently, really, to describe to them the command and how it was organized and what it was set up to do. We had the briefing team organized with principals and alternates so that if a man wasn't there, there was always someone to fill his part. We had about five speakers, and I was responsible for putting the whole thing together. We tried to have as many different uniforms on the platform as possible, so we would have the U.S. Navy, an RAF group captain, a French naval officer, and a Norwegian. We worked them all in, one after the other, with visual aids to describe the workings of the command and the problems.

It was a lot of fun, and we had to keep it current, keep it up to date. And there were many visitors, so we had many performances. That's why I say it took up a lot of my time. And then, from that start, I got into the business of running presentations each year over in Paris as a part of what Field Marshal Montgomery called his annual CPX, his command post exercises.*

---

*Field Marshal Bernard Law Montgomery of Great Britain.

Each year in Paris they would take as a theme some kind of a war—say, an all-out nuclear war in 1975—and put on a lengthy, two- or three-day presentation analyzing how this would be done. These things were done for a couple of years without any naval input to them, and Admiral Wright thought this was wrong. With great difficulty, he talked Field Marshal Montgomery into permitting the Supreme Allied Commander Atlantic to contribute to the CPX.

Q: It was actually Montgomery's show, wasn't it?

Admiral Waters: Oh, it was Montgomery's show and quite a thing. It was done in the movie hall. It lasted for two or three days, and you had to have at least three stars to get a seat. If you had less than three stars, you stood up, unless you were an actor in the show. It did a lot of skits and things like that.

We had a terrific time in our first performance there, because the field marshal would only give us an hour in his schedule, and Admiral Wright wanted to make a big splash to convince everybody that . . .

Q: And an hour's time was not sufficient.

Admiral Waters: An hour's time to fight a battle at sea in some kind of a presentation—a skit or something like that.

So we got a group of people together, a brainstorming session, and came up with various ideas. Admiral Wright was a man who was very much interested in this sort of thing. He has a great eye for detail and presentations and the types of visual aids and the colors used. So he was a very exacting and a very difficult man to work for in this particular capacity.

We did come up with scripts. We were going to do a three-part presentation in which we had three speakers. A British intelligence man on the staff would represent the Soviets and sort of cover the threat and what the Soviets were doing. I was to cover the U.S. operations of the fleets at sea, the task forces. Then the control and protection of shipping was done by a Canadian officer. That was the way it was finally sorted out. So each time we would do a run-through for the admiral, he would get ideas of more slides that he wanted to have in the thing. Since we were restricted to an hour, it finally got so that we had so many slides, that you had about three seconds per slide to get it on and off. That, of course, isn't long enough to look at the slide, really, and you really can't say anything while the slide is up there.

Q: You can't be very impressive with that speed.

Admiral Waters: He insisted that all of these things be

in, so in desperation, I turned to Ted Maynard, a civilian in the office of the secretary. He was a very talented gent at putting on presentations. He came down to Norfolk, and I showed him the script and showed him all the slides we had. He looked at it and said, "You know, what you have there is a motion picture."

I said, "Yes, I realize that, but I don't know quite what to do about it."

He said, "Let's make a motion picture, and we'll synchronize the speakers to the motion picture, but synchronize them live." So it wouldn't be a sound movie; you had to have living people there.

So I said, "Has it ever been done before?"

He said, "Not to my knowledge, but we'll give it a try." So we did. We converted our slides to a motion picture. This enabled us to throw in a lot of action shots of ships at sea to illustrate various things. We also used an animated cartoon to make points about describing different naval battles and that sort of thing.

Q: It sounds like a brilliant idea.

Admiral Waters: We did the script and put it on tape and then made a movie so that it synchronized with the tape. When we finally got the movie made, we practiced our speeches. We had three speakers, and we each had about three parts. You would have one part, and then the next guy would take over and then the next guy, and you'd come back to the first one and so on for about three times. We found, much to our surprise, that you usually read your script at the same speed each time, and that if you just sort of glanced around and had your eye looking for a certain mark, you could adjust the speed of your presentation so that it all tied in. I must say that if this hadn't worked, I don't know what we would have done. I probably would have resigned or something like that, because there wasn't time to do anything else.

Q: It certainly made for much less confusion, didn't it, than projecting the slides individually?

Admiral Waters: Of course, the idea was so novel that when we put it on, it made such a tremendous hit that it alienated the field marshal even more. He grudgingly let us in for an hour and we stole his show. Of course, Admiral Wright was delighted with the success of this thing. We had our problems, though. It was a terrific job doing this. For one thing, we made our original tapes of the voices and then flew directly up to Washington so they could start making the movie. We found that our tape recorder was at a slightly different speed from the playback thing they used, and so the timing was slightly off. So we had to fall out and fall back in again. It was a tremendous thing.

Q: Didn't you discover that there was a large contingent of the CPX boys who really were interested in this area?

Admiral Waters: Oh, yes.

Q: They had been deprived of it before.

Admiral Waters: Yes, very much so. Oh, there were various offshoots from this thing. In the animation that we used to show task forces, say, in the Norwegian Sea attacking each other--we adopted symbols for carrier task forces and for carriers and for ASW carriers and destroyers. And we had these little blue things move around on the ocean. Ours were blue, I guess, and the Russians were red. Everybody liked the symbols we adopted because they knew what was going on. And Junior McCain, when he was putting his sea power presentation together that he rode glory on, adopted our animated symbols.* He used some of our film, I think.

Q: Was this idea perpetuated?

---

*Rear Admiral John S. McCain, Jr., USN, became widely known for a sea power presentation that was given to many, many audiences.

O. D. Waters, Jr. #4 - 238

Admiral Waters: Yes, I did it for two years, and it was done a third year by my successor.

Q: Did you have more time in the subsequent presentations?

Admiral Waters: Yes, they relaxed a little bit and gave us a little bit more time.

Q: When did Montgomery give off being in control of these things?

Admiral Waters: It was after I left SACLant. I left SACLant in '56, and he was still there. He left in the next couple of years. It was quite an experience, and, of course, as I say, Admiral Wright was elated with the way the performance went off. He took us all to dinner and the theater, and we celebrated.

Q: And told you some stories, no doubt.

Admiral Waters: At the first performance of the Montgomery CPX, the audience were seated in bleachers on each side of the long room. At one end, in the worst seats, the performers who took part in the different parts of the CPX were allowed to sit. In our SACLant contingent we were determined that somebody was going to take notice of the Navy there. So the British captain and the Canadian captain and I got there early and got ourselves seats right on the front row of the performers' section and were very much in evidence in our dark blue uniforms.

One of the things that amused me was that during a break in the proceedings that morning--this was before we went on--Dickie Mountbatten was representing the Royal Navy, as Jerry Wright was the U.S. Navy.* I saw Mountbatten come over and put his arm around Admiral Wright and sort of motion over in our direction. I'm sure he was saying "Who are those chaps there, Jerry?" I had seen him while he was sitting in his seat.

One of the things given to you along with the program and everything was a seating arrangement with the identification of each person in the whole room. Each seat was numbered, and the names were down there, and, of course, in the performers' section, they weren't numbered. I had seen Admiral Mountbatten looking around and checking off each person there to be sure that he recognized that person and knew who he was. Then he looked around and saw these Navy types, and he didn't know us. That bothered him, so he came over and got Admiral Wright. The next thing I knew, Admiral Wright was bringing Admiral

---
*Lord Louis F. A. V. N. Mountbatten, RN, having served as Commander in Chief Mediterranean in the early 1950s, was appointed First Sea Lord in April 1955 by Prime Minister Anthony Eden.

Mountbatten over and introducing each one of us in turn to him so that he could catalog us away in his own little personal file of who was at the CPX. I thought this was some reflection of the thoroughness of the man in doing his job.

Q: Well, you then made your presentation on that occasion.

Admiral Waters: It was, fortunately for us, successful. We all came home celebrating. I think that just about winds up the highlights of my SACLant.

Q: Tell me the initial program which led into that, the presentation for the VIPs who came. Did this total program really smooth the way for the NATO setup? It was a job in public relations, wasn't it?

Admiral Waters: Yes, except that our part was classified. You know, we had the normal U.S. Navy classifications in NATO. The highest classification for NATO only is called Cosmic, which I always thought was a pretty good title. So you had to have NATO clearance to hear the particular presentation we gave.

There was another team which was really the public relations one who put on an unclassified briefing, the same sort of show for the headquarters. They performed at Kiwanis clubs and ladies luncheons and that sort of thing, wherever they were asked to spread the word about SACLant and explain this NATO organization.

In ours, we went really into operational plans and how the thing worked.

Q: Yours were intended for heads of governments and military leaders?

Admiral Waters: Military leaders and people like that and political figures. I gave the part on organization, which was a rather difficult one to give, because it's a very complex organization. Any Allied organization has to be complex. I always tried to explain it by showing how complicated it was and then reminding everyone that this organization had to be approved by 15 sovereign nations and. Therefore, there were lots of compromises in it, but that we felt that, certainly, there could be a better, more streamlined, and more efficient organization. But we also felt that if you really tried, you could make any organization work, and we thought this one would. That was the way we put it across.

Q: Well, from your experience with the organization in dealing with these other nationalities in time of actual

O. D. Waters, Jr. #4 - 242

conflict and in time of actual stress, what is your prognosis for it? Do you think it's a workable thing?

Admiral Waters: Well, I think you would start off with that organization and, hopefully, get by the first few weeks or the opening phases of any conflict. Just common sense would dictate changes when something didn't work. When you're actually in a war, it's much easier to change. In peacetime, when you're doing planning, these changes would have to be agreed to by every government and the NATO Council. When you get into an international organization it's surprising what small things will cause you problems.

Q: How cumbersome it is.

Admiral Waters: For instance, in our section we handled the boundaries between the different areas of command responsibility. Down in the southwestern corner of the Atlantic Ocean, we had a place where the NATO boundary had been agreed to as being in a certain place. However, the U.S. boundary for our U.S. Eastern Sea Frontier, which coincided with the other places, didn't quite jibe there. This had been an oversight or mistake, so we just put out a SACLant notice informing everyone that we were changing these two things to conform. Nobody paid any attention to it except the Danes. For some reason, still unknown to everybody, the Danes made a big fuss about it and said that the Supreme Allied Commander Atlantic had no right to change that boundary without referring it to the NATO Council and all the NATO nations.

Q: Did your duties in this connection involve you in the Mediterranean in any way?

Admiral Waters: Only in the business of coordinating our activities with the Commander in Chief Mediterranean, who was Lord Mountbatten at that time. Of course, at the Straits of Gibraltar, our commands came together, and we had to have all sorts of agreements on how you would pass over responsibility through the straits for shipping and that sort of thing. We maintained a liaison with their staff, but I think by your question you meant was SACLant responsible for the Mediterranean. It wasn't.

Q: Did you have any oblique relationships with the Organization of American States and their navies?

Admiral Waters: No. No. We didn't in our side of the compound there in Norfolk. Of course, as Commander in Chief Atlantic, Admiral Wright was involved.* Our staff

---

*In addition to his NATO job, Wright was also Commander in Chief Atlantic, a U.S. joint-service command, and Commander in Chief Atlantic Fleet, a strictly Navy command.

was entirely separate, and we stayed out of that. Getting back to that classified briefing, I think one of the more interesting little incidents that happened was when the Norwegian Storting, which is their Parliament, came over to this country for a visit, and they visited SACLant.

Q: You mean the members of their Parliament?

Admiral Waters: Twenty or so members of their Parliament were over here. They came to Norfolk, and we were supposed to lay on a briefing for them. We found out from our Norwegian staff members that they were mostly good, solid citizens--fishermen and industrial people--and they spoke nothing but Norwegian. This sort of stumped us.

Q: That's not the easiest language.

Admiral Waters: We had several Norwegians and Danes on the staff, and I didn't know until this time that any Scandinavian can understand any other Scandinavian, that is, if you're talking about Swedish, Norwegian, and Danish. They can all understand each other. It looks a little bit different and is pronounced slightly differently, but they get along all right talking to each other. Anyway, we got the Scandinavians on the staff, and they translated the scripts of the different speakers and then delivered it in

O. D. Waters, Jr. #4 - 245

either Danish or Norwegian to the Norwegian Storting when they came. It was very successful. I enjoyed it, because they translated it word for word, and, of course, I had given my part of it so often, I knew it by heart. It was very interesting to me to sit there and understand somebody speaking Norwegian.

Q: What proportion of your VIP visitors were Americans?

Admiral Waters: I would say a very minor proportion. We had many more visitors from the NATO countries overseas to the headquarters. There were a few Americans.

Q: How do you account for that?

Admiral Waters: Well, because mainly we were visited by the people from the other NATO countries. Our day-to-day relationships with the U.S. Navy were very close. We had a U.S. Navy liaison office right in the SACLant headquarters, where anything that we had to know that was going on in the U.S. Navy was available to us in that office, and particularly if it was in some sort of a classification that was supposed to stay within the U.S. Navy and not in any other navies. There were reading rooms where you could go and keep abreast of that sort of thing. We didn't think it was quite fair to smuggle that sort of thing in and huddle over it in an international combined staff office. So we would go into another office, which was entirely U.S., and keep abreast that way. The British had the same sort of a system; theirs was a little more cumbersome. Their naval attaché used to bring things down from Washington for them to read.

Q: It wasn't completely integrated then, as a NATO command?

Admiral Waters: No, it never can be, because there are certain things that, just from a practical standpoint, you like to keep under wraps, no matter what good allies you are. Everyone does it.

Q: What about your dealings with the press? Was this a complicated thing?

Admiral Waters: No, not so much so. We had a public relations section. Being in sort of a classified section of the staff, I didn't get into that very much. And, of course, our briefings were never to the press. The admiral was in the public limelight a great deal and had press conferences, that sort of thing.

Because of SACEur being in Paris and SACLant in Norfolk, the job on that staff involved a tremendous amount of traveling. I got to be sort of a transatlantic commuter because of working on these various presentations that had to be coordinated with Montgomery's staff. Then, when the time came around for the annual NATO meeting, which was usually in December, there would probably be two or three preliminary trips to coordinate staff papers and work on things with SACEur headquarters. So we had a combined position on them.

Q: What about the feasibility of CinCLant also being in command of the NATO forces? So much of his time necessarily is involved with the NATO elements. Is this a feasible arrangement for an American fleet commander?

Admiral Waters: Well, this has been, of course, a subject of discussion for a long time. I don't know how the situation is now.* In this particular respect I don't imagine that it's changed very much. It doesn't make it a very burdensome task for one man to be Supreme Allied Commander Atlantic and the Commander in Chief Atlantic under the U.S. flag. But the reason for it is that there is a very marked difference between the forces in the naval setup, the Allied Command Atlantic and the Allied Command

---

*At the time of the interview, one four-star U.S. admiral was simultaneously SACLant, CinCLant, and CinCLantFlt. In 1985 the commands were divided, with one four-star admiral serving as SACLant and CinCLant and another four-star admiral as CinCLantFlt and Deputy CinCLant.

Europe. The European Command is essentially an Army setup, which, of course, Eisenhower headed first.* That's because SACEur actually still has troops assigned to him under his command. So he has his resources right there. In case anything should happen, he could presumably push the button and start off into combat.

In the naval setup, no forces are committed ahead of time. They are all earmarked. On the declaration of war, they would pass to NATO command, so that the Supreme Allied Commander Atlantic has, under NATO, actually no forces to command until something happens, and then forces are put under his command. Of course, he does have them under his command when you have a big NATO exercise. They are passed over and come under his operational control. But until a war should start, he doesn't have actual command. Therefore, since the large part of his forces would be U.S. forces, it makes a good deal of sense for him to be the man who has them in peacetime so that there won't be a big wrenching change in case of combat commencing. That's the reason it's always been done that way, and that's the difference between the naval commander and the essentially Army commander, although SACEur does have some earmarked naval forces under him. His actual forces in being are there, and one of the things that came before Congress recently was to try to cut down the number of American

---
*General of the Army Dwight D. Eisenhower served as SACEur from 1950 to 1952, then successfully ran for President.

O. D. Waters, Jr. #4 - 249

forces that are actually assigned over there.

Q: In your time with the NATO setup, had the Polaris yet come into being?

Admiral Waters: No.

Q: Has that changed the situation any? The Polaris submarine is almost on a wartime footing constantly, is it not? Has this changed anything in the nature of the command?

Admiral Waters: No, because all of those nuclear retaliatory forces are under U.S. command and under the direct control of the President by law. In case of a nuclear war, they would be U.S. forces. It wouldn't make much difference what you call them. If the war started and somebody pressed the button, they would be used.

Q: As a part of a NATO command, did you have any relationship with the United Nations?

Admiral Waters: Well, only in that NATO was set up as one of the types of organizations that is encouraged by the United Nations charter. Regional organizations for security are encouraged by the United Nations charter, so there is a definite legal precedent for its having been started in the first place.

Q: Does this imply, then, that there was an active liaison with our United Nations representative?

Admiral Waters: I don't recall that there was, no. Certainly, if you mean do NATO matters get into the U.N. chain . . .

Q: Was our United States ambassador at the United Nations . . .

Admiral Waters: That's entirely separate, but it is important, I think, to realize that NATO was set up sort of under the auspices of the United Nations.

Q: Exactly, yes.

Admiral Waters: But it is not a part of the United Nations. Of course, the real reason for setting up NATO was as a shield for Western Europe against Soviet aggression and to keep it from spreading any further. It wouldn't make much sense to work through the Russians on something like that. No, the State Department chain is entirely separate. There is a permanent U.S. ambassador, who is the permanent representative of the United States in the NATO Council. Such people who represent each of the 15 countries of NATO run the day-to-day political business of the North Atlantic Treaty Organization. When you have special meetings, their places can be taken by anybody up to and including the head of state, usually not that far. There have been certain special meetings where the heads of state have represented their countries, but normally they don't go any higher than having the foreign minister or Secretary of State, or sometimes the Secretary of Defense.

Q: In that time with the NATO organization, were the naval forces ever plagued by the Russian submarines or Russian fishing trawlers, or what have you, out observing things?

Admiral Waters: Well, there was a little bit of it then, such as encounters on the high seas between NATO forces and Russians coming into close proximity to each other and the Russians refusing to give way and getting into close quarters. Nothing happened, but some incidents like that occurred.

Q: Was it a subject of discussion between the NATO nations?

O. D. Waters, Jr. #4 - 252

Admiral Waters: Oh, yes--what to do and not back down, that sort of thing. But there weren't nearly so many, because, of course, the Russian Navy was just starting to build then. They were much smaller and much less powerful.

Q: What was the established policy in NATO in terms of dealing with this?

Admiral Waters: Well, it was to avoid collisions and things like that in extremis but not to surrender your rights on the high seas, which is what we've always tried to do. It puts a captain in a pretty difficult position, defending national honor in such a situation and not letting another nation crowd you. How far do you go, and at what point do you take action to avoid actual collision? It's a tough spot to be in.

Q: We have a very interesting episode coming up in your career, your service in the Mediterranean at a time when something of some significance took place. You went to the Mediterranean command in September of 1956 and took over Destroyer Squadron Number Two, which was a part of the Sixth Fleet.

Admiral Waters: Yes, I actually went, I think, a little bit earlier than that, in the summertime. I came up for major command and was told I was getting a squadron of destroyers. Then I was assigned to relieve Lot Ensey as the Commander of Destroyer Squadron Two.* She was at that time in the middle of a deployment to the Med. Lot was ordered from DesRon 2 to be chief of staff of the Sixth Fleet. He was there the next year when he was selected for flag rank.

But it was a pretty good job to go to, because the prospective chief of staff of the Sixth Fleet was very anxious to have me relieve him as soon as possible. So the skids were all greased for me to get there in a very short period of time. I left Washington one day at noon on what was then called the blue plate special. That was before the jet aircraft.

Q: Was it a Constellation?

Admiral Waters: It was a Constellation or a DC-6 or something like that. Anyway, I flew directly from Washington to Paris. When I got to Paris, I was met by the assistant naval attaché with tickets and help of getting through customs and so forth. He gave me a ticket on Air France to fly down to Nice directly, which I did. At Nice I was met by the local naval representative and was taken to the Hotel Negresco, where they had reservations for me

---
*Captain Lot Ensey, USN.

and where I spent about six hours after getting some dinner. Then I was picked up bright and early the next morning and taken back to the airport, where I got aboard a COD plane off of one of the carriers, a carrier on board delivery plane, and went charging through the air across the Mediterranean to where the fleet was in the middle of an exercise. I landed on the Coral Sea. It was my first carrier landing and quite an experience.

Then from the carrier, I was helicoptered over to a Sixth Fleet cruiser which the squadron I was going to happened to be screening. I had lunch on board the cruiser, and then right after lunch, the Barton, which was my flagship, came alongside, and I went over by highline to the Barton.* In the course of about 40 hours, I had traveled from Paris to the Sixth Fleet operating in the middle of the Mediterranean and had used most conventional methods of transportation to get there, including the highline.

Q: This is a bit of a digression, but since you have said before that you had practically become a commuter when you were with the NATO command, a commuter back and forth across the Atlantic, did you ever experience any difficulty

---

*USS Barton (DD-722) was commissioned 30 December 1943 as a member of the Allen M. Sumner class. She had a standard displacement of 2,200 tons, was 376 feet long, and 41 feet in the beam. Her top speed was 34.6 knots. She had a main battery of six 5-inch guns and ten 21-inch torpedo tubes.

in this rapid transportation from one continent to the other and then being forced to participate in conferences, and what have you, very shortly thereafter? Did it serve to disorient you in any way?

Admiral Waters: It certainly did. I think what you're getting at is the effect you get from the time shift nowadays in jet planes. Remember, in those days we were still in the propeller planes, and it would take 12-16 hours.

Q: There was still a certain amount of it, wasn't there?

Admiral Waters: The way the flights were arranged, you'd leave here in the afternoon and get over there the next morning or about midday their time and be expected to rally around to the conference, not having had much sleep. I didn't have much success sleeping on planes, never have. By the time you'd finish half a day's work in Paris, you were a pretty tired fellow.

Q: Did you ever feel that you were at something of a disadvantage, I mean, being catapulted into a conference on that side and being forced to hold your own?

Admiral Waters: I used to try to stall them so that I

could get a night's sleep after I got there before I had to go do any work, but sometimes you couldn't do it. On one of these trips prior to a big conference, something had to be attended to in a hurry, and I remember Admiral Wright sent me over to do it. I left Norfolk on Sunday and got back on Thursday. That was pretty much of a killer. When I wasn't traveling, I was working.

Q: I understand it doesn't have the same effect when you are going north and south within the time zone.

Admiral Waters: No, I don't think it does. This time zone business sort of gets you all out of synchronism with what you're used to.

Q: Well, that was a bit of a digression. You reached your command in the middle of the Mediterranean.

Admiral Waters: Yes, I got there just about the time the exercise was winding up. The Sixth Fleet was accustomed in those days--and I imagine they still do it at the end of an exercise--to split up and go to various ports for liberty for a few days, maybe a week. We went down to Sicily and went into Palermo. I relieved Lot Ensey of command there. He went off to catch a plane and catch up with the Sixth Fleet flagship, and I took over the squadron.

The squadron usually stayed fairly well split up in the Mediterranean. There were eight ships, and there would be two or three of them assigned to one job and two or three to the other, a carrier screen or doing ASW or something like that. One of the things the Sixth Fleet did at that time was to supply four ships to the Red Sea-Persian Gulf area. There were always two coming, two going, and two there, so there was an average of about four ships in the Mediterranean. With each pair of ships, they always tried to have either a division commander or a squadron commander with them.

I guess it was September of that year that I went down with two ships of my squadron, the Barton and the Soley. The usual way to do it was to go into Athens and fuel and then go down and go through the Suez Canal. At that time, it was just after the time when the Egyptians had taken over the canal.* Of course, they had broken up the normal way the canal had been run by the old Suez Canal Company, where they had French and British pilots. They had pilots of all nationalities. We had a standing order from the Chief of Naval Operations, saying that under these conditions, when you went through the canal, you were not to permit the Egyptians to put a pilot aboard from a Communist country. Because there were then some pilots from Communist countries operating in the Suez Canal.

---

*On 26 July 1956 Egypt nationalized the Suez Canal.

Q: Was this for security reasons?

Admiral Waters: Security reasons, just not allowing them to get on our ships. And these were rather strict orders. So when I got to Port Said, we just tied up. We were not allowed to go ashore there, but the people from the naval attaché's office came down and came aboard to see if we had any requirements. I asked them about this pilot thing, and they said, "Oh, it's working fine. We have an agreement with the Egyptians. You have nothing to worry about."

So at about, oh, 4:00 or 5:00 the next morning, the convoy for going through the canal had formed up. You know, when the canal was opened up, we always went in convoys and kept the ships in groups together, because you can't pass in the canal except at certain places. The southbound convoy would make it to Great Bitter Lake and go off to one side and anchor while the northbound convoy came through from the other direction. So we started through, and we had Egyptian pilots to start with. Then you change pilots at Ismailia, when you're almost halfway through and just short of Great Bitter Lake. They do it on the fly; as the ships go by, the boats come out and the pilot who is on jumps in the boat and the pilot who's going to take you from then on jumps out, and you still stay under way at slow speed.

Q: How can you identify his nationality?

Admiral Waters: Well, you can't. That was my dilemma. Of course, these two ships, being men-of-war, were leading the convoy. My ship was first and the <u>Soley</u> second. As we got the pilot on the bridge, of course, the first things the quartermaster asked him were his name and nationality, signal number, and all of these things to put in the log. My pilot for the flagship turned out to be Yugoslav, so I blinked back at the <u>Soley</u> and asked them what was the nationality of their pilot, and it was Yugoslav too.

So then I hurriedly broke out my instructions and read them again, and they didn't say an Iron Curtain country or a Soviet-dominated country; they said a Communist country. I was in somewhat of a dilemma, because even though we were giving aid to Yugoslavia at the time, it was a Communist country. If you carry out the letter of your orders, you're not to permit him to pilot your ship. So I called the communication officer. There was no way of communicating with the Commander in Chief of the Sixth Fleet; we were out of communication with him.

Q: Who was he?

Admiral Waters: Admiral Brown, Cat Brown.* Any
----
*Vice Admiral Charles R. Brown, USN.

communication to Washington would have taken so long it would have been useless. We were on the Suez Canal communication channels, so I called the communication officer and asked what was the highest priority message I could send on this particular system. He said, "Well, there is one that means 'ship is in danger,' and the code word is so-and-so."

I said, "Well, use that one." So I sent a message to the Egyptian Suez Canal Authority, saying that my instructions were that I was not to have a pilot from a Communist country. My instructions were that they had been informed of this, and now my two ships were with Yugoslav pilots on board. The convoys were proceeding towards Great Bitter Lake, where we would anchor normally while the northbound convoy passed. I said, "I will proceed to Great Bitter Lake, but I will not get under way from Great Bitter Lake until the pilots are changed."

I didn't know what I was to do. I felt that I was in a terrific, embarrassing international spot. I had direct orders, and I didn't know what would happen, whether we'd be sitting there in Great Bitter Lake for a couple of weeks while we sent messages back and forth. Anyway, it worked, because we got to Great Bitter Lake, and a boat came alongside, and there were lots of apologies. The Yugoslav got off, and an Egyptian got on. I never did know whether this was a genuine mistake or whether it was being done to test the system to see if we would protest or not. Of course, I reported it all when I had a chance to. That was the last I heard of it. I passed the word around so that other people coming through the canal would know of the possibility, looking for trouble.

Q: At that particular time you went on into the Persian Gulf, did you?

Admiral Waters: The way we worked is that we would go down the Red Sea and stop overnight at Aden, which was still in the British control. We made a fuel stop there and then continued on around the other side to the Persian Gulf. The U.S. commander of the Middle East Force had his headquarters at Bahrain Island, about halfway up the Persian Gulf. That was Admiral Jack Monroe at that time.* From the Suez down around Arabia and up to Abadan at the top of the Persian Gulf is about 4,000 miles. People don't realize that it's that far, but it's a long journey, much longer than crossing the North Atlantic. So it takes you a right long time to do it.

Anyway, we got in there and found that we were scheduled to do a very interesting exercise. We were to go up to Abadan and join up with the Iranian Navy and work with them in a joint exercise, which would be reviewed by

---
*Rear Admiral Jack P. Monroe, USN, Commander Middle East Force from 3 August 1956 to 4 September 1957.

the Shah.* We had a great time in Abadan. There's a big Western European consortium there of oil companies, big refineries of Dutch and British and Americans in a big international community. The men on the American ships were really feted by these homesick Americans. They took these American boys in and fed them home-cooked dinners, and everybody had a wonderful time.

Then we joined up with the Iranian Navy, and they had some very, very old, slow ships, which were in a very bad state of repair. It was going to be a very difficult thing putting on any kind of an exercise with them. Of course, the Iranian officers were very much interested in impressing the Shah. They were trying to get more money for their Navy, and he was the man to impress. They wanted to do gunnery exercises and all sorts of things, and their guns wouldn't fire. I put a couple of officers and a couple of men aboard each one of the ships, and they managed as sort of liaison officers to make the communications work better. They actually went to work with the Iranians. They had horrible logistic conditions; for example, spare fuses for things didn't exist. If the fuse burned out, you either jumped the fuse, or you didn't use that piece of equipment anymore. But we worked with them, and they were a very affable people. Of course, I

---

*Mohammed Riza Pahlavi was Shah of Iran from 1941 until he was deposed in 1979 by forces loyal to the Ayatollah Ruhollah Khomeini.

had liaison officers from their ships over with me, and we had a lot of fun with them.

The Shah did come down, and by that time, with all of our hard work, we had gotten them so that they could hit a target at short range, and it looked really good. We went by a little island and did some shore bombardment, and everything worked fine. The Shah was aboard their flagship. Admiral Monroe was there in his flagship, and he had a dinner for the Shah, who is a very engaging man, very interesting. He's still not too old a man.*

Q: No, he's not more than 50.

Admiral Waters: He was fairly young at that time, very much of an athlete, you know, interested in skiing, water skiing, driving racing cars.

It was a very amusing dinner that Admiral Monroe had. Admiral Monroe's chief of staff and I were the two other U.S. officers invited, and there were the Shah and one or two of his people who were very senior in their Navy, very high-up admirals. Being an absolute monarch, he really was a commanding presence. The other two Persians sat very stiffly, sort of on the edge of their chairs, and kept their eyes cast down on their plates and only spoke when spoken to. It was not only rather impressive, but it made

---

*The Shah was born in 1919 and died in 1980.

it damn hard to keep the conversation bouncing around. Jack Monroe and I had the chief of staff thinking up things to talk about, like water skiing. The Shah was a very affable person.

Q: He's very adept at the use of the English language.

Admiral Waters: Yes. Well, anyway, that was a successful thing, and we hoped that the Iranians got some money. I think they did. When we left there and started back down to Bahrain, we got the news that the Suez incident had started, that the British and the French were attacking Egypt and the Suez Canal.* Of course, there had been lots of preliminaries and background on this, and it was expected, but it was sort of a shock that it actually started.

We got right back to Bahrain that same day and, of course, went on very much of a readiness footing, ready for anything. We evacuated a lot of people. A lot of people, including Admiral Monroe, lived in the town of Manama on Bahrain Island. Of course, the oil refineries there were under the British Petroleum Company, and they had a regular

---

*Israeli forces invaded Egypt's Sinai Peninsula on 29 October 1956. Britain and France then intervened on behalf of Israel in an unsuccessful attempt to secure the Suez Canal, which was damaged and closed to traffic. Rather than support the British and French, the United States asked for a United Nations resolution calling for an end to the fighting. A cease-fire took effect on 6 November.

Western European-American type of little city there for those people who worked in the oil compound and the oil refinery business.

We evacuated all of the Americans who weren't there over into the oil city, and they had housing and clubs and commissaries. There was a small amount of rioting there by some of the radicals. The British had a base in Bahrain. There was a British RAF pilot who was burned by the mob, but that was all. They didn't bother anybody else; they didn't bother any of our people.

Q: This was Arab reaction?

Admiral Waters: Arab reaction, plus the British were one of the nations who were attacking the Egyptians, so the Arabs took it out on the British. They didn't bother us.

The most serious thing about it was that the U.S. consul over in Dhahran, Saudi Arabia, sent a report in a very high priority message--flash or immediate or something. He understood that there was terrific rioting, burning, and looting in Bahrain. He was just making up a good story, but it came right in to Washington. Admiral Monroe, because things were so quiet, just sent off a priority message saying that everything was under control, because there wasn't really anything going on. We had these destroyers there. We were in position to do any shore bombardment or anything that might have been required. But, as I say, it wasn't. But the next thing poor Admiral Monroe knew was that he was on the carpet with the Chief of Naval Operations for not telling him about this horrible rioting. It took a day or so to get everybody calmed down, the fact that this fellow had gotten excited and put in the wrong kind of report.

My relief had cleared through the Suez Canal just before the trouble started; they sort of closed the Suez Canal on his coattails.

Q: He was in another destroyer?

Admiral Waters: He was bringing two of his destroyers in. He was Barney McMahon.* Barney came in and came on around. It took several days to get around that long route, through the Red Sea and then around up the Persian Gulf. He got there, so that meant that we had four destroyers plus the AVP which was the flagship of Commander Middle East Force.**

The Suez Canal was closed and things quieted down, and there wasn't much to do. Here I was with two of my ships; the other six were in the Med, and they were due to go back to the States. It was about time for us to end our

---
*Captain Bernard F. McMahon, USN.
**AVP--a small seaplane tender converted for use as flagship.

deployment and get back home before Christmas. So Barney and I got together and held a council of war. He said, "Admiral Monroe is probably happy to have four destroyers here now during this time. It's a good idea for him to have them, but he doesn't need two unit commanders for four destroyers. One of us ought to go." He said, "I don't know, but it's your turn. But if you don't want to go, I'll volunteer."

I said, "Wait a minute; you're second in line."

So we went and talked to Jack Monroe, and he agreed with us that it made sense. So he sent a message off to CinCUSNavEur to get permission to fly one commodore and his three staff officers out to rejoin with the fleet.* There was a little bit of a delay back in London about who was going to pay for this. They were still sending messages back and forth, when Jack Monroe--I always loved him for it--said, "Aw, hell. Go ahead and we'll buy you a ticket. Get on the plane and go."

We did go and it was a great idea, because we flew out from Manama on a BOAC or something up to Istanbul and down to Rome, and then took the rapido down to Naples and reported in there.** By that time, all of my ships, not counting the two that were still in the Persian Gulf, but the other six--of the other six, five had left for the

---

*CinCUSNavEur--Commander in Chief U.S. Naval Forces Europe.
**BOAC--British Overseas Airways Corporation.

States. There was still one left, and she was due in Gibraltar in the next two or three days and was going to join up with several other ships and go back. So they flew us to Gibraltar, where we joined up with the USS Strong, which was one of the ships in the squadron, and took off with her and with four other destroyers.

We were doing fine, sailing along, heading back for Norfolk. This was just after Thanksgiving. We ran into the sphere of influence of a very large force. It had several aircraft carriers and more destroyers than I'd seen in one place since World War II. I think there were 20 in the screen, fueling ships, and the whole works. We were ordered to join them, which rather dashed us, because we had been hoping to sneak straight into Norfolk. But we stayed out there with them for a few days while they ran back and forth and while the international situation quieted down, and then we finally got home.

Q: They constituted a fleet in readiness, did they?

Admiral Waters: Yes, they were just gathered from what was left of the Atlantic Fleet that was not in overhaul or not in early preliminary fundamental training, elementary training, and gotten ready in case they were needed in connection with the Suez crisis. Of course, it died down, and all of these ships went back into port, and we were very happy to get there.

Q: Since you were there and a part of that crisis, perhaps I should ask you what your interpretation of it is and preface the question by saying that there are some who felt that this was a watershed incident, that up to that point we had made it known to the world at large that we were prepared to use atomic weapons in emergency, and then on this occasion we backed down. In that sense it's been interpreted as a watershed because from that point on, the Russians took the ball and carried it. What is your interpretation of it?

Admiral Waters: I don't know that I'm qualified to comment on that particular part of it, on whether it was really a watershed incident or not. My feeling, sitting there in the Persian Gulf while this was happening, was that the French and the British didn't seem to be prepared to do what they set out to do. At the very outset they dropped in airborne troops, and then it was a matter of several days before anything else happened. We all felt that they didn't seem to have all of their ducks in line.

It still seems to me that if they had hit the canal and the Egyptians all at once with the air drop and with an amphibious force just off the beach at that time, that the whole thing would have been over. There wouldn't have been all of this arguing between the different countries and the fact that Eisenhower, our President at that time, refused to let the U.S. fleet have anything to do with it. It really would have solved the problem automatically.

Those of us in the Navy, sitting on the sidelines, couldn't understand why it was they didn't do it that way, and I still don't know. Of course, we did stand back, and it created a lot of hard feelings amongst the British. It was very difficult after I came out of there and went to Gibraltar to join my ships and to see friends of mine in the Royal Navy. I just tried not to talk about it, because I really didn't know anything about it anyway. But they felt pretty badly about having been let down.

Q: Their reaction was an immediate one.

Admiral Waters: Yes. I saw one of the officers there. He was commanding a squadron of their destroyers, an officer who had been on duty with me on the SACLant staff. I knew him quite well, and he was very bitter. We weren't very popular around Gibraltar at that particular time.

Q: Did you have any brushes with the French? I mean, how did they react?

Admiral Waters: No, I didn't see any French. Of course, I came just directly over from Italy to Gibraltar and then home. The two ships I left behind in the Persian Gulf, who were due home for Christmas from their six-month deployment, made it around the Cape of Good Hope and got home about February, I think. They weren't as unhappy as you might have thought; they got a very fine cruise down the East Coast of Africa and across. I think they even stopped in a South American port like Rio. This took some of the sting off of being away from home an extra few months.

Q: When were you able to free yourself and your destroyers from the flotilla in the Atlantic?

Admiral Waters: Oh, well, that went on for a couple or three days, and then the task force was dissolved. We probably went home to Norfolk by units; I've forgotten now. We didn't stay out there as long as we had feared. We could have stayed a long time, because they had plenty of fuel out there in the big task force.

After that we had a short time, which you usually get in port, like six weeks, from coming back from a deployment--through the holidays. Then we went into a very interesting phase where we worked for about six months with a hunter-killer task force, a hunter-killer antisubmarine carrier. My squadron was the screen on it, and we stayed together and worked together for six months.

Q: In the Atlantic?

Admiral Waters: In the Atlantic. Went down to the Caribbean during the winter months and had a lot of fun. We felt that we got to be a very good submarine hunting team by the end of six months. By that time we could all work together with a few orders and operate on doctrine and really get things done, at which time the group was dissolved. Then we were told to get ready to go back to the Med again and start screening the big, heavy carriers. So we deployed back early in July of '57 and went over. By that time I was senior enough to be the senior destroyer officer in the Med, so I was the screen commander for the Sixth Fleet. We worked in Task Force 66, the big carrier task force. We had a lot of fun in that respect. I enjoyed it a great deal, running the screen for the carrier task forces.

We encountered another international incident at that time. As I remember, there was trouble in Jordan, and the whole fleet gravitated towards the Eastern Med towards the latter part of our stay there. We stayed over in that area the whole time. Again, I got the duty of going down into the Red Sea and Persian Gulf. By that time the canal was open again. I must say that they were the same two ships, and there was a great deal of concern on the ships as to whether we were going to get back through or not; they thought maybe this was a bad luck charm and that it was going to be the same way as it was the year before, but it wasn't. It was a very normal cruise.

We again did some training with the Iranian Navy, but we came back on schedule that time.

Q: Had relations with the British improved in that period of time?

Admiral Waters: Well, yes, I think they had. As I remember, it was on that cruise that we did a joint NATO amphibious exercise in which we worked with British destroyers as a screen for an amphibious landing down in Sardinia, and our relationships with them were very good. Actually, the British officer was given command of the screen, and I worked under him. We had very good relationships. So that cruise went off more or less on schedule, except at the end of it this trouble in Jordan had the whole fleet over in the Eastern Med. That time we came back as a whole squadron, but we were about two weeks late leaving because of the crisis over there.

Q: In other words, we were somewhat edgy, were we not?

Admiral Waters: Yes, yes. But those Mediterranean deployments--I imagine they are still the same way--were a lot of fun, because you really operated under high readiness conditions, and you sort of felt like you were playing on the first team. When you first got there and joined up, you were a little rusty, but by the time you left the Med, you felt you had really well-trained ships that could really do their jobs.

Q: Did you feel, operating in the Mediterranean, especially vulnerable, a closed sea, when more often your experience had been in the open Atlantic or Pacific?

Admiral Waters: Yes, you did get a little bit of claustrophobia over there. You run out of ocean. One of the main features of the Mediterranean, I think, that's different from operating in the big oceans is that the weather can create bad sea conditions so rapidly, and also they can dissipate very rapidly. It's a very changeable place to operate in. It can be calm one day, and because it is relatively small, a storm system coming through can churn it up so that it gets very violently rough, and then it can get calm again in another short period.

Q: The physical circumstances of operating in the

Mediterranean are certainly in evidence, but there must be a mental attitude also that goes with it.

Admiral Waters: Yes, I think there is. And, of course, it's a very busy body of water. There's an awful lot of shipping in addition to the naval shipping. A tremendous amount of commercial shipping goes through there.

Q: Coast-wise.

Admiral Waters: Coast-wise and crisscrossing, so that from the standpoint of underwater sound operations, it's a very noisy body of water. There is a lot of acoustic noise under the water all of the time just from the ship traffic going through there. It's sort of an oceanographer's nightmare to predict the undersea characteristics of the Med, just because of the shape and size, the fact that you get lots of runoff of fresh water into a relatively small body of salt water in the rainy season. That changes the salinity and gives you layers which affect sound transmission. In the dry season, by the same token, you get higher salinity because you don't get enough runoff to replace the evaporation, and the water gets saltier. You have layering, and usually you can count on the Mediterranean to have very bad sonar conditions for catching submarines.

One of the interesting things I was on early in that cruise--on the second cruise to the Mediterranean--was in working over what was pretty obviously a Russian submarine. We had completed an exercise in the Western Mediterranean and, as was usual after the end of the exercise, the fleet would split up and go into different liberty ports. Just before you went into port, you always fueled and took on stores so that in case anything happened, you could pull out and be ready to go. So you always fueled before going into port by the fueling-at-sea process. And this was a busy time, particularly for the screen commander, because I was responsible for getting all of the destroyers alongside the right place at the right time and making sure that the schedule was carried out and not delayed.

We were just completing a very busy morning of replenishing and were just about to sit down and put our feet up and have a cup of coffee and go into port for a nice liberty. Then one of the destroyers that was lifeguarding astern of a replenishment ship spotted a submarine's periscope in the middle of formation. So he turned and picked him up on his sonar right away, and it was obviously a Russian submarine spying on the replenishment formation. So the submarine, of course, went down, and we put a half a dozen destroyers on it. I suddenly found myself as the scene-of-action commander of what was called a hold-down operation. The idea was to try to hold this fellow down by keeping in contact with him until he had to surface to renew his battery, at which time people said, "Well, what do you do now?"

I said, "Well, you render passing honors; you salute his flag. But you still have one up on him. You've made him disclose himself."

It has since been successfully done, as you know, but it hadn't been successfully done then, and everybody was very much interested in pulling one of these things off to get sort of a one up on the Soviets. We had this fellow dead to rights, but, as I said, the sonar conditions in the Med are very, very poor. From reviewing the records, I think we held this fellow for about 36 hours, and I believe he got away then when there was a very shallow layer. I had destroyers working him over, I had air support from Sardinia and patrol planes with sonobuoys and MAD gear and all sorts of things.* But after the time when I thought we lost him, we kept getting other contacts and had to check them out. We stayed out for about nine days on this.

Q: What was his potential for staying under?

Admiral Waters: Well, it's pretty hard to figure because if he was just lying doggo and not using his engines, he could have stayed quite a long time--probably a week, you

---

*MAD--magnetic anomaly detection.

know, if we weren't using up any of his battery. Or if he had gotten his snorkel up or something some distance away from us and we had caught him again, then he could have gone on for a longer period. But we eventually gave the thing up. They even sent a tanker out so we refueled, just so we could stay on the job. It was a very interesting operation, a very tough one. Of course, everybody in the whole Navy and all the way up to the White House were interested in this thing. We had to send a situation report every four hours on what was going on, and it went right directly to the top.

Admiral Burke was the CNO then, and he was most interested in trying to catch one of these guys, just to hold him down until he had to come up and holler Uncle. This fellow really was lying doggo on a layer, I think, and conserving his battery until he finally slipped away on us. He was fairly shallow. We even put a boat over with divers to dive down and see if they could possibly see him, to prove that we had what we had. We couldn't quite do that. We dragged a grapnel through the water and caught it on something and straightened up the tines of the grapnel.

So I reported all of these things that we were doing, and I kept getting encouragement from the CNO, and I knew who that was. It wasn't just some staff guy. Finally, after trying all of these things and getting pretty discouraged, I ended up one situation report with, "I have tried everything on this bird except salt on his tail." This, of course, went out secret, priority, and so forth. As I say, it went right back to the top.

About four hours later, I got a message in plain language from the CNO to me, and I knew who wrote it. It said, "Your So-and-so: Try salt." He finally slipped away on us, but they gave us an E for effort. We all went into Genoa, and they brought in the aviators from the planes and all of the destroyer people, everybody who had been in the exercise. We all got together, which was a very good idea of Admiral Brown to get everybody together and write down everything we knew about this operation while it was still fresh in everyone's mind. While we were doing this, we came up with the idea of proposed tactics for conducting such an operation, improvements in tactics.

Q: What you could do another time.

Admiral Waters: Lessons that we had learned. There were lots of things that came out. It was an entirely different thing from the normal submarine ASW tactic, where you go in and kill. You go in, you get a good contact, and you drop charges or fire ASROC or whatever.* You shoot your weapons at him to kill. Well, you're deprived of your ace card, because in this case you can't hurt him. You are not

---

*ASROC--antisubmarine rocket.

allowed to do that, so the advantage shifts very much to his side. All he has to do is lie around and get away from you. He's not trying to shoot a torpedo at you, and you're not trying to drop something at him. And he has the advantage of stealth and concealment.

Q: It's just sort of a hide-and-seek game.

Admiral Waters: There were lots of things. Instead of charging in at high speed, we found that the best thing to do was to form a kind of a fence around him with ships going very, very slowly so that he couldn't hear you. We were just listening for him; that way we could keep track of him a lot better. You didn't go at high speed so you made wakes in the water to give you an echo anyway from a sonar. So we proposed all of these tactics, and Admiral Brown thought they were great and he put them into effect right away as tactics for the Sixth Fleet. So it was fun—unsuccessful, but it was a good try. Of course, since then, we've gotten good enough that it's been done several times. They've done it to us too. Sailors always want to know, "What do you do if you make him surface?" Invite the skipper over for a cup of coffee if you're still friendly.

Interview Number 5 with
Rear Admiral Odale D. Waters, Jr., U.S. Navy (Retired)

Place: Admiral Waters's home in North Indialantic, Florida

Date: Friday, 4 December 1985

Interviewer: Paul Stillwell

Q: Admiral, to begin, I think one incident that we could pick up from your time as Commander Destroyer Squadron Two was when your flag captain was relieved rather unexpectedly.

Admiral Waters: Yes. That was in the summer of '57, when we were in the Mediterranean fleet. We had finished the competition year, and the flagship, the Barton, which was commanded by then-Commander Ray Peet, had won the E for excellence for the squadron. We were ordered, while at sea on an exercise, to approach the flagship for personnel transfer, and we knew what that meant; it meant that Admiral Brown was coming over to inspect us, Admiral Cat Brown then being commander of the Sixth Fleet. He came over to inspect us, but he also came over to present Ray Peet with the plaque for being first in the annual competition.

Within a couple of days, we received orders. It was during the night we received them. I remember distinctly I was in my cabin early in the morning, still asleep, when

Ray Peet burst in. He apologized for waking me up so early, but he said, "We've got a problem here. We've got to do something about it quick." He handed me a dispatch that contained his orders to report to Washington as the aide to the Chief of Naval Operations, who was then Admiral Arleigh Burke.

I read it over, and I said, "Well, you say we've got to do something, Ray. But I'll tell you something you're not going to try to do."

He said, "What?"

I said, "We're not going to try to stop these orders, because I know who wrote them--Admiral Burke himself."*

We had a difficult time. We had an officer on board who was fairly well experienced in submarines, but he had little time in destroyers. He was the executive officer. So I called him up and asked him if he thought he could take the command of the ship. We were at that time just about starting to make another run down through the canal to be a detachment of the Sixth Fleet, at which destroyers had to take turns. I was to take two ships, as I had the preceding summer, and go down through the canal and spend a month in the Red Sea-Persian Gulf area.

I can't remember his name, the officer who did this, but he did a good job. I called him in and asked him if he thought he could do it, and he said he'd like to have a try

---
*Admiral Peet's Naval Institute oral history records his memories of this same experience.

at it. I said, "All right, you've got it." As a matter of fact, it was about the only thing we could do--to promote the exec up to temporary commanding officer, or to commanding officer--nothing temporary about it. And he did a good job.

Q: How long did he keep that then?

Admiral Waters: I think he kept it for the better part of a year. He was, of course, not quite senior enough for it, and there were other people standing in line for destroyer commands, but he did well. The main thing I recall about that incident was that he said, "Yes, I'm sure I can do it, Commodore. Of course, you'll be here to help me."

I said, "Let's get one thing straight. You are going to be the captain, and I'm not going to be standing over your shoulder telling you what to do. You've got to do it all on your own, just as if I weren't here." Of course, that didn't actually happen, but it gave him a lot of self-confidence.

Q: How did it work out in practice?

Admiral Waters: It worked out pretty well. The only time that we had a little difficulty was going down through the canal. I don't know whether it still works that way, but in those days, you left about daylight from the northern end at Port Said and went in convoy south through the canal. At the same time a northbound convoy started from Port Suez down at the southern end, and we met sort of in the center at Great Bitter Lake. The southbound convoy would pull off to the side and anchor in the broad expanse of Great Bitter Lake and let the northbound convoy pass. Then you would go on down and exit at Suez. It took all day. By the time we got to the southern end, it was dark. The channel area was marked, but it was a little twisty. We were leading the other destroyer through it. That, as I recall, was about the only time that I ever stepped in. The new skipper was a little bit shaky, and he was going about two-thirds speed. There was some current, so I stepped in and advised him to increase his speed a little bit so the current wouldn't sweep us out of the channel. He was a little nervous, and I would have been, too, if I hadn't done it before.

Q: Did you have a pilot on that occasion?

Admiral Waters: We had dropped the pilot by that time. We had a pilot coming all the way through, but we dropped the pilot and then went heading on our own out into the Red Sea.

Q: Were there any noteworthy experiences from that tour?

Admiral Waters: No, there were no really noteworthy tours, except that so many of the crew had been on board the year before when we had been trapped in the Persian Gulf. There was a little bit of uneasiness amongst the crew about whether we would get back through or not this time. Everybody breathed a sign of relief when we did.

Q: Did you have any contacts with the Saudis during that deployment?

Admiral Waters: No. We didn't actually go into any Saudi ports. The base for Commander Middle East Force was Bahrain Island, which, as you know, is an independent sheikdom and under protection of the British. I presume it still is. Things change so much over there. But it wasn't Saudi Arabia, which was very nice, because Saudi Arabia was kind of tough to live in then. They enforced the Muslim laws of no alcohol and that sort of thing. That would have been very bad for the sailors' morale, not being able to get their beer. We didn't go into Ras Tanura or any of the other oil ports.

Q: How much time did you spend in port as compared with

under way?

Admiral Waters: Oh, I think it was probably about 50-50, as I recall it, or maybe more weighted towards being under way, because we didn't stay there very long, and it took you a long time to get there and a long time to get home. That maneuver of keeping at least two destroyers in the Persian Gulf-Red Sea area at all times involved six or eight destroyers. There were two on station, two leaving, two coming; six destroyers involved at all times.

Q: That's a pretty heavy commitment to maintain that presence.

Admiral Waters: Yes.

Q: Did you give the crews any special briefings on the customs in that area so they wouldn't make faux pas?

Admiral Waters: Yes, we did. They were given a briefing on the Muslim religion. I don't recall that we had any incidents at all. The places that we went, the natives that you came in contact with were always trying to sell you something, so they were very polite. The crew seemed to enjoy it. It was unusual. They brought back a bunch of junk, you know, brass and stuff like that, an Arab headdress.

Q: Then you were detached, I presume, and sent back to the Mediterranean before you went home?

Admiral Waters: Yes, we went back and joined the fleet, and I again took over the job as commander of the screen around the Sixth Fleet, which was a very important job. I always said there was the commander of the Sixth Fleet, the commander of the screen, and the commander of the logistics force, and they were the three most important guys there. Those exercises we had were a lot of fun. We were actually held over for about, oh, three weeks past our scheduled departure time, because there was a NATO exercise laid on in the Med. The British were flying aircraft that I believe they called Mosquitoes; they were the enemy. They were armed with nuclear weapons on this trip, and they were to try to destroy the Sixth Fleet.

My squadron was scheduled to leave, but somebody had the bright idea of using my squadron as a decoy. So I was called up for a conference I think they had at Rhodes, and they asked me if I thought we could make this squadron look like a carrier group. There were some scientific types there that had figured that if you put a radar reflector on something you could tow about 100 yards astern of the lead ship and have another ship keeping station right with this reflector, right on it, that it would look like a carrier. Then the rest of the ships were in a bent-line screen out ahead.

We looked it over, and I talked to my flag skipper, who said he thought he could do it. So we let another ship tow the spar, and the flagship took station just 100 yards astern of the other ship at fairly high speed, the way a carrier would go in that kind of an exercise. We practiced it a bit, and then we had the exercise. Of course, we didn't know what was going on; we just steamed along the way we were supposed to and kept station on this thing and quite successfully. We had to be very alert, because that's pretty close to steam up behind another ship.

The next morning, when the exercise was completed, I got a message from the fleet commander, saying, "Congratulations. You have absorbed about 50% of the enemy's nuclear power." And it ended by saying, "Hope you all have your lead-lined jockstraps on."

Q: That sounds like Brown.

Admiral Waters: So we were then dismissed with a "well done" and steamed back home.

Q: Did you do anything to simulate a carrier's electronic signature?

Admiral Waters: Some. We jabbered on the radio, but we didn't do much of that stuff. Of course, at that time electronic countermeasures were just starting. We had them in the ships, but they didn't work very well.

Q: What do you recall about Admiral Brown's operating style? He's been pictured as a very aggressive commander.

Admiral Waters: Well, he was very aggressive, and he was really hipped on the subject of having destroyers operate smartly and fast. When you're in a screening situation like that around a fast carrier task group, when you get a tactical message coming out over the voice radio, the destroyers don't wait for the execute. You get the message and see what it is, and it's going to take the destroyers usually longer to get to their new stations. If it's a change of course or change in the way the ships are deployed, the destroyers are supposed to move just as soon as they hear the message and not wait for the execute when all the big ships do. I told my officers--and this seemed to work pretty well; it seemed to satisfy Brown--I said, "When you get a message like that, even before you've figured out where you're going to go on your maneuvering board, ring 'all ahead flank' and put the rudder over one way or the other so you'll get some white water under your tail." And that worked great. We were congratulated for moving very fast; sometimes they were moving in the wrong direction for a few minutes, but that was all right.

Another thing was that Brown liked to see ships approach the fueling ship very rapidly. No destroyer people liked this because of what he wanted destroyers to do, and of course, actually did when we were working for him. You would get in position, two or three ships lined up astern of the tanker, and as soon as one pulled away, the other would start in. You'd start in at high speed, and when you got about with your bow overlapping the stern of the tanker, you'd back down. That was a little dangerous in case something went wrong in the engine room, but it looked really good. Ray Peet was especially good at this one; he made it look just great. Brown loved that, but as soon as we got a new Commander Sixth Fleet over there, they stopped doing that. I think maybe they had one accident. But it was a strain on the ship's engineering plant. As I say, if something went wrong and one screw backed and the other didn't, then you had a collision situation.

Q: Was there ever a tendency to operate in worse weather than might have been prudent? That's another thing I've heard about Brown.

Admiral Waters: Well, we might have been so, but as I recall, we were there in the summertime, and in the summertime you don't get much bad weather in the Med. When you do get bad weather in the Med at any time, it doesn't last very long. The seas can be really big and rough one day, but because the Med is so small, it smoothes out. So I didn't run into any of that with the old Cat.

Q: Are there any of your squadron COs that you especially remember other than Peet?

Admiral Waters: Now you're pushing an old man's memory. I can see them, but I can't remember their names. The skipper of the <u>Strong</u> was an awfully good officer, but I can't pull his name out of the hat. If I had a list, I could.

Q: After you out-chopped, how much longer were you in the squadron command?

Admiral Waters: Destroyer squadron commands were so popular then that I arrived home, as I recall, about the first of November.

We had an interesting trip home, because at that time there was some kind of trouble brewing, as there usually was, in the Middle East. The whole fleet was in the eastern side of the Med. Usually when your relief got to Gibraltar, that was the chop line; you could start going home. But they moved it then, because the bulk of the fleet was way over in the eastern Med, and we had to come through the Strait of Messina at Sicily, past the tip of Italy, before we chopped. So we were relieved when our relief got there, and then we started back. We had the whole trip across the western Med.

My orders were to fuel at Gibraltar and then proceed from there to Norfolk, if possible, stopping at Bermuda for fuel if necessary. In other words, it was sort of a challenge. So we got the skippers all together, and we decided on a way to see if we could get across the Atlantic. These were short hulled, 2,200-ton destroyers. It was going to be pretty close. It was close. Going across the western Med, we tried a formation that we worked out, where we put the ship with the worst record for fuel economy in the center as guide, and then we had a loose circular formation around him and set a constant speed--I forget what the speed was; it was the most economical speed, somewhere between 12 and 15 knots, I think. Of course, he steamed at that steady speed, which meant he steamed more efficiently than anybody else. But we also had a rule that we had them spread apart enough so that they kept a constant speed until they dropped way out of position, and then they slowly regained position. Some of the ones at the tail end of the circle were not too visible when you got up in the morning. That arrangement seemed to work pretty well.

We had high hopes. We got into Gibraltar and got full fuel and started off. But we ran into the usual bad weather that you run into between the west side of Europe and the Azores, and that used up some fuel. We were steaming into head seas and winds. We kept figuring and figuring and figuring, and finally we got to the point where I had to make a decision. I said, "Well, I'd sure love to do it, but I would sure hate to get almost to Norfolk and have to have fleet tugs come out and tow us in." So we, at that point, changed course to the south, went to Bermuda, and fueled. As it turned out, we could have made it, because we had nothing but beautiful flat, calm weather the rest of the way. But if we had had just one storm without fueling, we couldn't have made it.

Q: Better to be prudent in that situation.

Admiral Waters: Yes, yes. Of course, everybody was disappointed, because they wanted to get home for Thanksgiving.

But to continue on with your question about leaving the squadron. When the squadron came in to the destroyer piers at Norfolk, of course, there were big crowds of people there. We had a band, and all the crews' and officers' families were there. There was a very good friend of mine, George Washington Pressey, who later became an admiral too.* He was standing on the pier to meet me, because he had orders in his hands to relieve me and was looking forward to it. He relieved me in about three weeks, I think.

Q: Then you went to Yorktown. I've interviewed one of your predecessors in that job, Admiral E. K. Walker.** He had been a destroyer squadron commander earlier, and he said he thought that was even more challenging than running a single large ship. I wonder how you would make that comparison.

Admiral Waters: Well, it was different, of course. There were different problems, but it was a very interesting job. I'll tell you the personal side of that. I got a letter before we started across from P. D. Stroop.*** Have you interviewed him?

Q: He's in our collection. My predecessor interviewed him.

---

*Captain George Washington Pressey, USN.
**Rear Admiral Edward K. Walker, USN (Ret.), whose oral history is in the Naval Institute collection.
***Rear Admiral Paul D. Stroop, USN.

Admiral Waters: Well, he was an aviator, but he was assistant chief of what was still called BuOrd then.* It was just about to be changed to BuWeps.** But he was assistant chief, and he was also an ordnance PG.*** I got a letter from him saying that they were looking for somebody to command the Naval Mine Depot in Yorktown, and that he would like very much to have me to take the job. Oh, my God, a wonderful job and it's a beautiful station. The quarters were built back in the early Twenties, and they were built like quarters were supposed to be built. The captain's quarters sits on a broad expanse of lawn overlooking the York River, with the other officers' quarters stretching on down the line. But the captain's quarters were big enough to look good with big southern pillars out in front, that sort of thing.

Q: Admiral Walker described the house as being built as solidly as a fortress.

Admiral Waters: Actually, they were reinforced concrete, and they were supposed to withstand an explosion if you had it on the ammunition storage part of the station.

At any rate, I got home and talked it over with my

---
*BuOrd--Bureau of Ordnance.
**BuWeps--Bureau of Naval Weapons. Stroop became the first chief of the new bureau when it was established in 1959.
***PG--Postgraduate.

wife. I said, "Here's the situation. We can accept this job which P. D. Stroop has offered, or we could say no, and I could try for a job in the Pentagon." I was a senior captain at that time. I was 47 years old and had had my major command. I was coming under the gun for flag. Actually, some of my class had already been selected when we started that early dipping-down business, including Francis Foley.*

So I said, "If I really want to try to make admiral, I should probably go to the Pentagon, but it will be the sort of a job of showing yourself, getting visibility, and really you don't have the responsibility and authority there. You sort of shuffle papers around from one committee meeting to the next and that sort of thing. Yorktown is pleasant living. I probably wouldn't make admiral from there, but it would be probably the pleasantest living we've ever had. Besides that, I wouldn't be bored with the job, like I would be if I were commandant of a naval base again or commandant of a naval district, where you spend most of your time watching parades and that sort of thing."

So we talked it over and decided we'd go for Yorktown. I did, and I never regretted it. I got there, and I relieved a captain who was embittered because he had had a heart attack and wasn't able to have a major command or a

---
*Rear Admiral Francis D. Foley, USN (Ret.), is the subject of a two-volume Naval Institute oral history.

chance at flag rank. Pierce Chilton was his name, and he didn't take too much interest in the station.* Maybe I shouldn't put this on the record about another officer. He was a capable guy, but I can understand how he felt, because he had had a real good chance to go on up. Anyway, I took over from him.

We had a fine bunch of officers. I had about 3,000 civil service employees there. As you probably know, it was the big mass detonating storage place for the Atlantic Fleet. Yorktown was and still is the main storage for what they call mass detonating explosives. It got its name from the fact that the mines are actually filled there with explosives. They stored large bombs and just about everything except gun ammunition, which was then stored in a little ammunition depot down near Norfolk, called St. Juliens Creek. I think that's since been closed, but I'm not sure.

Q: I'm not sure either.

Admiral Waters: Anyway, we were the mine depot. Also by the time I got there, we had a big missile facility for the three T's.

Q: Tartar, Terrier, and Talos.**

---
*Captain William Pierce Chilton, USN.
**The reference is to three types of naval surface-to-air missiles that entered the fleet in the 1950s.

Admiral Waters: Yes, and we stored them and adjusted them and repaired them. At what they called Skiff's Creek Annex, we had a nuclear facility, where we actually had all of the nuclear weapons for both the Atlantic and Mediterranean fleets. We were allowed to say that we had a nuclear capability there, but we were not allowed to say whether we did or did not have any nuclear weapons. Under me I had a commander as officer in charge of that facility. That had very special security. Because of the missiles and the nuclear weapons, we had the largest Marine barracks in the continental United States for security. It's 13,600 acres, a huge place, and beautiful, a forested place. Of course, it was ideal for magazines because there were a lot of hills and valleys. I don't think that an ordinary conventional magazine would have hurt much of anything if it had blown up. I used to tell Harry Cox, who was the officer in charge of Skiff's Creek, that if he had any nuclear accidents over there, he was the one that had to go up and tell Mr. Rockefeller that he couldn't use Colonial Williamsburg for the next 2,000 years, because that was only 13 miles away.*

At any rate, with all of this activity there, it kept me busy and, as I say, it was something I was interested

---

*Commander C. Harry Cox, USN. The Rockefeller family, which amassed its fortune from Standard Oil, provided the philanthropic support for the restoration and maintenance of Colonial Williamsburg.

in. We had a big loading pier, and many ships came in. Particularly destroyers and cruisers came in to get missiles and bombs and that sort of thing.

Q: That was really at the beginning of the missile era. Was there a Pacific counterpart yet on the missile storage?

Admiral Waters: Yes, I think that was at Seal Beach, California. I think that was Seal Beach NAD.*

Anyway, it suddenly occurred to me that here I had all of these fine young officers who were working for me, and they were getting fitness reports that were headed "Naval Mine Depot," which really didn't reflect the mission; it was sort of old-fashioned. I think I led the parade in the name-changing thing. I proposed this, and the bureau went along with me, and we changed the name from the Naval Mine Depot to the Naval Weapons Station in 1958.

That was an education in itself. You say, "Well, let's change the name." Sure, you change the name, you change the stationery, or you do what we did--blank it out and stamp over it. You get into things like changing the post office, because we were an official U.S. post office. You've got to get into letter-writing with the postal department. That wasn't really hard to do. Then we had to

---

*Seal Beach Naval Ammunition Depot, near Long Beach, California.

work with the State Highway Commission to change all the road signs. They got the road signs changed before we changed the name.

Q: Who had to approve the change itself?

Admiral Waters: I think the bureau, and then I believe it probably had to go over to CNO, but it was all approved. I'm trying to remember whether we did it on the 40th birthday of the old Naval Mine Depot or not; we may have or may not have; I'm not sure. We had a big ceremony and had the bureau chief down and changed the name. After that, a lot of people followed in changing the names of their stations.

Q: One thing that Admiral Walker remembered from his tour was the ceremony associated with Yorktown Day each year.

Admiral Waters: Oh, yes. You learned all about the pecking order in all of these organizations connected with the Revolutionary War, such as the DAR and the SAR.* I didn't know anything about that until I got there. The thing that did impress me was that that occurs on October the 19th, and it had been customary for many years for the

---

*DAR--Daughters of the American Revolution; SAR--Sons of the American Revolution.

Navy to furnish a military parade consisting of the Marines at the Marine barracks. We didn't have very many sailors attached to that station; we had an awful lot of Marines. They would put on a beautiful parade. Then they would have all kinds of dignitaries over in the village of Yorktown in the reviewing stands.

When I was there, I tried to find out who was supposed to be the reviewing officer, but they didn't know about that kind of thing. So everybody took the salute. There were the Sons of Cincinnati, the Friends of Lafayette, and various other outfits that I had never heard of, and they were up above the Sons of the American Revolution in the pecking order. Sons of Cincinnati, I think, had to be descended on the male side from people who were on Washington's staff.

Q: Pretty exclusive.

Admiral Waters: Pretty tough, yes. But it always seemed to me that a lot more should have been made of Yorktown Day, October the 19th, because that was the day that the country really began. That was when Cornwallis surrendered and made it possible for us to be the United States of America.

Q: I would guess that being from Virginia didn't hurt you

O. D. Waters, Jr. #5 - 302

at all at Yorktown.

Admiral Waters: No. There was another funny thing that happened. When they first established Yorktown in the early Twenties, the mine depot bought a lot of land. We tried to exclude as many of the old historic spots as we could, but there were just some that were impossible. There are some wonderful examples of 17th and 18th century farmhouses. There was one in particular that was back in the ammunition storage area, the restricted area, where you had to have a special pass to get in. A retired doctor, an old man from Richmond, was the descendant of the people who had owned that house, and he would come down about once a year to have a look at it. He would never tell you when he was coming. Fortunately, the crew had been in there and had run the mowers through, and the grass was all cut, and the place looked good. Apparently, the previous time he had come it was sort of a wilderness. He showed up one day, and so I put him in the car and took him out to the ammunition storage area. When we got back to the office, he said, "Well, it's easy to see we've finally got a good Virginia man in here running this place."

Q: Did he still have ownership, or what was the situation?

Admiral Waters: He didn't have ownership, but there was an

agreement that the house would be preserved, and it was. We patched it up and kept the roof tight and that sort of thing.

Q: What determined your inventory? Did the Bureau of Ordnance control how much of what things you would have?

Admiral Waters: Well, actually, the initial determination would descend from CNO to the fleets, then come to the bureau and down to us. The operating people would determine what they thought they needed, and we might change that a little bit to have a little safety margin.

Q: There was a manufacturing capability as well as storage, wasn't there?

Admiral Waters: Yes, yes.

Q: How much manufacturing did you do?

Admiral Waters: We did a fair amount, particularly in the manufacturing of some of the large bombs and the mines. The mine cases, we filled an awful lot of them there. During World War II they had had a big explosion there that wiped out a whole mine-filling plant, and people were a little leery of that kind of an operation. But that is where the danger occurs with ammunition; it's when you're making it or when you're moving it around. If you can leave it in one place, leave it. We had revetments where we could keep a railroad car, a boxcar, full of ammunition and store it there until we got ready to tow it down to the pier and around. We had railroad tracks running all over the station.

There was another thing I was instrumental in getting started; it wasn't completed while I was there. We had an L-shaped pier, and the traffic was a problem when a ship was alongside being loaded or off-loaded; you'd meet yourself coming back. So we finally got it made into a rectangular pier.

Q: You'd had much or nearly all of your experience up to then exclusively Navy, military organizations. Now you had this vast civil service organization to manage. What did you have to do to be capable of doing that?

Admiral Waters: Well, you had to learn something about civil service and their rules. I very fortunately had an excellent director of civil service personnel, and he taught me a lot. I had to learn an awful lot about civil service regulations, and what you could do and what you couldn't do. Bill Davis was his name; he was a grand guy. I used to get him every now and then when we'd have some crisis come up with the civil service. I'd say, "Bill, I wish we could go back to the days of Andrew Jackson."

He'd say, "What do you mean, Captain?"

I'd say, "To the victor belongs the spoils. We ought to throw all of these guys out every four years and get a bunch of new ones."

An interesting thing that happened while I was there was that President Kennedy agreed that the federal employees could be unionized.* They never had been permitted to unionize before. We had a pretty good setup where we had a monthly meeting of the leaders of all the different groups, and anybody could come who wanted. We had it in the auditorium, and I would conduct it, and we'd keep notes. It was a formally conducted meeting, but then everybody had a chance to stand up and speak his peace. The people were quite happy with it, so that when the first union came in to try to organize Yorktown, they met a cold shoulder. The people didn't want it. They didn't want to pay dues. They were happy; they were getting treated right, and they liked it the way it was. So all the unions were able to attract to their side were the sort of wackos who wanted to make a name for themselves in some way.

This culminated in an incident one day when I was visited by the head man of the union that was trying to

---

*John F. Kennedy (1917-1963) was the 35th President of the United States, serving from 1961 until his assassination on 22 November 1963.

organize us. He came into the office, and he was indignant, because the notices about the meetings for union organization that he had put up over in some of the offices of the ammunition factories had been torn down by the employees. He was indignant and wanted to know what I was going to do about it. I said, "Well, you are trying to organize these people, and if they don't want to be organized, it seems to me that's your problem. What are you going to do about it?" That's the way it stood. I don't think they ever got a union while I was there, but they did later on.

Q: Did your work force come largely from the local area?

Admiral Waters: Practically solidly from two rural counties in Virginia, York County, which surrounded us, and right across the York River from us was Gloucester County. They all came from there. You'd find names of the same families.

Q: Different generations?

Admiral Waters: Yes, different generations, brothers and sisters. I remember one of the big families in York County was the Hogge family. We had a lot of Hogges there.

Q: Was there any reluctance about this potentially hazardous sort of work?

Admiral Waters: No. No. We'd had, really, so few accidents, and the place had been there long enough, so we had pretty well developed safety precautions that were adhered to and strictly enforced.

Q: What are some examples of safety precautions to prevent this sort of tragedy?

Admiral Waters: Well, one of the things that we were afraid of was having a fire start near the ammunition magazines, which were built in these valleys and wooded ravines and so forth; they were all surrounded by thick trees, leaves, and so forth. That would be the number-one danger. One of the ways of preventing that from starting was that there was a box at the entrance to this restricted area, and anybody who smoked had to put his lighter or his matches in there. If you were caught back in there with anything that would start a fire, usually you'd go out the front gate.

Q: So it was really comparable to going in a magazine on a ship.

Admiral Waters: Yes. That's right. That's right. One thing I had to change when I got there was that we had a fire whistle, a big, huge whistle that you could hear all over the place, and we had automatic devices in the magazines. Sometimes if the water pressure in the mains would get low, the fire whistle would go off automatically, and we'd have a false alarm. When that happened, all the senior officers were called up and told what device had been set off, and they would stream to that.

So they all had pickup trucks that were assigned to them for their regular duties, and they took them home with them at night so that if one of these false alarms went off during the night, which they fairly frequently did, everybody would come charging in with lights blinking, charging towards the fire. So I opined that even if we got a real fire some time, probably the biggest danger was having automobile collisions of everybody going to the fire. If everybody went to the fire and it really was a blow-up, who would be left to run the place? I elected that I was going to stay home and not go to the fire, and the exec would take charge. I designated certain people to go and the others to stay back to be called. It worked a little better; it kept you from going out at night so much.

Q: Was there any concern about sabotage?

Admiral Waters: Not at that time. Not at that time. Of course, we had the sentries, the Marines, not only at the gates, but we had sentry posts. They had just disbanded the horse Marines when I got there. We had actually had a group of horse Marines, stables and horses, because the best way to patrol the perimeter fence was on horseback. The roads didn't get close enough so that you could see things. By the time I got there, they had built roads and we had gotten jeeps. So we did patrol the fences and that sort of thing.

Q: Was sabotage the concern? Is that why you had so many sentries?

Admiral Waters: Yes.

Q: You wound up having your cake and eating it, too, in that you went to this job that you liked and got selected for rear admiral as well. When did you get the news?

Admiral Waters: Well, I went there in '57. Actually, I relieved on New Year's Eve of '57. I was selected in July of '60 and left in the fall. I got orders in August. One of the reasons, I'm sure, that I was selected was that P. D. Stroop liked to hunt and fish. He turned out to be a good friend and supporter of ours, and liked the way we did things, obviously, in changing the name and all that sort of thing, and then the work record. We had a herd of deer down there, and he would come down when we had our deer drives on Saturdays, which we worked in conjunction with the Virginia State Game Commission, so we did everything legally. We could only do it on Saturdays, because it was back in the working areas, and we couldn't shoot back in there when the men were working.

At that time there was a tendency, a trend, to promote people to admiral from people who had been in the Pentagon, as I mentioned previously, in higher visibility, who got to be known by the three- and four-star admirals in OpNav. When Stroop came down to some of those deer hunts, he told me, "You know, a lot of these guys who get selected are doing jobs up there where they have no responsibility for their actions. If they write a bad paper, they can say, 'That's a bad paper,' and rewrite it, whereas all of you people out here running these ammunition depots and things like that, if the thing blows up, there's one fellow responsible, and that's you."

I said, "I realize that."

He said, "I think you ought to get a little more credit for it." Well, I was glad to hear him talk that way. He called me up when the selection board met. He was an aviator, and there were four aviator admirals on the selection board. The CNO always had a party on Sunday before the selection board met on Monday in those days. I suppose they still do. There were four aviators and five blackshoes.* He called me on the phone on Monday morning, the day the board met, and said, "Muddy, we had a party last night. Talked to a bunch of brownshoe guys. Do you happen to know a couple of blackshoes in this august group?" That meant to me that he'd pretty much convinced his fellow aviators to vote for me. Of course, as somebody once said, once a selection board meets, your record goes out the window; all you need is one thing--that's six votes. So, sure enough, in a couple of days the word came down officially.

Q: He had some added clout by then in that he was the bureau chief for the new Bureau of Naval Weapons.

Admiral Waters: Yes, yes. I'm sure he didn't do anything but just chat at the cocktail party, but Massie Hughes was Commandant of the Fifth Naval District then.** We came under him as the area commander. He was on the selection board. The tip of the peninsula where we were was in the Fifth Naval District. Of course, he had Norfolk and all that other side. So things like the blood bank and collecting for the United Givers Fund and all that sort of

---
*Blackshoe is a Navy term for a surface officer who has specialized in cruiser and destroyer operations, as opposed to a naval aviator, who is known as a brownshoe.
**Rear Admiral Francis Massie Hughes, USN.

thing, he got me over there and he said, "Now I want you to take charge of the peninsula, and I'll take the rest."

I said, "Aye, aye, sir," and we did pretty good. So we got to be friends, and when we were at the opening of the new hospital in Portsmouth, he told me that he was on the selection board. That's when he said, "You know, all this record and everything goes out the window. All you need is six votes."

Q: It certainly helps to have your friends there.

Admiral Waters: Yes, it did. I think most flag officers will admit that the primary requirement is that you certainly should have some capability of doing your job, some professional capability, but luck plays a certain amount.

Q: It certainly does.

Admiral Waters: Just where you are and who's on the selection board. Because looking at it another way, there are so many really good people who don't make it. I was, of course, very much buoyed up by being selected, but at the same time, I was very unhappy that my friend Sam Moncure didn't make it.* You feel both ways.

---
*Moncure was a Naval Academy classmate of Waters.

Q: Admiral Foley told me that he was a protege of Admiral Anderson, the CNO.* Anderson had been grooming him for promotion by bringing him along in various billets. But then Anderson had only two years as CNO, so Foley didn't get what might have been the next rung up the ladder.

Admiral Waters: Yes, that's right. Francis didn't get above two stars, did he?

Q: No, sir. Did you have any connection with the Polaris program when you were at Yorktown?

Admiral Waters: No. We had a bunch of submariners who had a spot way back in the woods, where they had a missile they were working on to shoot off of a submarine.

Q: Regulus?

Admiral Waters: I believe it was Regulus.

Q: Then you got ordered back to another destroyer command after that. That must have been a satisfying assignment.

---

*Admiral George W. Anderson, Jr., USN, whose two-volume oral history is in the Naval Institute's collection, was Chief of Naval Operations from 1961 to 1963.

Admiral Waters: That was probably the best job in the Navy for a fresh-caught flag officer, and it was highly sought after. As a matter of fact, an awful lot of guys that went on up much higher than I did had it, including Rivets Rivero.* He had that job when he was selected. Bill Leverton had it; he would have gone on up, except for having had a heart attack. I relieved Bill Leverton.**

Q: He's a real gentleman. I've talked to him.

Admiral Waters: Yes. He married my wife's first cousin. Bill and I were shipmates. He was on the Augusta for four years; and I was on her for three years. He was an usher in our wedding and met my wife's cousin, who was maid of honor, and they were married a year later. We've been very close. I relieved him. The only trouble about that job was that every destroyer officer knew it was there, and everybody wanted it. So you really had to fight to hang on to it. I took over just before Christmas in '60, and I got relieved in February of '62, so I had it about 15 months.

Q: How many squadrons did you have in your flotilla?

---

*Rear Admiral Horacio Rivero, Jr., USN. Rivero retired as a four-star admiral; his oral history is in the Naval Institute's collection.
**Rear Admiral Joseph W. Leverton, USN.

Admiral Waters: There was one squadron that was home-ported in Yokosuka, Japan. The rest of them were deployed out in the Pacific Fleet. They told them six months; usually it went eight or nine. I usually had around 36 destroyer types to worry about. My flagship was a tender, and that was also deployed for six months at a time. The _Dixie_, the _Prairie_, and the _Piedmont_ took turns. One nice thing about that job was that the tender came out with a band that was furnished by ComDesPac, so I owned a band.* That made me very popular. I got invited to every party in Yokosuka, because they wanted to use part of my band. My favorite tender was the _Dixie_, because they had a band, a very good band, and whenever I would come into a party, they would play "Dixie."

Q: So you were in Yokosuka for a while then?

Admiral Waters: Yes. I had my family with me. That was why it was such a good job. It was the best of two worlds, because you had the number-two house right next to Commander Seventh Fleet's house up on top of what the Japanese charts call Unnecessary Mountain, at the top of Halsey Road, and lived side by side. We could go through a garden gate to his house. Then down at the foot of Halsey Road was a pier, and that's where the tender was tied up.

---

*ComDesPac--Commander Destroyer Force Pacific Fleet.

Q: What do you remember about the Seventh Fleet commanders? I think probably Admiral Griffin was there.*

Admiral Waters: Admiral Griffin was in command. I liked Don and still do. He was a hard man to work for.

Q: How so?

Admiral Waters: Well, he was very strict about having everything that any unit of the Seventh Fleet did attributed to the Seventh Fleet. As I had destroyer units, either divisions or squadrons, usually divisions, deployed out, they would come into Guam and either come on up to Yokosuka or go down to the Philippines. I would fly out to Guam and meet them, meet with the captains and brief them. That was one of the first things I explained to them, that Admiral Griffin was a little bit touchy on the subject of Seventh Fleet getting credit for what Seventh Fleet units did. "If you rescue a Japanese fisherman or anything like that, if you can mention Seventh Fleet three times in the first paragraph, do it. Then put the name of your ship in the second paragraph."

---

*Vice Admiral Charles D. Griffin, USN. Griffin retired as a four-star admiral; his oral history is in the Naval Institute collection.

Q: How was he operationally?

Admiral Waters: Operationally he was fine, and he was a good friend, but that's the only sort of peculiarity. Everybody has peculiarities, and that was one of his. It was a good idea.

Q: What were some of the incidents that came up during that period?

Admiral Waters: One that I especially remember--I think it was in the fall of '61. They had a big SEATO amphibious exercise, the Southeast Asia Treaty Organization--Taiwan, the Philippines. The British still had a fair representation of ships at Singapore. They came up and were in it. They had a British admiral. We, of course, had a lot of ships, and we did a landing on the west coast of Borneo. They designated me to take my destroyer tender down and house all of the press and the VIPs, which I protested loudly. I pointed out that this would take them away from doing their primary job of keeping destroyers on the line, and I was having enough trouble doing that anyway. That was always the first thing in the morning meeting, "Who is having troubles? Who needs to be fixed?"
    Johnny Gannon, who was Commander Taiwan Patrol Force,

had a big seaplane tender as his flagship.* I tried to get them to give that job to Johnny, because he didn't have anything else to do. But Johnny was senior to me, so I did it.

Q: What do you remember about the exercise?

Admiral Waters: Well, the exercise went off all right. We had the damndest collection of people on board. We had a lot of press, and then we had seven-star generals from the Philippine Army. We managed to get through it and take care of it all right.

Q: Was there a fair amount of cooperation among the various nations?

Admiral Waters: Yes, it was very good, and the exercise went off pretty well. I don't recall any serious incidents. Being with all of the PR people, we had a guy on board who was doing the PR for the Seventh Fleet, and he got the grand idea of comparing this to a bullfight. All of these messages went out saying that the bull was in the arena now, and all of the people were getting ready to attack--a lot of real far-out stuff. Finally, the British admiral, who later on was--I think he was first Sea Lord,

---

*Rear Admiral John W. Gannon, USN.

and I've forgotten his name now, but he was a very clever man--he finally came up with a dispatch that said, in effect, "It seems to me that the bull is having some problems with his alimentary system." [Laughter] And those messages stopped.

Q: Had the coolness which you had experienced before with the British gone away?

Admiral Waters: Yes, yes, it had subsided then, and we worked together very well.

Q: Were they the most professional of all the navies you worked with on that, would you say?

Admiral Waters: Yes, I'd say so, except for one thing. Given a chance, the Japanese were very fine sailor men, and we had a lot of close cooperation and work in that job with the Japanese, because they were based right in the same basin with us. Of course, they were and still are called the Maritime Self-Defense Force, which really irked them. There was nothing that could happen that would raise the morale of those people more than being called the Imperial Japanese Navy again, and they were trying at that time. I knew a lot of those Japanese admirals, and they were really wonderful people.

Q: I take it there was no residual hostility.

Admiral Waters: No. We would have parties together, and you'd find yourself talking to a Japanese, and the conversation would be, "Where were you at so-and-so, and did you shoot at me, and did I shoot at you?" That kind of thing.

Q: I know Admiral Burke had a lot of those exchanges with Japanese officers.

Admiral Waters: But you had to admire the Japanese for their professional capability. The small ships that they were allowed to have, they ran very smartly and very well. We did things like have softball games with them. A Japanese admiral would play on their team for a while, and I would play on our team for a while. We'd have beer and so forth.

Q: They had a very proficient ship repair facility there at Yokosuka also.

Admiral Waters: Yes, very good. Yokosuka was a wonderful base and probably the best harbor I've ever seen for sheltering from a typhoon because the cliffs were so high.

I've never seen many harbors that I would want to stay in if I had a chance to get out.

But as the flag officer on a tender there, I was in port most of the time, except when I got under way and went south to inspect the ships down in the Philippines. I took trips out to Guam by air and always stopped in Hong Kong on the way down and back so I wouldn't have a mutiny on my hands. As such, I was in port most of the time, so I was SOPA admin: senior officer present afloat, administrative.

Whether there was anybody senior to me in port or not, I was responsible for all kinds of things, the worst of which was that I was responsible for the conduct of the forces afloat when they were ashore. The worst people we had to deal with were Admiral Griffin's aviators off the carriers. When the Coral Sea would come in, you could expect that there was going to be something, because there were so many of them and they'd been at sea for so long.

One of the things, when I would meet my destroyers in Guam, was to advise them very seriously to tell everyone, "When you go ashore, don't hang around those places at the waterfront, because the shore patrol's all over the place, and that's where you get in trouble. Get out to the outskirts of town." I even had the name of a few places I would give them to go. They got along pretty well, but the big horde of aviators would come in, and they would trash a bar or something. Of course, the Communist press in Japan would make a big thing of that. It was one of my problems as SOPA admin.

I had a young legal officer, Maitland Freed, who later became a captain in the Judge Advocate General's Corps.* He had a wonderful sense of humor. Every morning at 9:00 o'clock, I had an operational conference with the different heads of departments. Maitland's turn was always last. You know, we went to the operations officer saying what was wrong with what, and then to the material officer saying what they could do about it, and where the spare parts were bogged down that we needed, and that sort of thing. Then Maitland would report particularly on the conduct of the forces afloat. I'll never forget, one day he said, "Well, we had kind of a bad night last night, Admiral. You know, the Coral Sea came in. One young aviator, in a fit of boyish exuberance, broke the end off a beer bottle and struck a Japanese national in the face with it." Those were the problems you had to sort of fight your way out of.

Q: I take it that Admiral Griffin didn't want the Seventh Fleet mentioned three times in the discussion of that incident.

Admiral Waters: No, no. He didn't want the name of the ship that the man was attached to mentioned either.
_____
*Lieutenant Maitland G. Freed, USN.

O. D. Waters, Jr. #5 - 323

Q: How close a relationship did you have with the Commander Fleet Activities Yokosuka?

Admiral Waters: Very close. I had a close relationship with him. And then we had Commander Naval Forces Japan, another admiral. He didn't live on the Yokosuka base. He lived in the old palace that the princes who had high rank in the Imperial Navy lived in out the other side of town--Admiral Withington.* I had close relationships with him. He used to get me into golf games with Japanese admirals, and that was really a riot. They loved to play golf, but they hadn't had a chance to play when they were younger, and they were just starting, but we enjoyed it.

Q: One of the events of that time there was the restoration of the battleship Mikasa.** Did you get involved in that at all?

Admiral Waters: Yes. I wasn't too closely involved in that, but Kemp Tolley came over after all the contributions were made and she was all done over again.***

---
*Rear Admiral Frederic S. Withington, USN, whose oral history is in the Naval Institute collection.
**A pre-dreadnought that served as the Commander in Chief Japanese Combined Fleet's flagship during the Russo-Japanese War of 1904-05. She is revered by the Japanese in much the same war Americans treasure the USS Constitution.
***Captain Kemp Tolley, USN, whose two-volume oral history is in the Naval Institute's collection.

Q: He had commanded Fleet Activities Yokosuka previously.

Admiral Waters: Yes. I don't know whether they commissioned her or made her into a national monument, or whatever it was they did. He came over for that. Kemp had been a first classman when I was at the Naval Academy and one of the ones that "spooned" on me, so we were old friends, and it was good to see him again out there.

Q: We have his oral history, and he describes that. The Japanese didn't want him to leave when it came time for him to retire, so he was very popular there.

Admiral Waters: Yes, he was.

Q: Did you have relationships with the Japanese local dignitaries and so forth?

Admiral Waters: Oh, yes, very much so. We had an official relationship with the mayor, but he was a little wimpish sort of a fellow, and he didn't really have much authority. The man who really ran the town was the chairman of the chamber of commerce. He had a gingersnap factory in Yokosuka and a hell of a lot of money, and he was the strong man. Before I was detached, after I got my orders, he gave a big party for me out over on the Izu Peninsula at a big golf course. I offered to pick him up and take him over there in my car. I had a very good driver, and he thought that was fine. We also had a Nisei interpreter at NavFac, who came along. The old gentleman spoke a little bit of English, but his English was not that good.

This was a golf game and then a banquet with geisha and playing all the games, you know, running around, sitting on pillows and taking the pillow away each time, and all those crazy things they do, with all the saki and beer and so forth. The next morning, I had the honor of being invited for breakfast with the chairman. That was an experience. On the way over, the interpreter explained to me that we would like to go by the railroad station, because the chairman wished to pick up a lady friend of his. He said, "The chairman wants me to explain to you that you gentlemen like to play golf, but he has other hobbies." We picked up this girl, and she was a beauty. She also could play golf. She played golf with us. There was rather a large crowd.

But the next morning when I had breakfast, it was a Japanese-type breakfast with peculiar things like radishes and pickles, and I had a little bowl of things that I thought were bean sprouts, and I was eating away at them.

They were supposed to be a great delicacy. So I turned to the interpreter, and I said, "What are these, bean sprouts?"

He said, "No, those are freshly hatched eels." When you looked at them, they were little teeny things with blue eyes.

Q: I remember that they sold packages of eel just as you would get potato chips or popcorn or something like that.

Admiral Waters: Yes.

Q: How much touring did you and Mrs. Waters do in Japan?

Admiral Waters: We went up to the big shrine north of Tokyo.

Q: Kamakura?

Admiral Waters: No, we lived almost at Kamakura. See, it was just across the peninsula from us. The modern shrine, which the older Japanese look down upon because Kyoto is the real place for shrines, but this was up north of Tokyo. You took a drive up there, spent the night, and you had to drive up a mountain road to get to it. There were so many S-curves. Somehow or other the Japanese didn't have collisions on these things, but you would change sides of the roads. We went up there.

My wife and I had the two smaller girls with us; the other two were in school back here. When I was off on a cruise to the Philippines at Easter time, a Japanese admiral and his wife went along with my wife and daughters as their hosts and conductors. They drove down to Nara and Kyoto and had a wonderful time.

Q: That's a beautiful area of Japan.

Admiral Waters: They did that while I was gone, in my big old Mercury station wagon that I had shipped over there. They used our good Navy driver, who liked to do things like that. He got to go on the trip too.

Of course, I got down to Sasebo; I don't think my wife got down there.

Q: Did you get to sea in destroyers at all during that time?

Admiral Waters: No. I would maybe take a run on trials with some of them after they'd been overhauled, something like that. The main thing we did, and this was a very good idea of my wife's--we were supposed to cultivate friendships with the Japanese Navy. Of course, I had done my part with the ball games and getting together for golf and that sort of thing. They had lunches and dinners, and we did too.

I believe it was the <u>Dixie</u> or the <u>Prairie</u>, one or the other--we decided to have a dependents' cruise, because the home-ported squadron had a lot of dependents out there. So she got the idea of inviting the wives of the Japanese admirals to go out. Of course, they had never done anything like that--never been aboard a ship.

Q: Their culture just wouldn't permit it.

Admiral Waters: Yes. They were delighted and just seemed to have a wonderful time. We laid in a big supply of orange soda; that's their main drink. They had a great time; it was a nice day. We went out into Sagami Wan and back again.

Q: One of the traditional jobs of a type commander or immediate superior is conducting inspections. Do you have any recollections from doing those?

Admiral Waters: No, not specifically. I did an awful lot of them. I can't remember any examples of anybody being really badly down. They had been put through a course of sprouts before they deployed, and they were usually in pretty good shape.

Q: How much contact did you have with the type commander back on the West Coast?

Admiral Waters: I had very little except for mail and messages. The most contact that we had, as I say, was trying to run down spare parts and get them there. They were a big help in that. We had special priorities on communications to get through, and sometimes we'd have to have stuff specially flown, but things worked out pretty well.

Q: I recall that demonstrations by the local people were popular. Did you see any of those?

Admiral Waters: Oh, yes, yes. We would get word in advance that there was going to be a demonstration and were advised not to leave the base. There would be crowds around the entrance to the Yokosuka naval base. One other thing, which really worked to my advantage, was that neither my wife nor I was permitted to drive an automobile off the base. Therefore, when I wanted to go off the base, that made taking an official driver legal. It pleased me fine, because I didn't want to drive in that Japanese traffic anyway.

Q: Not with that station wagon.

Admiral Waters: Well, I'm talking particularly about official cars. The reason for it was that if a flag officer had been involved in an accident, it would have made the Communist press, and they'd have probably invented somebody who had got horribly mangled in it or something like that. So it just wasn't done. It worked fine.

The Japanese ceremonies and events were always so punctual that it was very bad manners not to be there exactly on time, preferably a couple of minutes early. This driver I had was so good. When we had to go someplace up near Yokohama, for example, he would make a dummy run at the same time of the day so he would catch the traffic. We would be on our way to the Prince Hotel, which was off the main road up towards Yokohama, and Decker would pull over to the side. "I'm about 40 seconds fast, Admiral. Do you mind waiting?" So we'd kill 40 seconds, and then we'd get there right on the button. He had it all figured out so that when we turned in, it would be the proper door of whoever exited first.

Q: Admiral Nimitz liked to have things done that way too. I've heard that about him.

Admiral Waters: It's a great deal if you can get a man who does things that way. It makes you look good; it makes you look sharp.

Q: And that is very important in the Japanese culture.

Admiral Waters: Oh, yes, particularly the way they observe the punctuality.

Q: Just as you're talking about the accident, you are representing our nation, in just a little thing as when you get there.

Admiral Waters: Yes.

Q: Anything more on that tour of duty that you especially remember?

Admiral Waters: I don't believe so.

Q: From there you did go back to Washington. Was that something you had sought?

Admiral Waters: No. There again, I got caught up in the problem of loyalties. When I left there it was pretty obvious that, never having served on the E-ring in the

Pentagon, I should go there for promotion and pay.*
Again I got a letter from P. D. Stroop, whom I figured had a great deal to do with my being a flag officer in the first place. The Navy had changed BuOrd into BuWeps, and he was the Chief of BuWeps, and he wanted me to come and be Assistant Chief for Administration and Inspector General. Unfortunately, that was the worst job they had. I just felt I had to go if P. D. wanted me, and he did, so I went.

Q: You owed him that one.

Admiral Waters: Yes, I owed it to him, and I went. It was a bag of worms. I had all of the nasty jobs to do. I was in charge of all BuWeps personnel worldwide, including all the ones in Washington. I was in charge of office space, parking, of which there never was enough, all kinds of great things like that. In the inspector general thing, I never liked to do that kind of inspecting, anyway. That wasn't anything that I would call really pleasant. Then the worst thing that happened was that disciplinary problems with officers were on my plate too. There was a captain whom I knew very well and liked very much. He developed alcoholism, so we had several discussions with him and took him up to the chief. Finally, he reached the

---
*The Pentagon has lettered corridors, going from A at the innermost to E at the outermost. E-ring offices, which go around the perimeter of the building, are considered the most prestigious.

limit one day when he passed out at his desk. So we let him resign. But those things were very . . .

Q: Personally troubling, I'm sure.

Admiral Waters: Yes, troublesome to me.

About the best thing in that job was that we had a big computer setup in BuWeps, and that came under me. I got very much interested in that. That was my first introduction to computers. We had the computers there and whatever computers there were at that time--there weren't too many--at stations underneath us.

That was the time when they decided to create the job of Chief of Naval Material over top of all the material bureaus. I was violently against it, as were most of the people in the bureaus. Why should we put another layer of supervision when we're getting along pretty well the way we are? I call this Waters's 20-25 year law. Things I took a violent viewpoint on about 25 years ago are turned around the other way now.

Q: They've abolished that earlier this year.

Admiral Waters: Yes, that's right.

O. D. Waters, Jr. #5 - 334

Q: What were some of the things you did in your role as inspector general?

Admiral Waters: I went out and inspected ammunition depots and ordnance plants, that sort of thing, gave them a going-over. Mainly, as I saw the role of inspector general, it was to go out and not just inspect these people, but to get the skippers and the senior officers together and listen to their problems, write down their problems, and go home and see what we could do about it. That's what we did. Fortunately, I had a senior captain as assistant inspector general, and so he was able to take care of a lot of that part of the job.

Q: Do you remember any of these problems that you were able to solve?

Admiral Waters: No, I really don't. I don't think we had any real major ones, but some of them we did solve. But there again, usually you came up against civil service problems. Civil service problems are difficult to solve; they've got themselves so entrenched that it's very difficult to do anything about a civil service person who is so protected by rules and regulations of civil service.

If you have one who is absolutely worthless and you want to spend about six months to a year, you can get rid of him, but it takes an awful lot of time and expense to do it, to take the various steps and the grievance committees. We did that to one person back when I was at the Naval Ordnance Laboratory, and we kept at it. It took us a year, and figuring the time and salaries of people and the time they put in, it cost us over $50,000 to get rid of this guy, but we finally got rid of him.

Q: I'm sure there are others who realize it's that difficult and take advantage of it. And that must be especially frustrating for someone such as you who had come up in a background where you tell someone to do something, and he does it or else.

Admiral Waters: Yes, that's right. That's right.

Q: In your inspector general role, did you get into any of the investigative type things, looking into problems that might have occurred? I mean, hypothetically, had there been an explosion, it would have been investigated.

Admiral Waters: Yes, that would have come under me, but fortunately we didn't have anything bad that required that much. Maybe we had a few boards of investigation and that sort of thing, but nothing really serious.

Q: The Bureau of Weapons then included both the Bureau of Ordnance side and aviation. How much did you get into the aviation part of it?

Admiral Waters: Just as much as I had to.

Q: Did you go to air stations?

Admiral Waters: No. I didn't get involved, really, in air stations. Somehow or another, I've forgotten how now, but the air stations weren't part of the inspector general's job. They had a different inspector general, maybe OP-05 or whatever.*

Q: Did you have any contacts with the aircraft manufacturers?

Admiral Waters: Some with the aircraft manufacturers and quite a few with the ones that made missiles and ordnance and that sort of thing. I recall when Mr. McNamara issued his order that you couldn't accept anything from a manufacturer.** You couldn't go to lunch with a manufacturer if you were a contracting officer. Well, I wasn't a contracting officer, so I went to lunch with

---

*OP-05--Deputy Chief of Naval Operations (Air)
**Robert S. McNamara was Secretary of Defense, 1961-68.

manufacturers. My philosophy was that if I were going to sell out, my price was a hell of a lot higher than lunch.

Q: That was the time of the great TFX squabble that the Bureau of Weapons was involved in.* Did you get involved in that at all?

Admiral Waters: No, I didn't.

Q: The Navy had essentially thought that Boeing would get the contract, and then it wound up going to General Dynamics instead. There were a lot of investigations and so forth.

Admiral Waters: Yes. Well, that was an experimental plane in development. That came under RDT&E, and that was Dick Ashworth's.** Dick Ashworth really had a rough time with that one. He had to testify, I remember, and he really carried the ball for the Navy. A lot of people had it in for him, but somehow or another, other people knew what a good man he was and what a job he'd done. When he left Washington, he got a better job and went on up to three

---

*TFX--tactical fighter experimental, which became the F-111. The issue was whether it should be adopted by both the Navy and Air Force. The Navy never did adopt the F-111 but a much modified version that became the F-14.
**RDT&E--Research, Development, Test, and Evaluation; Rear Admiral Frederick L. Ashworth, USN, who has been interviewed for the Naval Institute's oral history program.

stars.*

Q: Anything else you remember about him?

Admiral Waters: Well, he'd been a good friend of mine for a long time, and I liked him very much.

Q: He had been in the atomic business early on, too.

Admiral Waters: Yes. Dick was sort of right-hand man to Deac Parsons, whom I had known well.**

Q: What are your recollections of Parsons?

Admiral Waters: A great man, a great officer, very, very thorough and meticulous, very smart, very intelligent, knew his job, very quiet and unassuming. I had known him when I was just finishing the PG course at Annapolis and was sent down to Dahlgren as part of what they called the Cook's tour in those days. He was experimental officer then, and he was sort of over all of us and lived right up the street. I liked him very much. Later on, when the atomic business was going so big and the missile thing, he and

---
*Ashworth later served as Commander Sixth Fleet and Deputy Commander in Chief Atlantic Fleet.
**Rear Admiral William Sterling Parsons, USN (Ret.). In 1945 Parsons was the weaponeer for the atomic bomb dropped on Hiroshima and Ashworth for the one dropped on Nagasaki.

Butch Parker were together in some division of OpNav.*

I was on Admiral Wright's staff then as captain, and they asked for me to come up and join them up there. Admiral Wright was out of town, and the chief of staff agreed to it. I wouldn't quite have served my two years on Admiral Wright's staff, and he got back and countermanded the order, as he usually did in his emphatic way. He said not only was I required to serve my two years, but he needed me for an extra year. So I stayed three years on that staff and never did get to go up with Deac Parsons and Butch Parker, which I would have loved at the time.**

Q: What do you recall about working with Admiral Stroop during that period when you were up in BuWeps?

Admiral Waters: He was a delightful man to work for, a good leader, not highly excitable, always calm. He had his hand on the helm all the time, but was a nice, pleasant man to work for.

Q: Any specific incidents you recall in working with him?

Admiral Waters: No. That's a long time ago. Earlier I was recalling the captain who turned alcoholic. I had to

---
*Rear Admiral Edward N. Parker, USN, whose oral history is in the Naval Institute collection.
**Parker was deputy commander of the Armed Forces Special Weapons Project from 1952 to 1954.

confer with Admiral Stroop a lot on that sort of thing, and he always had a very, very intelligent, I thought, reaction to what we should do. Also, it was quite evident that he would back me up in whatever I did about it.

Q: That's a delicate thing. You have to balance the interests of the individual against those of the service.

Admiral Waters: Yes.

Q: Anything else on the administrative side? How much did you do in that as opposed to the inspector general role?

Admiral Waters: I did more on the administrative side than the inspector general. As assistant chief for administration, for example, I was assigned the job which was officially called liaison with the working group that was setting up the Chief of Naval Material staff. Privately, over in BuWeps, we referred to my job as protecting the bureau to keep it from getting stolen blind, but they did take a lot of our good people. That was a tough job.

Q: Do you remember any specific incidents along the way as it got closer to setting up the Naval Material Command?

Were there milestones to go through in disestablishing one and setting up the other?

Admiral Waters: Oh, yes, there were things like that. One of the things that made the job easier was the fact that Vice Admiral Bill Schoech was a very wonderful officer, I thought. Having him as the new Chief of Naval Material helped things out, because he had been assistant chief of BuWeps, as I recall.* As a matter of fact, when time was coming up for me to get out of this administrative job in BuWeps, which I was not too fond of, Admiral Schoech wanted me to come over and be his sort of number-two man over there.

Q: That speaks highly of your work.

Admiral Waters: I felt very flattered by it, but at the same time, I had been talking with the people at BuPers, and because of my previous work in the mine recovery business way back in World War II, they had me lined up to become ComMinePac with the second hat of Commander Naval Base Los Angeles.** I much preferred that to staying on in Washington. Schoech was such a nice guy that I went over and talked to him about it and some family matters,

---
*Vice Admiral William A. Schoech, USN, Chief of Naval Material from 1 July 1963 to 20 April 1965.
**ComMinePac--Commander Mine Force Pacific Fleet.

and so forth. He said, "Okay, Muddy, I'd like to have you come over, but I understand your problem. I'll let you off the hook."

Q: You didn't owe him as much as you had Stroop, I take it.

What effects, if any, did you feel in the Bureau of Naval Weapons from the McNamara regime?

Admiral Waters: The biggest effect I got from the McNamara regime was, of course, that everybody went through that business of flag officers can't ride first class anymore, even though the British still do it to this day; they wouldn't lower their standards. But we went through all that stuff, which was a bit annoying.

The main thing I remember was in my next job when I went out to the Pacific Coast and was ComMinePac. I reported to that job in February of '64, and I was there until August of '65. The Vietnamese War got started while I was there. Well, McNamara had made several trips out to Vietnam, and on one of his trips, somebody introduced him to the naval mine. He went crazy about the naval mine because it's such a cost-effective weapon. As everybody knows, it's relatively cheap to make, compared to other weapons, and you don't have to blow up a single ship for it to be worth using, because it can cause the enemy to go to

O. D. Waters, Jr. #5 - 343

such great lengths to avoid it or counter it, and that sort of thing.

McNamara got so taken up by it that he decided that we should mine in Haiphong, and the orders were issued. Tom Moorer was Commander in Chief Pacific Fleet then, so the orders came down from him to me to start making these plans and making the auxiliary plans.* This was tough because we had to get the mines out of storage, mostly in Yorktown, had to get them out to Subic. We had to comb the fleet to find minemen that were capable of doing these jobs, and they were getting harder and harder to find. Then we had to convince the naval aviators that dropping mines from an airplane was different from dropping bombs. They didn't want to do any mine training. Of course, the mine comes down in a parachute, and it's a different undertaking.

Q: And it doesn't make a big bang when it hits.

Admiral Waters: No. Besides that, you get shot at just the same, but you don't get any credit for hitting anything. I did manage to get the fleet commander to let me arrange a practice range down at Santa Rosa Island and had some of the planes from Miramar, I guess they came from, make runs over that, dropping dummy mines.** When

---
*Admiral Thomas H. Moorer, USN (Ret.), whose three-volume oral history is in the Naval Institute's collection.
**Santa Rosa Island is off the coast of Southern California, near the Santa Barbara Channel. Miramar is a naval air station near San Diego.

they missed the target by three miles, they were convinced. Moorer was convinced, and he issued the orders, so we started seeing that the aviators were properly trained. We got the mines out to Subic, we got them aboard the carriers. We had minemen aboard the carriers to adjust them. Of course, we had the plans made for the minefields, which had to be designed according to the hydrographic information we had and the oceanographic information we had. Everything was set to go, and we actually were on six hours' notice to mine Haiphong. That must have been in '64.

Q: Would this have been after the Gulf of Tonkin incidents?*

Admiral Waters: Yes, I believe it was. I felt convinced that this mining would quite likely bring a quick end to the war over there, because all the supplies were coming in through the harbor at Haiphong and then on down the roads. Well, we were on six hours' notice when apparently some people in the State Department started kicking up their heels against this, saying we might inadvertently mine a Soviet ship. Of course, they hadn't read the Geneva Convention or anything like that, because mining is

---

*North Vietnamese patrol boat attacks on U.S. destroyers in the Gulf of Tonkin occurred on 2 August and 4 August 1964, although the latter is in dispute.

perfectly legal in warfare, and you put up notices. If ships then go into these mined waters, it's their fault. There were also some ships going into there bringing supplies that I was led to believe--I don't have any proof of this, but I was led to believe were either or both Canadian- and British-owned, if you traced their ownership back, and the State Department didn't want to offend them. At any rate, it was canceled. Our morale went down like this.

The war went on, and I came back and was oceanographer and was retired. Then eight years later, in '72, they again decided to mine, and they did it that time. They did a damn good job and just completely closed that harbor down. As a matter of fact, they did it so well that nobody else could sweep them. We had to go back and sweep them up after it was all over. But, at any rate, I sat down and wrote Tom Moorer. By that time I was retired and was a professor here at FIT; he was Chairman of the Joint Chiefs.[*] I wrote him a little note and said, "Dear Tom, I'm delighted to see that the plan to mine Haiphong was finally carried out. Of course, I'm not privy to classified information anymore, but knowing that there were probably no people around who were experienced enough to draw up minefield plans, I would be willing to bet that they used our plans to do it."

---
[*]Florida Institute of Technology.

He wrote me back a nice little note and said, "It's nice to hear from you." He, too, was glad to see we finally mined it. He ended by saying, "You're a pretty good guesser."

Q: What do you recall about the plan that you developed back in '64? How thorough was its coverage?

Admiral Waters: It was thorough enough to close it off, using mainly aerial-dropped mines and mixing them up between acoustic and magnetic and pressure. I don't think we had any idea of using moored mines of any kind. We didn't have to because of the depth of water; it was shallow enough. The proof in the pudding was that it worked in '72. It closed everything out of there.

Q: You said mainly aerial drops. What other types did you have? Did you have some brought in by submarines, for example?

Admiral Waters: Yes, we had submarine-laid mines, and also, of course, the old pre-World War II days and during World War II, there were minelaying ships. But to use minelaying ships, of course, you've got to have control of the air and not get in too close to shore batteries.

Q: Right. So that would have been pretty well ruled out.

Admiral Waters: Yes. I don't think we had any minelayers in commission then; they'd all been decommissioned.

Q: There were a couple, I think. The Ozark and Catskill, maybe, had been converted to mine countermeasures ships by then.

Admiral Waters: Yes.

Q: Did you intend to use submarines against Haiphong also, or was it strictly aerial?

Admiral Waters: I really have forgotten. I think it was aerial. It must have been all aerial, because I know we concentrated on getting the mines into the magazines aboard the carriers and getting the minemen there to adjust them and get them ready for laying. That's the ticklish part of the thing, because you have to really know what you're doing so it will work.

Q: Were some of these men called out of retirement to do this?

Admiral Waters: They may have been, because we didn't have too many minemen to begin with. We used to say of the mines we had in World War II--it was somewhat of an exaggeration--that you had to have a Ph.D. to put them together. But by the 1960s we had the new family of mines. They had been engineered to the point where if you wanted to use a magnetic mine, you just put in one kind of a black box and connected the terminals, and if tests on it failed, you pulled that out and pulled another one off the shelf. If you wanted acoustic, you could put an acoustic mechanism and that sort of thing.

Q: Were these relatively new mines, then, that you would have put in Vietnam?

Admiral Waters: Well, they had been built since World War II. Right after the war ended, I was at the Naval Ordnance Laboratory, and Dr. Roy Weller, who recently died, was the chief of engineering, a very brilliant guy. He got together everybody that knew anything about mines, and we had a group of people who worked on what the future mine should be. That set the whole program from then on.

Q: I think they developed still another generation for the actual use in 1972. That was my understanding.

Admiral Waters: Yes. They had by then. They had developed and built these newer mines. Now we have an even newer generation.

Q: Well, that was part of your job. You also had all of the minesweepers working for you. What do you recall about that part of it?

Admiral Waters: I used to know the number of minesweepers I had. I had the seagoing class, the MSOs, oceangoing minesweepers. I had the MSCs, the smaller ones, and we had some minesweeping boats, so there were lots of units but few people on them.* As I recall, with all these ships we had about as many people in uniform in the Mine Force as were required to man one of the big new fleet carriers.

That was an interesting job. We did training there, trained them in all kinds of minesweeping. And then we had a unit which was permanently deployed over in Sasebo, Japan. That was a really nice thing, because I got to go over there and inspect them. And we had some down in the Philippines too.

Q: I think the old Epping Forest was in Sasebo as a flagship there.

---

*MSCs--coastal minesweepers.

Admiral Waters: That's right. That's right. Who was the great Navy football player? He was a jaygee, and he finally did his time, and they offered him so much money to come back and play for Boston.

Q: Joe Bellino.*

Admiral Waters: Joe Bellino. He was out there one time when I went out to inspect.

Q: I think he was exec on one of those minesweepers.

Admiral Waters: Yes, and he was highly respected. He was a real gentleman and a hell of an officer. He was a very good officer and had a good reputation. We were sorry to see him go, but we couldn't blame him. They kept calling him on the phone and raising the ante of how much money they'd give him just to run back kickoffs. He worked ashore with the men on softball teams, football teams, and that sort of thing and did a real good job.

But we never had any real minesweeping jobs to do. When the Vietnamese War started, we got caught up in the fact that the Viet Cong were being supplied down the coast

---

*Lieutenant (junior grade) Joseph Bellino, USN. He had won the Heisman Trophy as the nation's top collegiate football player while playing for the Naval Academy in 1960. After he left the Navy he played professional football for the Boston Patriots and Cincinnati Bengals.

by junks and small boats, and the U.S. Navy didn't have anything to counter them. So we used minesweepers for that. They weren't very well designed for that purpose, but that was all we had for about a year or so down there. Market Time was the name for that operation.

Q: They persisted for some while after that. I remember working with them in the late Sixties on that patrol. They put LSTs in there and some Coast Guard boats and little riverine craft.

Admiral Waters: Yes.

Q: Did you get over to Vietnam yourself?

Admiral Waters: No, I never got over there. Of course, we kept a close report on them, and I saw some of the ones that had been there when I went over on inspection trips to Sasebo and the Philippines. That was a very interesting job, that Commander Mine Force and also the two-hatted thing. I had two headquarters and two complete staffs. They called it the Naval Base Los Angeles, which made the people in Long Beach mad as hell, because it was in Long Beach, but the area that it covered included Long Beach. The Commandant of the 11th Naval District--of course, that came within his district, but he and I were old friends.

He said, "Look, Muddy, you take the upper part of Orange County and all that stuff up around you, and I'll take the rest."

That setup worked very well. What it amounted to was really public relations, being on the reviewing stand for Veterans' Day and all that sort of thing.

Q: Did you have dealings with the movie groups if they were making Navy movies?

Admiral Waters: I surely did. That was one of the interesting parts of the job. We had a PR section up in Hollywood to keep contact with the movies. And as the Commander Naval Base/MinePac, whenever they had VIPs visit Washington who also wanted to come to the West Coast, CNO would send them to me. The only good thing about it was that they always sent an escort along who had a pocketful of money that picked up the tab. So we pretty soon got used to this, and we got together with the PR guys up in Hollywood who had close working relations with all the studios up there. We got in with an ex-Navy man who was one of the top men down at Disneyland.

It was obvious that these people were not interested in looking at a little old naval base with a shipyard and that sort of thing; they'd seen those before. There were two things they wanted to see on the West Coast: they wanted to see Hollywood, and they wanted to see Disneyland. So we'd set it up that way. They had a red-carpet treatment that we would work around, where they would be taken over to Disneyland. Instead of going in the front door, they'd go in the back door and not have to stand in line. It worked just great. Then we were welcomed on the set of their various movies and television. One of the ones that was nicest to deal with was the "Bonanza" crowd.

Q: Some of the actors were Lorne Greene, Michael Landon, and Dan Blocker.

Admiral Waters: Yes, we got to know all those people very well. They were all nice people. Michael Landon was a little standoffish, but the rest of them were very, very personable, especially old Dan Blocker; he was great. The guy who is now Trapper John, he was Adam, I think, in the first series.* The other one that welcomed us on board, and the authorities in Washington kind of took me to task one time for taking people on the set, was "McHale's Navy." But they treated you so well, and they went out of their way if you had guests there.

Q: Who were some of these VIPs that you remember escorting around?

---
*Purnell Roberts played Trapper John in a later television series.

Admiral Waters: The one that I remember most vividly was an admiral from the Brazilian Navy. He was the equivalent of the chief of our Bureau of Ordnance. I had met him before, I guess, when I was back in Washington. He came out, and he was a very dignified man and quiet. I was explaining the schedule we had laid out for him, and he was indignant that we had decided to take him to Disneyland. "A child's playground," he said.

I said, "Well, I'd like for you to reconsider, because knowing your bent as an engineer, I'm not taking you down there for the rides and exhibits and things. But the thing is so beautifully engineered and done, I would like you to see that part of it. We can get you behind the scenes to show you how they do some of these things."

So he finally acquiesced and said he would go. Well, we had a red carpet treatment for him, and part of that was that they usually furnished a good-looking little girl guide who spoke the language of the person who was being given the treatment if he was a foreigner. They had this real good-looking little Brazilian gal who spoke Portuguese. Well, the old boy took to that right away. You know that he overturned the whole schedule by insisting on taking her to lunch. He was about an hour late for a reception we were holding for him.

Q: Typically were these naval-type VIPs?

Admiral Waters: Usually naval types, yes.

Q: And mostly foreign?

Admiral Waters: Yes, mostly foreign people that Washington really didn't know what to do with and wanted to get them out of town somewhere.

Q: Were you involved in any of the making of movies or TV shows to provide technical advice or Navy assets?

Admiral Waters: Well, actually I never provided any technical advice, but when Otto Preminger made In Harm's Way, they had the premiere showing up at Grauman's Chinese theater. They came to me and said, "We want to make this a really naval thing. Could you have naval people there in uniform, and could you furnish bunting and rig flags for us outside the theater?"

I said, "Sure." So Otto Preminger then made me his guest of honor. Suze and I went up, and we had a wonderful time. He had the typical Hollywood reception, where you had lots to drink and even sat down at a table and ate these very heavy hors d'oeuvres. Then we went upstairs and had a big dinner. But the place was crowded with movie celebrities at the time. It was a very wonderful thing. I made no contribution other than helping him put on his show.

Q: What do you recall about relationships with the cities of Long Beach and Los Angeles? Mayor Sam Yorty, for example, was a colorful guy.

Admiral Waters: He was a very colorful guy, and I got one up on him. He was the mayor of Los Angeles, and I was Commander Naval Base Los Angeles. When I got there and got in the job, I said, "Do these guys ever call on you?"

He said, "No."

I said, "I'm going to call on you."

"Is that right?"

I said, "It may not be right, but I think it would be fun to do."

So we went through all these arrangements, and Yorty was tickled to death. I went up in uniform, of course, with my aide, and went down this long corridor in city hall. There were more people there with holstered guns than you ever saw. We got to his office, and they apologized and asked me to please sit there for a moment. Then they ushered me in. Yorty was all over the place. "Admiral, how nice of you to come to see me. Because you have come, I have got a special surprise for you. Here!"

And there was this blonde movie actress, Mamie Van Doren? She was very well-upholstered. He had her in his office to meet me. That was my special reward for calling on him. He was quite a guy, and I think he later on came to a change of command or something like that.

Our relationship with the city of Long Beach was just wonderful. Ed Wade, who has since died, was the mayor then. And the Small Businessmen's Association and the Chamber of Commerce were very, very helpful to the Navy.

Q: They depended on sailors' business.

Admiral Waters: Yes. It was about 180 degrees from the way I remembered it as an ensign when I was stationed there on my first ship. At that time the people of Long Beach sort of looked down their noses at these sailors who were thugs and would rape their daughters and that sort of thing. But by the Sixties, when I got there, this had all completely turned around. As a matter of fact, they were so anxious to please the Navy that they gave us a big Navy landing there that we didn't need and didn't want. We took only part of it and quartered the shore patrol in there. Because by the time they had this landing built, we had piers where we could tie up practically everything except an aircraft carrier, and we didn't have many aircraft carriers in Long Beach. The piers at the naval base proper would take the cruisers and destroyers and, I believe, the amphib ships.

Q: How much relationship did you have with the naval shipyard there?

Admiral Waters: Commander Naval Shipyard came under me. I mean, he was not a tenant; he was part of my command. Of course, he got his technical direction from BuShips.* That was Jamie Adair, a wonderful ED officer.**

We had a hospital ship tied up there that furnished our medical facilities, plus a pretty big dispensary. While I was there, we managed to get through a program to build a hospital. You know, we closed down Long Beach after World War II, and we had a huge naval hospital up there that we turned over to the Veterans Administration. Then when the Vietnamese War was coming along, I was looking around because I knew we were going to start getting wounded patients and going to tax our capabilities. I went to the Veterans Administration to see if they could help us out, to keep from having to take people down that "blood alley" to the hospital in San Diego. They said, no, they didn't have any space. So we put in for a hospital then. I was there for the ground-breaking, and it's since

---
*BuShips--Bureau of Ships.
**Captain Admiral Jamie Adair, USN; ED--engineering duty.

been built.

Q: In your civic capacities did you have any relationship with any of the sports teams in L.A., of which there are many?

Admiral Waters: No, I don't believe I had any of that kind of relationship. I was, of course, an honorary member of Rotary. Being honorary was a good thing because you didn't have to go every week unless you wanted to; you didn't have to make up some place or pay a fine.

One of the nicest perks of the job was that as the commander of the base, I was made an honorary member of Virginia Country Club, which was an old, old, beautiful golf course, almost in the harbor of Long Beach. That was a great thing, a wonderful golf course to play golf on, manicured by hand.

Q: An unusual name for it.

Admiral Waters: Yes. It's on Virginia Avenue.

Q: I see. Back when you'd been with the fleet in the Thirties, didn't that focus more on the San Pedro side rather than Long Beach?

Admiral Waters: Yes. See, they didn't have the big breakwater there then. That came in the late Thirties. But when I was there in the early Thirties, we anchored behind a little stretch of breakwater at San Pedro. The line started there. The flagship was behind the breakwater, and then we anchored on up, so we were closer to San Pedro. But you could also get shore boats to Long Beach, or you could take a shore boat into San Pedro, which was a shorter ride, and if you had transportation, get across to Long Beach.

Q: So was it the breakwater that really shifted the interest more to the Long Beach side?

Admiral Waters: Yes, I think so--that and the fact that they built the shipyard in there.

Q: You mentioned these two different staffs for the two separate responsibilities. How did you keep track of what you were doing in each one?

Admiral Waters: It was pretty simple, because I had two excellent chiefs of staff. One was Fletcher Hale, Flick Hale, who was at the naval base, and my chief of staff on

MinePac staff was Steiny Steinmetz.* Both of them knew their jobs, so it was easy to keep things separated. Actually, the running of the naval base was really a public relations thing, unless something kind of sticky came up. And I could depend upon Flick Hale to detect that sort of thing.

The accommodations up at the naval base were much nicer and more spacious and more commodious than the ComMinePac headquarters, which were in the old control tower for Reeves Field that had been an airfield during World War II. Even though MinePac had kind of small offices, I spent most of my time there. That's where I would go every day to start off the day. Then about two to three days a week, I would go up to the other office. Or if anything came up, Flick would call me, and usually I'd call him and say, "You got anything that needs to be signed?" I'd say, "Get it together, I'll be up in half an hour."

Q: Was part of that the fact that you had a stronger interest in the Mine Force?

Admiral Waters: Yes, I suppose it's fair to say that, but also the mine force was an operational command and things were going on every day that you had to deal with--

---
*Captain Fletcher Hale, USN; Captain Everett H. Steinmetz, USN.

casualties to ships, and that sort of thing.

Q: Did you have operational control of the ships?

Admiral Waters: I had operational control of the ships while they were there with me, and that was most of them and most of the time. I had operational control of them while they were training, and I had a training officer, an operations officer, a full staff. Of course, the ones that were deployed came under the operational control of someone else.

We used to pride ourselves on those deployments. The longest hop was between Long Beach and Honolulu. We had these big rubber tanks to carry extra diesel stacked on the fantails, and that's the way they did it. But we never had any trouble going out, because usually the prevailing winds and currents helped the ships get to Honolulu. But when an outfit was coming back from deployment, when they got to Honolulu, we had a division standing by, ready to go out with these tanks to meet them in case they ran out of fuel on their way home. In the first place, it was a matter of pride in not asking for help, and in the second place, it would have been very, very uneconomical to get any kind of a tanker out there for the small amount of oil that those little spitkits would take.

O. D. Waters, Jr. #5 - 363

Q: In a sense you were a preserver of a dying art there, weren't you?

Admiral Waters: Yes, yes.

Q: It seems to be making somewhat of a comeback now, but there was a real nadir there for a while.

Admiral Waters: Yes. Of course, Korea frightened us for a while. The use of the old-fashioned moored mines by the North Koreans held up the landing at Wonsan for three days and made the Navy look really bad. The North Koreans, with the ChiComs helping them, sowed that harbor so full of mines in all kinds of different directions, no pattern to it at all, that it was just practically impossible to sweep them.* They had that many in there. It was a really tough job, and somebody could still do it to us today, and we probably wouldn't be able to do anything about it.

Q: Was there any development work yet on helicopter minesweeping while you were out there?

Admiral Waters: Oh, yes, yes, that had started. That's a pretty tough thing to do. You have to have awfully big, strong helicopters, and they're kind of peculiar things

---
*ChiComs--Chinese Communists.

anyway. They can break down, and they're complicated. The maintenance of them is a tough job.

Q: The Navy is now finally coming out with some new mine countermeasures ships, new construction.

Admiral Waters: Yes. That was one thing that I pushed for when I was in MinePac, countermeasure ships, because that was for use against the so-called influence mines, the bottom mines. We needed some kind of a countermeasure ship that could detect something out ahead of it and not have to run across it and send things out on cables or wires, wire guided, to destroy them.

Q: One traditional thing in the personnel area was that the cruiser-destroyer people usually got their pick of the litter. Did this cause a disadvantage for you in MinePac?

Admiral Waters: Well, I suppose you could say that, although it's pretty difficult to judge. A lot of officers, particularly those coming out of OCS and ROTC, requested small-ship duty.* Of course, the skippers you got were usually pretty good. They would probably come from destroyers and be sort of outstanding shiphandlers and get an early command that way.

---
*OCS--Officer Candidate School; ROTC--Reserve Officer Training Corps.

Q: So it wasn't a problem that you perceived, then?

Admiral Waters: No, it really wasn't. The personnel wasn't a problem. I didn't have any with them.

Q: Anything else about that before we head you back to Washington?

Admiral Waters: No, I don't think so. While I was there, P. D. Stroop, who was ComNavAirPac, got an airplane and gathered up all the loose flag officers he could on his way up to San Francisco.* There we attended Admiral Nimitz's 80th birthday, which was quite an affair and an honor to attend.

Q: What do you recall about that occasion?

Admiral Waters: Well, I recall that I was a little bit embarrassed, because Admiral Nimitz kept singling me out to remind him of things that had gone on on the _Augusta_. So a couple of times there we found ourselves the center of everything. I felt like I was kind of monopolizing the show, but it was wonderful to see the old man.

---

*ComNavAirPac--Commander Naval Air Pacific. Stroop was then a vice admiral. Fleet Admiral Chester W. Nimitz's 80th birthday was 24 February 1965. He died 20 February 1966.

Q: I would think that would be a very touching occasion, 30 years after that earlier association.

Admiral Waters: Yes, yes. They had built a special elevator into the quarters there on Treasure Island, where they had the Nimitzes. Mrs. Nimitz descended in what she said was her "gilded cage." She had arthritis very bad at that time, and she descended and greeted us all.

Q: After you finished out up in Los Angeles, you headed to Washington to be Oceanographer of the Navy. What do you recall about taking over that job?

Admiral Waters: The first thing I recall is when I found out I was getting the job. See, at that time we hadn't started training anybody as oceanographers. We didn't have an oceanography PG course, for example. People who'd had the job were, as I used to say, customers of the oceanographers; they had either been in submarines or destroyers and had known a great deal about surface layers and that sort of thing. So I was sitting in my office at ComMinePac one morning, and I had a problem about a very good enlisted man who had gotten into some sort of difficulty with BuPers. I forget exactly what it was. But I called the assistant chief of BuPers about this, and he said, "Oh, that's easy. I'll take care of it."

I said, "By the way, Joe, if you see my card coming towards the top of the pile there, take it out and put it at the bottom, because I think this is a good job, and I'm having a good time here."

Q: That's just the way to get yourself transferred.

Admiral Waters: He said, "Whoop! The chief wasn't here yesterday. I went to a scheduling conference. And I think your name came up. Let me check." So I heard him go, squawk, squawk, squawk, on the squawk box, and he came back and said, "Yes. There were three names proposed as Oceanographer of the Navy, and you are leading the list."

I said, "Oceanographer of the Navy? What the hell is that?" That's the way I found out, so we came back to Washington.

At that time the Oceanographer of the Navy was stationed at Suitland, Maryland, at the Naval Oceanographic Office, which had formerly been the hydrographic office. You know the title of Oceanographer of the Navy and the oceanographic office were both proclaimed by act of Congress without reference to the Navy, because oceanography had gotten to be so popular.

Anyway, the oceanographer at that time was at Suitland. He was also commander of the oceanographic office, which included all the hydrography and charting and that sort of thing. Plus we had oceanographic divisions doing various types of oceanographic work, including ocean currents, salinity, gravity fields, magnetic fields. The oceanographer reported to the Assistant Chief of Naval Operations for Administration, up through him to CNO. It was a very awkward thing, because usually the Assistant CNO for Administration didn't know much about what was going on out in the oceanographic office and couldn't really care less. He had a lot of other things he had to worry about.

Q: Was that Admiral Roy Benson then?*

Admiral Waters: He succeeded Jim Dempsey.** Benson was much easier to deal with. He was very interested in these things, and you could tell him about it and then it would pass on through for the CNO's signature, or whatever was required. Dempsey you usually had to go about three rounds.

About that time it was decided at the CNO level that the Oceanographer of the Navy should be higher up in the rank structure. The Navy should put more importance on oceanography and try to bring together all of the little scattered pieces of it spread throughout the Navy, just as they were spread throughout the federal government in other departments. That later resulted in NOAA being

---
*Rear Admiral Roy S. Benson, USN, whose two-volume oral history is in the Naval Institute's collection.
**Rear Admiral James C. Dempsey, USN.

established, which didn't help the situation too much, because it didn't bring enough of them together.* But that's a different story.

In the Navy, they formed a task group under Admiral Rivero, who was the Vice Chief of Naval Operations then, and I was in on the group.** We sat around the table, and in about a week we thrashed out how to pull all of these things together. There was a certain amount of important basic research being done under the Chief of Naval Research, at ONR, and at various universities they had projects being done. Then there was the development work that was being done under the Chief of Naval Material, and under him by the Director of Navy Laboratories. Also, the Chief of Naval Weather Service had a great interest in the ocean because it affected the weather.

Just fortuitously, I happened to be senior to the Chief of Naval Research; to the Director of Navy Laboratories, who was an Assistant Chief of Naval Material; and to the Chief of Naval Weather Service. They were all very capable people and easy to work with. They didn't care so much about the pecking order and so forth. So they were in on the thing, and they became Assistant Oceanographer for Ocean Science, Assistant Oceanographer for Research and Development, Assistant Oceanographer for

---
*NOAA--National Oceanographic and Atmospheric Administration.
**Admiral Horacio Rivero, USN, served as VCNO from July 1964 to January 1968. His oral history is in the Naval Institute's collection.

Meteorology, and they all reported to me for the broad thing. I was supposed to overlook the whole setup, particularly the budgets. That meant getting in and fighting for the weak places and cutting out the places that shouldn't be there.

The oceanographer was then taken out from under the Assistant Chief of Naval Operations for Administration, and I reported directly to CNO.

Q: When did that change come about?

Admiral Waters: That change took place in early 1966. In addition to these arrangements that were made and approved by CNO, I was also told that the Oceanographer of the Navy should have higher visibility. I should move out of Suitland over in Maryland, but they didn't have room for me in the Pentagon. I should form a staff and rent a place for it to have offices. So I formed a staff; counting everybody--mail room and all human beings on it--I think the total was 75 people. We managed to find a very convenient building that we just about filled up. It was a fairly new building, a small building, and it was at the north end of Washington Street in Alexandria. That made it very nice, because I was not having anybody in the Pentagon breathing down my neck, but if something happened, particularly in the budget business, I could get there in ten minutes. That's what the change amounted to.

Oh, they also told me that every command that was worth anything had an advisory panel, and I should have an advisory panel. So I started looking around, and I sounded out Admiral Arleigh Burke, and he accepted very gracefully and enthusiastically, actually.* I also had Admiral Savvy Sides, who had just retired, and had some very good scientific people, like Dr. Ralph Bennett, who had been the technical director at the Naval Ordnance Laboratory.** I had a very good group. We met fairly regularly, and they religiously attended, particularly Burke. It sort of puffed me up a little when I finally left after five years, Burke also left the advisory panel.

Q: Now, in putting this staff together, how did the setup change from what the situation had been out at Suitland?

Admiral Waters: Well, the setup at Suitland was that instead of having a staff to look into all of the different functions, I used the working departments at Suitland to do that for me. For example, one of the expensive parts of doing oceanography for the Navy is the oceanographic surveys you make. Of course, you make two kinds of surveys: you make hydrographic surveys to make the charts,

---
*Admiral Arleigh Burke was then retired, having completed his term as Chief of Naval Operations in 1961.
**Admiral John H. Sides, USN (Ret.).

and the oceanographic surveys go out and get various kinds of data on the oceans. One example is on the sea bottom for reflectivity of sonar to increase the range and all that sort of thing.

What I had to do was to pull people out of these departments and bring them over and have little staffs like that to overlook the whole thing. I had an R&D liaison man, and sometimes I used people from these other outfits' staffs as part-time members of my staff, like people from the Naval Research Laboratory or the Office of Naval Research.*

Q: I would think this would give you a greater degree of control, having them directly under you.

Admiral Waters: Yes, it did. It did give me a greater degree of control. I had meetings with the assistant oceanographers, and we discussed our problems, particularly the budget problems. I didn't actually control a lot of those budgets after we had gotten them; they went to different channels, like the ones in development went to the Chief of Naval Material. The others in science went through the Chief of Naval Research. But we were the ones that got behind them and justified them and asked for them and tried to fight our way through to get them.

---

*R&D--research and development.

Q: You probably had a working relationship with the Military Sea Transportation Service, because they were running your survey ships.

Admiral Waters: Yes, we did. They were running some of our survey ships. When I took over, we still had some Navy crews on ships, but I think by the time I left, the Military Sea Transportation Service had them all, some with uniformed crews and some under contract arrangements.

Q: Then it's up to you to provide the scientific personnel, isn't it?

Admiral Waters: Yes. We provided the scientific teams, and that was why having my own staff helped. The operations office was responsible for that. It was a great thing to do away with the Navy-manned ships, because a Navy-manned ship, on the average, spends only 50% of its time at sea. That's because of overhauls and because of morale problems for the men, getting them back to their home ports.

When we went to civilian-manned ships, the crews were, of course, paid higher, but they had no home port. I mean, it was up to MSTS to take care of overhauling. We had agents stretched around the world where they could get supplies and that sort of thing. So all we had to worry about was changing the research teams and the seagoing teams of oceanographers and their helpers and technicians and things. This worked fine. As a matter of fact, we would watch the operation of these ships, and if any of them dropped below 70% time at sea, then we'd start looking into why. So it made a great difference economically to do it that way, and you didn't have to bring the ship all the way from South Borneo. We flew the teams out to the nearest place and they boarded. It changed that way. Practically all the heavy instrumentation was mounted in the ships, but a lot of the fancier stuff, we just flew that along.

Q: Could you describe the operations of both types of ships, please, both the mapping and survey ships and the oceanographic research ships?

Admiral Waters: Well, they are quite different in a lot of ways. The hydrographic ships that do the mapping and surveying are ships that are equipped with sounding boats, as they call them from the old days. Now they're equipped, of course, with echo-sounders, and they are lowered over the side. They go out and run lines in certain patterns relative to the beach to establish the bottom. The single most important thing here is navigation, because it doesn't do you any good to say, "It's 50 feet deep here," if you don't know where "here" is. So we got more and more sophisticated types of navigation equipment as it became available. Eventually we got satellite navigation in the mother ship. I suppose by now they have laser control of the boat so that knowing where the ship is, they know exactly where the boat is.

While I was there, we developed a system of computerizing the hydrographic data. We had a big computer on the mother ship, and the data would come in and be fed into the computer, and you could really run off a chart right on the spot. It would be rather rough, but that rough data would eventually find its way back to Suitland and be gone over by the specialists who would make corrections on the contours, knowing the way that contours normally ran, and in that way produce a really finished chart.

Q: Do you do this because the bottom changes? Why would you make a new chart?

Admiral Waters: You do this because the bottom changes. The best example I can give you of that is that soon after I took over as oceanographer, the Vietnamese War was on, and one day a rather indignant dispatch came in from the commanding officer of a destroyer, and it was passed along to me for action from CNO. This officer was commanding a bomb-line destroyer, which stayed even with the line of battle of the troops as they shifted up and down close to the beach. He was supposed to supply gunfire support on call to the people ashore. He had found out that the 100-fathom curve was three miles farther out to sea than it was on his chart, which was rather dangerous, because if he got in close, he could run aground.

Now, the chart he was working from was made from Japanese surveys that were made during World War II. The Japanese are good hydrographers, and you could depend on their charts. But he was operating somewhere near the Mekong Delta, and all of this sediment came out in the deltaic material and had just filled in at the mouth of the river and up and down the beaches. So I called my staff in, and I said, "We have two choices, I think. One is to set up a big operation and resurvey those areas there that we're using as soon as we can, which would be a big operation, or you guys can just go and take shovels and go out there and shovel that sand back."

We actually did set up a rather costly operation and a very intensive one. We took three of our best survey ships and based them in Subic. They relieved each other on station out there. They would go out and keep running these bathymetric lines, then relieve each other and get time in port and get fixed. That's the way we did it. We resurveyed that whole area.

As I said, the important thing was to know where you were. At that time we had no satellite navigation, and we didn't have any Loran C stations in that area, of course, because it was pretty unfriendly ashore there.* You had to set up these small towers so you could do accurate navigation by getting signals back from the towers. Raydist was one that we used. They had various trade names for this short-range, high-accuracy navigation.

Of course, the boys in the boats never knew whether they were going to run into Charlie or not when they got on the beach and set these things up.** We were very lucky. A few of the towers were blown up by grenades, and one boat had bullet holes in it, but we never had anybody hit in doing this survey.

But because of this shifting sediment you have to keep resurveying. Now, in a place like the coast of Maine or the Norwegian Coast, those surveys are probably good forever.

Q: How do you know when you've got enough information to make up a new chart?

---

*Loran--long-range aid to navigation, an electronic system that emitted signals from shore stations. Ships used receivers to pick up these signals and plot lines of position that could be used in obtaining fixes.
**The enemy was the Viet Cong, abbreviated VC. In the phonetic alphabet, those letters are Victor Charlie, so the Viet Cong were known in the slang of the day as "Charlie."

Admiral Waters: Well, there are rules that you go by that come from experience, of having a certain frequency of depth soundings per area, and you can also tell from the variation in them. If they stay more or less the same for a long ways, you know you've pretty much got a plane in there, and a lot of times in shallow water the way to keep from having to survey the whole thing is to drag wires across it, and if it doesn't catch on anything, then you haven't got a pinnacle.

Now, the oceanographic surveys were entirely different. They could be done for a variety of reasons. One would be to determine the distribution of the warm and cold water in the ocean. We'd always try and figure out how to predict. It's just like predicting the weather. You have fronts in the ocean just like you have in the atmosphere, and you lower instruments over the side that give you salinity, depth, and temperature. Temperature is the easy one. They plot these things, and they draw inferences from them. They publish atlases. Now, I think, they've gotten it to a point where it's computerized, and it goes into centers that send it out very rapidly, and the operational forces can get data on the water they're in and where the layers are most likely to be and that sort of thing.

O. D. Waters, Jr. #5 - 379

Q: You have a program of chart corrections, too, don't you?

Admiral Waters: Oh, yes. That's a tremendous thing, and it has to be meticulously done.

Q: Where does the information come from for those?

Admiral Waters: Well, it can come from a variety of places. It can come from people who have run a survey in that area or close to that area. Usually it comes from shipping, either from the Navy or from merchant ships who, running their fathometers, have found something that doesn't agree with the chart. Then you go out and investigate it. Of course, a lot of the changes to navigation are changes of the location of navigational lights and buoys that get displaced by storms. That's sort of an automatic thing.

Q: Do you coordinate the Notices to Mariners also?

Admiral Waters: Yes.

Q: What are some examples of those?

Admiral Waters: That could be anything. It could be the

fact that somebody is going to run a minesweeping exercise in such and such an area, and people with lobster pots and things like that should not be there. Many times that worked in reverse. People with lobster pots would say they had lobster pots there, and then make claims against the government. That's the way the game goes.

Q: How much international cooperation was there in the work you did?

Admiral Waters: A tremendous amount of international cooperation, both in oceanography and in the hydrographic business. There's been cooperation in hydrography ever since about 1922, when the International Hydrographic Bureau was formed with about a membership of 40-some nations, I believe. I forget the exact number. That was set up for the purpose of exchanging hydrographic information and charts between nations, because it's so expensive to make, and in that way you could save each other money. It was set up as an international organization in Monte Carlo and is still there.

For some reason or other, they changed the name to the International Hydrographic Office, but it is still an independent organization supported by the countries that belong to it. Three directors head it up, and one of them is elected the presiding director, or the senior director, or the president—I forget what they call him. Those people are elected every five years at a big meeting. I had the fun of attending one. I think it still holds that there's always been an American as one of the directors. It's a very nice job to go to if you retire; you get to live in Monaco for five years at a tax-free salary, which isn't all that great, but it's a pleasant life.

Q: Did you find that the direct access to CNO helped your working relationships?

Admiral Waters: Oh, very much. Very much.

Q: In what ways?

Admiral Waters: When Moorer was CNO, he always had a meeting on Thursday morning, I remember, at 9:00 o'clock. Various people at that level directly under the CNO attended. I was one of the standard invitees there, and I always got called upon to bring up anything I wanted to that affected me. That helped. Then, of course, by virtue of reporting directly to the CNO, it meant that I had direct access to him if I wanted to take it. I didn't very often take it, because I knew he was awfully busy, and I only took it when it was very important, and then I got in to see him immediately because he knew I wasn't crying "wolf."

Q: What particular cases do you recall that had that kind of urgency attached to them?

Admiral Waters: I recall one that was rather dramatic to me. I had known Senator Magnuson, who was chairman of the Merchant Marine and Fisheries Committee of the Senate, under which the Subcommittee on Oceanography was a part.* I had met him there. He was a very pleasant gentleman. He was also a friend of my brother's, and I had met him socially too. He was very much interested in oceanography, and he kept tab on what we were doing. Unbeknownst to me, he dropped a bill in the hopper one day; it said that the Oceanographer of the Navy should be a three-star admiral. He had a man working for him who was a very good friend of mine. He was one of his administrative aides but particularly looked after the oceanographic and fisheries side of things. He called me, and he said, "Did you know the boss has dropped a bill in the hopper on you?"

I said, "No. Tell me about it." So he did, and I said, "Oh, my God, he just did it and didn't say anything to the Department of Defense about it?"

He said, "Nope. He just thought it was a good idea."

---

*Warren G. Magnuson, Democrat from Washington state, served in the U.S. Senate from December 1944 to December 1980. He had been a lieutenant commander in the Navy.

So that was when I called Tom on the phone, and I said, "Tom, I want to tell you something." I told him that I had been told that Senator Magnuson had proposed that the oceanographer be a three-star admiral, and I said, "I just want you to know that I had no knowledge in advance of this. I know nothing about it. I'm not trying to get myself promoted by the Senate."

He said, "Okay, Muddy, that's fine. Don't worry about it. It will be taken care of in the Department of Defense."

Of course, nothing more was ever done or heard about it, but I was glad I had that access to him. It could have reflected on me as, in an underhanded way, trying to get myself promoted.

Q: When did the move come about consolidating with the Defense Mapping Agency over in Fort Sumner?

Admiral Waters: That came about after I left. This was done by one of the paper-pushers over in the Department of Defense who was looking for, I always felt, a way to set up a lot more civil service jobs, because it was tacked on as an amendment to some bill. It established the Defense Mapping Agency. The reason for this was so that there would be better cooperation between the Army, the Navy, and the Air Force, all three of which had their own mapping agencies. So their duties were very clearly defined. The Army did their mapping just for Army purposes, because the Continental United States hydrographic charting was done by the Coast and Geodetic Survey, which it was called at that time. It's now under NOAA, called the NOAA Corps. The Navy was responsible for the rest of the world as far as hydrographic surveys were concerned. The Air Force did their own air type charts required by aircraft flights, which was different from the other three. There was great cooperation between all three of them. As a matter of fact, when I was at Suitland, and the Army's mapping agency was way out northwest of Washington around the beltway, we had, I think, about at least three round trips a day of station wagons between us and the Army Mapping Service, exchanging data and carrying stuff back and forth. There was no reason for the Defense Mapping Agency to be set up.

Q: How much of a relationship did you have with the Coast and Geodetic Survey while it was still in existence?

Admiral Waters: We worked pretty closely with those guys and had good relations with them in the mapping part of it. Of course, they had to furnish us with the land part of charts that we made for special naval purposes. They furnished us with that sort of thing, because we made a certain number of charts for our training areas that you have at sea near Norfolk and Newport, for example.

Q: Short of covering the command in general, I wonder where the requirements came from. Who gave you direction on what things to do?

Admiral Waters: The requirements on things to do were pretty well hashed out, as far as charting was concerned. That's a long-term, look-ahead program, and that was pretty well agreed to in advance, unless something special came up.

Q: So the Vietnam thing would be an exception?

Admiral Waters: Yes, it was an exception to that. You just went around and covered places that you knew were going to need to be covered in a few years.

We had a different type of surveying that was highly classified, and we had three special ships to do that. That was surveying the ocean bottom for the missile submarines. I won't go into that, because that's probably still highly classified. But we had three great big ships that were specially configured to do that, and they did an excellent job of it. As a matter of fact, they invented a system called the Harris array, where they just spaced a whole array of transponders under the bottom of the ship. With that system you could sweep a wide path and survey a whole area of the ocean bottom at one time. This was deep-ocean stuff.

Q: So you were really doing a contour map of the ocean.

Admiral Waters: Yes, yes. Another thing that was a constant task for us was mapping the anomalies in the magnetic field of the earth. That changes enough so the mapping has to be done over about every seven years. So it takes you seven years of flying these airplanes all the way around, and then you have to start over where you started in the first place.

Q: Does this tie in with sunspot activity?

Admiral Waters: They don't really know completely what causes it, but it's sunspot activity. It also has something to do with the wobble of the earth. That's getting worse or better, I forget which--one or the other. When I was there it was called Project Magnet, still is, except they use much better airplanes now. It used to be hard to do, because we had these old Lockheed three-tailed planes.

Q: Constellations?

Admiral Waters: Yes, Constellations. They weren't quite long-legged enough to cover as much as we wanted to cover on certain flights, so they had to fly over too much water. So now they have the P-3s.

Q: That's the patrol plane, antisubmarine plane.

Admiral Waters: Yes. I think that's what they have now. They keep flying around and around the earth, collecting magnetic data on magnetometers.

Then we had a program which had to do with the earth's gravity field. That, again, was very important to missileers, because that tells you which way is up. If there's an anomaly in the earth's gravity field at a certain point, these machines that detect which way is up will be thrown off by this anomaly. Then, of course, the aim of your missile or projectile will be thrown off by that much.

Gravity is much more difficult to measure than magnetism, because it takes a much more accurate and finely tuned instrument to measure it. When we started off doing it, we had a gravimeter, they call it, that would only work on a stable platform, so we got one submarine and had it designated to the gravity program. It went round and round the world at various places where, for strategic reasons, we wanted to check the gravity field. We had it manned entirely by bachelors so it didn't make any difference where they were Christmas. Just so it was a fairly decent port, so they could have a good time. That worked pretty well. Finally, the instruments have now been developed to the point where they can be flown in aircraft, and it makes it a lot easier. The submarine has long been decommissioned.

Q: Do you remember which one that was?

Admiral Waters: I should, but I don't recall.

Q: Probably a conventional submarine.

Admiral Waters: Oh, yes. It wasn't nuclear. It was a conventional submarine. Of course, they just had to get down deep enough so that the waves weren't bothering them. If there wasn't a very big swell going, they didn't have to go down very far.

Q: You talked of your slight befuddlement at the beginning when you heard about being offered the job. Did you work out some program to develop a training course to move people up toward this?

Admiral Waters: Oh, yes, yes. I became the father of that. You know, each course at the Navy PG School has a sponsoring officer. I guess Ed Stephan, who was one of my predecessors as oceanographer, may have started it.* But we have up to a master's degree in physical oceanography, chemical oceanography. They had one in ocean engineering. Now, whether they still have it or not, I don't know. There was some talk about stopping it. I don't know why, because it seems to me it's very important, but maybe they figured that the civil engineers ought to be ocean engineers too. Maybe that was the reason. At any rate, we had this ongoing program there that's still going on, and I was the sponsor for it. My staff and I surveyed it and looked at what they were teaching them, to see if they were teaching them what we thought they ought to be taught.

Q: So there's a more systematic method now for training specialists in this?

Admiral Waters: Yes. We even have some Ph.D.'s now in captain's rank. We've got a lot more knowledgeable people now. You don't have to go and start reading the textbooks and get your department heads to come in and explain things to you the way I did.

---

*Rear Admiral Edward C. Stephan, USN, was Oceanographer of the Navy from June 1960 to April 1963.

O. D. Waters, Jr. #5 - 390

Q: It's a shame that Don Walsh retired, because he looked like a rising star.*

Admiral Waters: Yes, he was. I had something to do with Don's coming up. He was a lieutenant commander when I first got to know him. He was down at Texas A&M taking a master's course in oceanography. We had these graduate courses both at the PG school and, as we do in other branches of sciences and engineering, we have them go to other colleges and universities as well. We had a very good course there at A&M, and Oregon State had a very good one. Don went down there, and he worked like the devil, did very well. I went down to A&M, because they were having a big inner-space festival, or something like that, in the middle of the winter, and I was one of the speakers.

Don took advantage of this and had a little party and got me off to one side. He's a pretty persuasive fellow and very intelligent. He persuaded me to step in with the Bureau of Personnel and see if I could get him extended for another year down there. We managed to do that, and he got his Ph.D. In addition to that, I think Don has either a business or a law degree. I believe he's got a law degree,

---

*In January 1960 Lieutenant Don Walsh, USN, together with Jacques Piccard, descended seven miles to Challenger Deep, the deepest point in the world's oceans, in Project Nekton. A 1954 graduate of the Naval Academy, Walsh retired in 1975, soon after being promoted to captain.

too, that he got on his own. He's very intelligent. After that, I recommended him, and they got him into the old job that Ed Snyder had had as Special Assistant to the Assistant Secretary for R&D in charge of oceanography.*

Q: What was your relationship with the secretariat in that job?

Admiral Waters: I had direct relationship with ASN R&D, who, most of the time I was there, was Bob Frosch.** When Frosch came, I went over and made an arrangement that every two weeks on a certain day, Thursday, I would have an hour with him at 10:00 o'clock in the morning. Sometimes it didn't work. Sometimes he just couldn't do it, and we'd put it off until the next week or whenever. But we kept the schedule as well as we could so that my staff knew that I was going to see Frosch on such and such a date, and they would bring things in to me, things for the Secretary. I would have a list of things to take up with him. This kept us closer to each other by seeing each other frequently and at regular intervals. I would take these things up, and we'd have about an hour's discussion. I'd get in my car and flip back to the office. As I'd walk in the door, I'd

---

*Captain J. Edward Snyder, USN, who later, as a rear admiral, served as Oceanographer of the Navy.
**Assistant Secretary of the Navy (Research and Development) Robert A. Frosch.

say to the secretary, "Call the boys." She'd call the boys and they'd come in, and I'd go down the list: "He said no on this. He said yes on this."

Q: What kinds of things did you bring to the Secretary, as opposed to the CNO?

Admiral Waters: Well, mainly things concerned with money. I don't know whether it's still true, but at that time the Assistant Secretary of the Navy for Research and Development was the only assistant secretary in any of the armed forces that had any control over money. He had the whole research budget under his control, which made it very nice. He was my boss on the civilian side, whereas Tom was on the Navy side.

Q: What kinds of things would you report to Admiral Moorer about?

Admiral Waters: I would report to him about things that we wanted to get. I was thinking the other day--I know that I used the term "catch-up football." We were trying to get another ship to survey the contour of the ocean bottom. We were starting to build one of the new classes of missile submarines, and I said, "The areas are going to change, and we're going to need these surveys. Now is the time to get the ship, not after we find out that we need it and have to wait a couple more years to play catch-up football." That's the kind of thing I would bring to him.

Q: So things that affected the Navy type requirements.

Admiral Waters: Yes.

Q: How much relationship did you have with the civilian organizations such as Scripps or Woods Hole?

Admiral Waters: Scripps and Woods Hole both worked for us, in the sense that they did a lot of research projects and operational projects for us. We were responsible, while I was there, for supporting about 60% of Woods Hole's operational commitments, their projects. We were responsible for about 40% of Scripps. The reason for the difference between the two of them was not because we liked one better than the other, but because Scripps is a part of the California State institutional system, and they got some money from the state, and Woods Hole was private. So we divvied it up that way, and everybody was happy. We had a very close relationship with them and had projects there that we kept track of. I'd been to both places quite often; they had some awfully good people. They are the two centers of excellence, as far as I'm concerned.

Q: I've heard that Emperor Hirohito of Japan has an interest in this area. Did you ever hear from him?

Admiral Waters: No, I never heard from him. He's a marine biology man. While the Navy employs quite a few marine biologists, we are interested in marine biology in sort of a highly specialized way. One example is the prevalence and habits of whales, which can look like submarines, and where they go and where they're likely to be in large numbers and fool you into thinking they're submarine contacts. Nowadays I imagine that sonars are so good that they can tell which is a whale and not a submarine--that is, if you read Hunt For Red October.*

Q: Did you do any research on the recovery of mineral resources from the ocean?

Admiral Waters: No, we didn't as such. It really wasn't the Navy's business. We knew a lot about it, and I had big manganese nodules sitting behind my desk that our ships had dredged up while doing other jobs. We kept abreast of the development in that, but we didn't have a mission in that sort of thing.

---

*A novel by Tom Clancy that engages the Soviet and American navies in a race to find an errant submarine. Published in 1984 by the U.S. Naval Institute Press.

Q: Did you have any role in teaching line officers oceanographic information that would be of value to them? Such things as the thermal layers could affect the operation of their ships.

Admiral Waters: My people wrote some textbooks, which I presume we used at training schools. Also, some of them wrote articles that were published in magazines like the Scientific American. I'm sure we furnished materials for the Officer Candidate School and places like that.

Q: I've heard--I don't know how true it is--that submariners have a better grasp of oceanography than surface ship officers.

Admiral Waters: That's probably true because they have to. They're immersed in it a little bit more than we are.

Q: It's a matter of staying alive.

Admiral Waters: Yes, more than the surface boys are. You have to understand surface layers and how you hide under them and what causes them, a little bit more than the surface boys do, although I think that they're getting pretty well aware of them in the ASW business. They certainly ought to.

Q: You mentioned Ed Snyder. What do you remember about him?

Admiral Waters: Well, Ed was a very intelligent guy whom I first met when he was a special aide to the Assistant Secretary for R&D. He was very helpful in keeping me informed in what was going on in that office as it affected me in my work. He was just an excellent liaison man there. Later on, when he became Oceanographer of the Navy quite a few years later, he did a great job in running the oceanographic office. It's now been somewhat downgraded and split up again. I don't know how that happened but it did. The former oceanographer is now Chief of Naval Research.

Q: Admiral Mooney.*

Admiral Waters: Yes, Brad Mooney. He's a good man. I used to have a great deal to do with him when I was oceanographer and he was over in OP-31, the submarine desk in Naval Operations. What came under his wing then were the small submersibles. That's another thing we were very much involved in. We were involved in both oceanography

---

*Rear Admiral John Bradford Mooney, Jr., USN.

and ocean engineering in the small submersibles that were so valuable in going down and doing certain things. You could get the human eyeball down to see things that you just had to imagine from up above or interpret from a TV camera or something like that. So we were much interested in building those things.

Q: Were you involved in that Sea Lab program, having people live on the ocean floor?

Admiral Waters: Very much so, yes.

Q: What do you recall about that?

Admiral Waters: I first got involved in it before I even knew I was going to be oceanographer. This was when I was in Long Beach and was ComMinePac. They made an arrangement with us to bring in all the people that were going to be in Sea Lab, the aquanauts. We gave them an old hangar and a place to put their gear, a place to train and do whatever they had to do, gave them a place to operate and train in. One of them was Scott Carpenter, whom I got to know quite well at that time.*

---

*Lieutenant Commander Malcolm Scott Carpenter, USN, was one of the nation's original seven astronauts in the Mercury program of the early 1960s. In May 1962 he was the second American to make a successful orbital flight of the earth.

Q: What do you remember about him?

Admiral Waters: Very, very interesting guy, very easygoing, good-humored fellow, hail fellow well met. It maybe had something to do with his undoing. He became an aquanaut because he wrecked himself riding a motorcycle, and he couldn't be an astronaut anymore. Yes, I liked Scott. One funny thing I remember about Scott was that he came over and paid me a call before they left. He was in my office, and we were talking about the difference between being an astronaut and an aquanaut. I said, "You know, Scott, in my opinion--and you probably won't agree with this--in many ways being an aquanaut is more dangerous than being an astronaut."

He said, "Why do you say that?"

I said, "Because you're down there, and every time you go down a foot, you get a half a pound more of over-pressure on you. In space, all you've got to contend with anyplace is the absence of 14.9 pounds of pressure. In space, there are no little animals that come and bite you and corrode things. Space is not corrosive on the things you depend on to live in or to ride in, and things like that."

He never did say he agreed with me, but when he came up from his 30-day stay below the sea, that's exactly what he told the newspapers. It was sort of a direct quote from what I had told him.

Q: I guess there was a man lost in that program that sort of set it back, didn't it?

Admiral Waters: Yes. Scott was in Sea Lab I. We lost a man in Sea Lab II. It was one of those unfortunate things. They got carried away with keeping to the schedule and let that become more important than the safety precautions. They dived in the dark and cold when they shouldn't have. And it was too cold. The men had already dived once before that day, and they were tired. The cold and the fatigue got one of them, and they weren't able to get him out before he was killed. That really set the program back. But by that time, we had really gathered enough data to realize that we didn't need all that big, expensive habitat to live in. All we needed was just a little chamber down there so we could short cut it by that much.

Q: What was the ultimate objective envisioned in that program?

Admiral Waters: The reason for it was that when a diver goes down to great depths, anything over 100 feet or 150 feet, you can't breathe just ordinary air anymore, because the air has to be at the pressure that you are at. If you are at 150 feet, you've got 75 pounds over-pressure on you, which is quite a bit per square inch. When you can't breathe the air anymore, you have to breathe a mixture of gases, oxygen and helium, because the nitrogen in regular air has a narcotic effect on people and gives you what they call the "rapture of the deep." So you substitute helium for that. Then you can dive on down to perhaps, we think, 2,000 feet.

Coming back up, the decompression gets longer and longer the deeper you dive. It takes a long time, because all of this stuff under pressure goes into your lungs and then into your bloodstream and into your tissues, and you have to slowly release the pressure while that comes out. If you do it too quickly, it will make a bubble, make an embolism, and either kill you or give you the bends, which is very, very painful. So the decompression is done in a decompression chamber, very slowly, and the guy is watched, his blood pressure is taken, his temperature, and so forth.

Now it turns out that it doesn't really make any difference how long you stay down there. That doesn't affect the decompression time very much; it's how deep you go. So the reasoning goes like this: if you are going to have to go down to 500 feet and work on a job, and it's going to take a couple of days to do it, then instead of having people go down for a day's work and then go through that long decompression, and then after that, go down again and come back and do the long decompression, wouldn't it be more sensible to have a place that they could live in down there and just do the job and do the decompression once? That was what the whole thing was all about, and that's still the name of the game.

Q: One thing that happened while you were oceanographer was the loss of the USS Scorpion.* Were you involved in looking for that ship?

Admiral Waters: I was not directly involved in it, but I was very much following it. We had a special technical group formed that sort of acted as detectives in trying to find it, and who actually did find the general location. Then the Trieste, one of the ships in this submersible fleet that I had fought for, went out on that search and found it.** They found it in 1,500 feet of water way

---

*The USS Scorpion (SSN-589) was commissioned 29 July 1960. She operated into May 1968 with the Sixth Fleet. On 21 May, during a transit to the East Coast, she reported her position to be about 50 miles south of the Azores. Six days later, she was reported overdue at Norfolk. At the end of October, sections of Scorpion's hull were located about 400 miles southwest of the Azores, the cause of her loss a mystery.

**Trieste II, a research bathyscaph, was successor to Trieste I, which had been used by Walsh and Piccard for their dive in 1960. The wreckage of the Scorpion was discovered by underwater cameras from the USNS Mizar (T-AGOR-11) in late 1968, then examined in detail by the Trieste II in 1969.

southwest of the Azores. There's an awful lot of ocean out there. That was really a feat to find that thing.

Q: Well, there's another feat that happened recently, the discovery of the Titanic.* You must have had an interest in that.

Admiral Waters: Yes, I did. That man from Woods Hole who invented the remotely operated vehicle that went down and took all the pictures--I've never met him, but I've shown a lot of movies of him in my lectures. He's quite a guy. He's a lot prettier than Jacques Cousteau and wears a blue and white stocking cap instead of a red one.

Q: Anything else on your tour there as Oceanographer of the Navy?

Admiral Waters: Well, we've touched on the submersibles, we've touched on the general oceanography, gravity, magnetism. One of the things that I spent a lot of time doing as oceanographer that I probably should include here very quickly is the fact that so many other departments of the government had some interest in the oceans. It's

---

*The SS Titanic departed on her maiden voyage from England on 10 April 1912. She sank--with an inestimable loss of lives and riches--just five days later, having struck an iceberg in the North Atlantic. Her wreck was discovered by a Woods Hole expedition led by Dr. Robert Ballard.

surprising the number of departments that are doing work in the oceans. I made it a point to establish contact with those people in those departments and to work with them whenever we could.

When I first went there, before they formed NOAA, we had the Bureau of Commercial Fisheries and the Bureau of Game Fishing and Wildlife; they were in the same department, the Department of Commerce. They didn't speak to each other, but we got to speaking to both of them, and we could feed information to them which was helpful to them, and they could give us information about their work that was helpful to us. We did an awful lot of cooperative work.

Like the geological survey, which is a small but very elegant outfit; they're good. They were interested in the sea bottom of the Gulf of Mexico for traces of oil deposits. We were interested in it from its reflection of sound waves and antisubmarine work. We were going to do a cruise down there and invited them to go, so they came piggyback with us. We both used practically the same data, but we interpreted it in different ways. That was one thing that I did, work with a lot of those people. The Coast Guard was very much interested. As a matter of fact, I got the Commandant of the Coast Guard to assign one of his good officers as a liaison; he was on my staff permanently. When we got into all this diving business, I got the Chief of Medicine and Surgery to assign a doctor part time to my staff.

Q: That was in their interests also.

Admiral Waters: Yes. He was interested in hyperbaric medicine, and it was great having him. A funny thing, the first day he showed up, he came over with his boss. I said, "Of course, you know you've got to bring your little black bag and give out aspirins too."

By golly, when he showed up, he had his little black bag with him, and he said, "You thought you were kidding, didn't you? I wasn't kidding about it. Anybody need a prescription for anything?"

Q: I'd also like to touch on your role on the Naval Institute editorial board and the board of control, since we are representing the Institute here. How did you come to be on the board?

Admiral Waters: Like everyone else, except the *ex officio* members, like the Chief of Naval Operations and the Superintendent of the Naval Academy, I was elected. I found it a most interesting and pleasant job. It took some time, but it got you away from the office for half a day and got back down to Annapolis, and you felt like you were back in the Navy again. We read an awful lot of interesting material, got a lot of free books. Every book that was published, I got a copy.

Q: You have a chance to do something good for the entire Navy there, which I think is useful.

Admiral Waters: Yes, I think so too. I think the Proceedings is a wonderful publication. We were very proud of it. I'm still proud of it. It has a reputation, I think, well-earned, of being the best professional military publication in existence. I'm sure that's true. I know the Royal Navy looks up to it. I think it's a great magazine.

Q: What are your recollections of Commander Bowler and the board meetings?*

Admiral Waters: I thought Bud Bowler was a great fellow. The board meetings were always run most efficiently. Of course, we had our homework to do, readings to take home with us. Everything that was published in that magazine was read by at least several of the board of control members, and the others had enough knowledge of it to vote

---

*Commander Roland T. Evans (Bud) Bowler, Jr., USN (Ret.), was secretary-treasurer. He ran the organization on a day-to-day basis.

on it. Most of it was read by everybody. But the biggest assignment, the toughest assignment, was judging the essay contests once every year. It begins before Christmas and used to end in January, as I remember.

Q: What do you remember about that, other than the big work load?

Admiral Waters: I remember one particularly tough choice we had to make one year when we had an article submitted called "Against All Enemies," which is a phrase taken from the oath to defend the Constitution of the United States against all enemies, foreign and domestic.* The domestic part was underscored, and the essay was written as a criticism of our own people, particularly politicians, who were undermining the security of the United States by doing certain things that weakened the military forces. It was a very well-written piece, but it criticized some politicians openly and by name. So, therefore, it would have been a very hot number. It particularly criticized Senator Fulbright.** It's not fair to just say Fulbright and no others, because there were some others that were criticized. At any rate, it seemed to me to be the best of

---
*Captain Robert J. Hanks, USN, "Against All Enemies," <u>U.S. Naval Institute Proceedings</u>, March 1970, pages 23-29.
**Senator J. William Fulbright, Democrat from Arkansas, served in the Senate from 1944 to 1974. He was especially well known as the chairman of the Senate Foreign Relations Committee during the Vietnam War.

the articles. We had our meeting that year to make the final decision on the winner down at Patuxent Naval Air Station, and we had a long discussion over this. It seemed that most everyone thought it was a very fine article, but also most everyone was a little bit afraid to publish it, because it might get the Naval Institute into hot water.

Two of us there, Admiral Mack and I, sort of got together as a minority and made speeches to the effect that the Naval Institute is not an official publication of the Navy, and that its charter says that it shall publish articles of interest to the professional naval officer that may be controversial.* In other words, it isn't just a rubber stamp for what the present CNO believes. After some discussion, we decided that the man who would have to take the heat on this was Admiral Tom Moorer, who was the Chief of Naval Operations, and ex officio, the president of the Naval Institute. Of course, he wasn't in on the selection job. But the blame would be put on him, so we decided we would pass it up to him to decide whether he was willing for it to be the winner of the essay contest. If he decided that he didn't want to back it, the others which we had ranked behind it would fleet on up, and this article would just be thrown out.

When it was shown to Tom Moorer, I understand he said,

---

*Rear Admiral William Paden Mack, USN, whose two-volume oral history is in the Naval Institute's collection.

"That's damn good, but it ought to be a lot stronger." So it became the winning essay. It seems to me that there was about two weeks' lag time before anybody realized that the Naval Institute had published anything like this, and then it hit the newspapers. It flared up for about a week and then died down when people were educated into the fact as to what the Naval Institute really was and how this wasn't the Navy taking potshots at Senator Fulbright and others. It was an institute of people who were just allowed and permitted to discuss questions of interest to the professional naval man or military man.

Q: Were you impressed by the quality of the imagination and the original thought in those essays?

Admiral Waters: Oh, yes, I was. They were difficult to judge, and a lot of hard work went into them. It was a great honor more than anything else. The remuneration wasn't all that great, but it was rewarding.

Q: Did the board put an emphasis on the idea of the _Proceedings_ as a forum, that people could agree with Captain Hanks on "Against All Enemies" or disagree, and that the Institute itself didn't take a position?

Admiral Waters: Yes, of course. I mean, that's the whole idea. Let everyone, anyone have a crack at being for him or against him. But it certainly would have defeated the purpose, I think, of the whole Institute, to have the Institute have an official position. We couldn't afford to.

Q: Are there any books that came out during that time that you especially remember?

Admiral Waters: I remember the new Dutton, which I prize very highly.*

Q: Do you have any recollections of the annual meetings of the Institute?

Admiral Waters: Well, my only recollections are generally pleasant ones, of seeing old friends there, like Admiral Wright, whom I'd worked for. You always see a collection of people like that at the annual meetings, and for that alone it's worthwhile going. It's good to hear the CNO express himself rather forthrightly at the meetings, and I enjoyed the ones I've gone to.

Q: One change that was made during that time was taking

---

*The Naval Institute Press periodically publishes new editions of <u>Dutton's Navigation and Piloting</u>.

the Naval Review from being an independent publication and making it one issue of Proceedings. Do you remember the deliberations on that?

Admiral Waters: I don't recall the deliberations. I don't remember there being very much opposition to it, because it was a laborious thing to put out. I think it would have really strained the staff to have to publish that in addition to a regular issue of the Proceedings.

Q: A thing that accompanied that was the change in the page size of the Proceedings so that it became the same size as the Naval Review. Was there concern about a break with tradition there?

Admiral Waters: I don't think so. I remember that. The only thing was that facetious remarks were made about "now I'll have to get the space between my shelves changed for the old back issues." But, as I remember it, it improved the appearance of the magazine so much, and it was, if I recall, quite a bit cheaper than that old process, letter press. When they went to offset, it was cheaper and easier to read, I believe.

Q: What do you remember about the financial health of the

organization while you were on the board?

Admiral Waters: Well, as I recall, the board never was very rich, neither was it very poor, but it couldn't afford to get very rich because of the tax-free situation.

Q: You can provide more for the members then.

Admiral Waters: Yes.

Q: That's the pleasant situation the Institute has now after The Hunt for Red October.

Admiral Waters: Yes, I imagine so.

Q: Are there any of the full-time staff members that you especially remember from then?

Admiral Waters: Frank Uhlig.* Is Frank still alive?

Q: He's up at the Naval War College now.

Admiral Waters: I knew he had left the Institute. Yes, I remember Frank very well. That used to be his baby, didn't it, the Naval Review?

---

*Frank Uhlig, Jr., served in various positions at the U.S. Naval Institute from 1960 to 1981. He is the editor of the book Vietnam: The Naval Story (Annapolis: Naval Institute Press, 1986).

Q: Yes, it did. I took that over from him when he went to the War College.

Admiral Waters: I wrote an article for that while I was oceanographer. I was in the Naval Review one year.* And way, way back yonder, I once published an article on leadership.**

Q: What do you recall about the period when you were winding down and you spent some time at NOAA right after you left the job as Oceanographer of the Navy?

Admiral Waters: Going over to NOAA was a little maneuver on my part to stay active in the Navy a little longer and not retire until another pay raise came in that I was told was coming, which would have been foolish to miss. Then the secretarial side of the Navy was not averse to having me go over and at least pretend to be an adviser to National Oceanographic and Atmospheric Administration as they were starting, because as the Secretary pointed out in his letter, I had reorganized the Office of the Oceanographer, and perhaps I could be of some help to them.

---

*Admiral Waters's article was "The Ocean Sciences and the Navy," published in 1969 Naval Review, pages 234-253.
**Commander O. D. Waters, Jr., USN, "On Serving One's Country," Proceedings, February 1953, pages 168-169.

I don't think they wanted me; I don't think they wanted anybody from the Navy telling them what to do, but they couldn't very well refuse it, so I went over.

There were some very nice people over there that I got to know, particularly Admiral Nygren, who's now retired.* He would have been an admiral in the Coast and Geodetic Survey, but they changed that to the NOAA Corps. He and I used to sit and shoot the breeze a lot. They had some very good people at NOAA, and they had hired some ex-Navy people, some who had been in the Polaris project.

I enjoyed my tour there, but I don't think I accomplished very much. They kept thinking up difficult tasks for me to do. One was that they asked me if I would get together a group from the former Bureau of Commercial Fisheries and the former Bureau of Game Fishing and Wildlife, which had been sort of enemies in the Department of Commerce for years and work out how we were going to coexist. One of them was left in the Department of Commerce, and one went with NOAA; that's what happened when they had the split. They wanted me to get them together and work out their differences. Well, I didn't know fish from anything, anyway, except a little bit about whales and about the deep scattering layer, but it was sort of fun conducting these meetings. We really didn't get very far with it. There were some nice people on both sides of the

---

*Rear Admiral Harley D. Nygren was Director of NOAA.

table there.

Anyway, after trying to do a lot of rather futile things like that, my time there came to an end, and Bob White, who was the administrator of NOAA, called me in the day before I left and had a conference with me on what I thought about the way they were going. I had prepared myself for this and gave them a list of suggestions I had about doing this and doing that, and I don't think any one of them was adopted.

Q: What had precipitated this move? You weren't due to retire statutorily yet. Why had you made the shift from oceanographer to NOAA?

Admiral Waters: Well, I shifted from oceanographer to NOAA because I was ordered relieved by Admiral Zumwalt, who wanted younger officers in all of the top jobs in Washington.* I'd had the job for five years. I really had no argument on that score, because three years is usually a long tour in any job, as you know. And five years is phenomenal.

Q: I think you mentioned before we started the tape that that made you the second longest Oceanographer of the Navy.

---

*Admiral Elmo R. Zumwalt, Jr., USN (Ret.), was Chief of Naval Operations from 1970 to 1974.

Admiral Waters: Yes. Matthew Fontaine Maury was oceanographer for 19 years, from 1842 to 1861. He was actually called hydrographer in those days. The reason that he stopped was to become a member of the Confederate States Navy. They immediately promoted him to commodore. He had been a lieutenant for about 20 years.

Q: Why did you not choose to go to another Navy job at that point?

Admiral Waters: Well, I didn't want to go to another Navy job and stay in one for a normal tour of duty, because, in the first place, I wasn't offered anything but sort of pasture jobs that weren't very interesting and I felt I would be bored in. In the second place, I was very much interested in oceanography. I had worked pretty hard at trying to learn something about it, and I wanted to stay in it. I didn't want to just retire and quit. I think I'm correct in this--that one is much more desirable as the recently retired Oceanographer of the Navy than as the recently retired Commandant of the Fourth Naval District, who at one time was Oceanographer of the Navy.

Q: Why had you stayed in the job so long? Had you not expressed a preference for another change of duty?

Admiral Waters: I had not expressed a preference, because I liked the job very much, and I liked the people I was working with and for. At that time, Tom Moorer and Bob Frosch and those people seemed to like what I was doing, and so I thought, "You know, some day they might make me a three-star admiral. You can't tell." But that really wasn't the reason I was hanging around; I was hanging around because there were so many interesting things going on, and I wanted to see them through.

Actually, when I was told rather abruptly that I was going to be relieved, I had the plans all made to make a trip up to Point Barrow in Alaska, because close to there, you know, we had a floating ice island with experimental work going on on the ocean, under the ice, as well as seeing all those oil fields and the offshore oil businesses they were considering. I had plans all made to go up there. When I was told I was going to be relieved, I canceled them, because it was going to cost a bit of money, and I thought if I was going to continue being oceanographer, it was a good idea for me to go. If I wasn't, I would like very much personally to go, but it wouldn't do the Navy any good.

Q: What have you done in the years since you've retired?

O. D. Waters, Jr. #5 - 417

Admiral Waters: While I was still over at the Department of Commerce, at NOAA, I had been down here in Florida at the Florida Institute of Technology, which was started back in '58 and accredited in about '62 or so, to provide higher education for the young engineers and scientists at the Cape for the space program, because we're only 20 miles from there. I had been invited down in '66, when they started a department of oceanography. I was invited to give the commencement address that year and install the new department. That's the way I had met the president, Jerry Keuper.*

Fortunately, he had bestowed a doctor of science honorary degree on me that year. So when I retired, he came up and said the head of his oceanography department was leaving. He heard I was retiring--wouldn't I come down and head up the Oceanography Department? My wife and I had both discussed very strongly going to the La Jolla area of California. As a matter of fact, she had even looked at a house out there. I had once been heard to say that I would retire in Florida when they built an air-conditioned golf course. But he managed to send a VIP plane that he borrowed from the Harris Corporation here, and flew us both down directly from Washington and put out the red carpet. We stayed in the VIP houseboat that they have down here. They said, "We hear you are a golfer, so we've arranged a

---
*Dr. Jerome P. Keuper.

golf game."

I said, "You're trying to persuade the wrong person. Mrs. Waters is a fisherman. Have you got any fishing?" We went deep-sea fishing and had a lot of fun, caught a lot of rock.

Anyway, it was not a very high-paying job. I was head of the department. But we liked it here, and I just couldn't resist the temptation to try another career for a little while, so we came to Florida.

Q: How long were you with that institute?

Admiral Waters: I was there for four years, and then I had a health problem. I had an occluded artery. Fortunately it wasn't in my heart; it was down in my belly. But it required the same sort of cardiovascular team and the same sort of operation that sets you back. I was 65 then, and I figured it would be a good idea to take it easy.

Q: You have very pleasant surroundings here.

Admiral Waters: Fortunately, we came here at a good time, in 1971, when real estate like this was affordable. I'd hate to have to pay for it now.

Q: Have they made any progress on getting golf courses you

can use?

Admiral Waters: Not air-conditioned ones, but I've gotten acclimated, so the heat doesn't bother me, particularly on golf courses around here close to the ocean. You usually get a breeze. It's not bad at all.

Q: Natural air-conditioning.

Admiral Waters: Yes. It's worked the other way on me. I've just come back from visiting children and grandchildren up in Northern Virginia, and I find that my blood has gotten thinned out. I can't stand the cold weather at all.

Q: Admiral, can you offer any thoughts to sum up your life and career in the naval service, looking back at some of the high points and satisfactions overall?

Admiral Waters: Well, I suppose that the most fortunate thing that ever happened to me in my naval career was to be a junior officer commanded by Captain Chester Nimitz. I think that's one of those things you write on the luck side of your career, because if a junior officer has the good fortune to serve with a man like Nimitz, a little bit of that leadership ability can't help but rub off on you by osmosis or something like that. That was one of the high spots of luck and good fortune in my career.

Another thing I considered a triumph was to be selected to go to PG school in ordnance engineering, which at that time was difficult to do. That was when it was very prestigious, and they took people with the good records, both academically and at sea.

And, of course, getting command of a destroyer. I think commanding a destroyer is the high point of anybody's career. From there on it's sort of downhill in some ways. As the captain, you're sort of king of all you survey. You don't have that much to survey, so that you can get very knowledgeable of it and close to it and your people. At the same time, one of the low points of my career was when I was commanding that same destroyer and was in a collision. I thought my career had gone down the tubes, but again I survived it.

I think one of the most unusual things that happened to me was just finishing the ordnance PG course in 1940, and going over as an assistant attaché and joining the British and getting put on this business of recovering enemy mines. I was just a general ordnance PG, and the other officer who went with me, a classmate, Stephen Archer, was a specialist in mines. So I said, "Let me wear your mine specialist badge." We both went over and did that, and that was a tremendously interesting thing to do.

We were both young enough to think some of it was fun, when it really was pretty damn dangerous. I mean, even just spending the night someplace was dangerous, because the Germans were always coming over dropping those unfriendly bombs.

Q: We're fortunate to have both your recollections and Admiral Kauffman's in the collection, because you were pioneers in those areas.

Admiral Waters: Yes. Admiral Kauffman was in bomb disposal, and that was a branch that was both naval and Army, and they did nothing but dispose of bombs. They mostly did it by the numbers. There weren't as many of the mines, and so the British could afford to train people into why this mechanism did this. So the people that went out to work on mines knew a lot more about what they were tampering with than the people who were recovering unexploded bombs. They didn't have any "press button A, press button B" thing to do.

One thing that I had impressed on me by the British when I was ordered back to organize mine disposal was not to mix it up with bomb disposal. Of course, that's the first thing anybody thought about when we got back here, was that mine and bomb disposal went together. I fought like hell, and I was just about to lose the battle. I was going to have to take over mine and bomb disposal. They are combined now--explosive ordnance disposal is what it's called. You can do that in peacetime, but in wartime you've got to separate them out, because you take some kid you bring in and train to do it, you can't train him in both of those things; they're too complex and complicated, so you have to separate them. That's what I was trying to say, when all of a sudden, Draper Kauffman saved our lives. He showed up on leave from the Royal Navy, but his daddy was an admiral, and he got him transferred into the U.S. Navy. So we said, "Here's your man. He's a bomb disposal expert." So he started a separate school, and they stayed separate all during the war, and then came together after the war was over.

Q: Just down the road from here at Fort Pierce.

Admiral Waters: Fort Pierce was where they took cadres of people who had been trained in mine disposal and in bomb disposal and turned them into underwater demolition, UDTs.

Q: Any other thoughts to sum up?

Admiral Waters: Of course, the other big highlight in my career was the day that the word came down from Washington to Yorktown, where I was in command, that I had been selected to be a rear admiral. The word had gotten around to expect this. A chief warrant officer with whom I had served since he was under me in mine disposal as a second class electrician's mate was stationed there. By this time he was chief warrant officer, and he had made arrangements with the people over at the power plant, where the fire whistle was, a very useful thing to have around an ammunition depot. When the word came down, he had them blow "secure" on the fire whistle, which was three blasts, which I thought was one of the best salutes I'd ever gotten.

I was selected in July, and because I wasn't selected ahead of time or anything, my name was right up within one of the top of the list, so I made my number pretty rapidly. I made my number when Admiral Dan Gallery retired, who has been an old friend of mine.* When he retired, I got to take his place, and I made it on the first of October. That was another big day. My mother was still alive. She put one shoulder board on, and my wife put the other shoulder board on. And we had the Marine Drum and Bugle Corps in the barracks there at Yorktown. I read my commission, and they broke my flag. That was the first time that Yorktown had ever been commanded by a two-star admiral. That only lasted for a month or two.

I guess that's about it, Paul.

---
*Rear Admiral Daniel V. Gallery, Jr., USN (Ret.), whose oral history is in the Naval Institute collection.

Q: Well, I'm very grateful to you for finishing this up. It's been a long hiatus between the beginning and the end, but on behalf of the Institute, I certainly want to express our thanks for your having made this contribution. This will be a worthwhile thing for scholars now and in the future. It gives your career a lasting heritage. We thank you for that.

Admiral Waters: Thank you for the opportunity.

Index to

The Reminiscences of

Rear Admiral Odale D. Waters, Jr.,

U.S. Navy (Retired)

Air Force, U.S.
The attack transport Glynn (APA-239) provided supply support for the construction of an Air Force radar system in the Arctic in 1952, 202-215

Alaska
In 1970 Waters planned to visit oil company sites in Alaska, but the trip was called off because of his impending retirement, 215, 416; an oil company sent the ice-strengthened tanker Manhattan through the Canadian Arctic around 1970, prior to the construction of the Alaska oil pipeline, 216-220

Alcohol
Waters got involved in getting rid of a BuWeps officer who had an alcoholism problem in the early 1960s, 332-333, 339-340

Anacostia, D.C.
Navy-owned land across the river from the Washington Navy Yard was used in the late 1940s for testing a new antisubmarine weapon, 157-158

Antisubmarine Warfare
Aircraft operating from Brazil conducted ASW operations against German U-boats in the South Atlantic in 1943, 85-86; in 1945 the U.S. Atlantic Fleet staff got reports that the German Navy was experimenting with guided missiles on submarines and made plans to counter them, 95-97; role of the Tenth Fleet in World War II, 97-98; intuition was sometimes better than operations analysis, 99-100; role of convoys, 101-102; Weapon Able was an antisubmarine rocket developed on a high-priority basis at the Naval Ordnance Laboratory in the late 1940s, 155-158; U.S. destroyer operations against a Soviet submarine in the Mediterranean in 1957, 276-280

Archer, Lieutenant Stephen M., USN (USNA, 1932)
Served as a naval observer in England in 1940-41 to acquire knowledge about German magnetic mines, 48-53, 420-421; in 1941 helped open and run a mine disposal school at the Naval Gun Factory in Washington, D.C., 53-54, 64; went to Pearl Harbor shortly after the Japanese attack in December 1941 in order to aid in explosive ordnance disposal, 70; had a desk in OpNav during World War II in connection with ordnance disposal, 81

Arctic
The attack transport Glynn (APA-239) provided supply support for the construction of an Air Force radar system in the Arctic in 1952, 202-215; a young reserve officer on board the Glynn did valuable survey work in the Arctic, 211-212; radar on board the Glynn was useful for navigation through ice fields, 212-213; an oil company sent the ice-strengthened tanker Manhattan through the Canadian Arctic around 1970, prior to the construction of the Alaska oil pipeline, 216-220

Armed Forces Staff College, Norfolk, Virginia
Overview of the joint services course, as conducted at the school in 1950, 170-176; because of his amphibious experience, Vice Admiral John L. Hall was an ideal officer to serve as commandant, 171-172; usefulness of contacts with classmates, 174-175

Army Air Forces, U.S.
Was designated in 1945 to shoot down German missiles if they were fired by submarines, 96; many people believed that the use of atomic bombs against the Japanese in 1945 was unnecessary because the U.S. mining campaign was so successful, 163

Army, U.S.
There was a close relationship between the Army Mapping Service and the Naval Oceanographic Office in the late 1960s, 384

Ascension Island
The light cruiser Memphis (CL-13) was involved in anti-German blockade operations between Brazil and Ascension Island during World War II, 84-85; served as a convenient intermediate stop for Allied aircraft going from South America to Africa during World War II, 86

Ashworth, Rear Admiral Frederick L., USN (USNA, 1933)
Testified to Congress in connection with the TFX aircraft in the early 1960s and wound up being promoted, 337-339

Asiatic Fleet, U.S.
When the cruiser Augusta (CA-31) was reassigned from the Atlantic to the Asiatic Fleet in the early 1930s, married officers were permitted to transfer to other duty, 24; the Augusta's officers dealt with diplomatic personnel during a tour of duty as Asiatic Fleet flagship in the 1930s, 27-28

Atlantic Fleet, U.S.
The USS Vixen (PG-53), formerly a private yacht, served as flagship in 1944-45 for Admiral Jonas Ingram, who had a small staff as Commander in Chief Atlantic Fleet, 92-93; the flagship had excellent communications facilities, 93-94; functions of the fleet staff, 94-95; in 1945 the U.S. Atlantic Fleet staff got reports that the German Navy was experimenting with guided missiles on submarines, 95-97

Atomic Bombs
Role of the destroyer Laffey (DD-724) in doing oceanographic work in connection with the atomic bomb tests in the summer of 1946, 133-134; description of the bomb tests themselves, 134-140, 145-148; radioactive contamination of ships, 138-143; research and development work on atomic bomb fuzes at the Naval

Ordnance Laboratory in the late 1940s, 155; many people believed that the use of atomic bombs against the Japanese in 1945 was unnecessary because the U.S. mining campaign was so successful, 163; planning in the mid-1950s for possible use of nuclear weapons by NATO nations, 225-226; nuclear weapons for the U.S. Atlantic and Mediterranean fleets were stored at Yorktown, Virginia, in the late 1950s, 298

Augusta, USS (CA-31)
Steaming was limited in the early 1930s because of restriction on fuel use, 19-20; the ship had top-notch enlisted men in the 1930s because the Depression allowed the Navy to be quite selective in recruiting and retaining quality individuals, 21-22; warlike intentions of the Japanese in the early 1930s led to the reassignment of the ship from the Atlantic to the Pacific, 22-24; married officers were permitted to transfer to other duty, 24; had wonderful leadership from various skippers in the early 1930s, 24-26; training of junior officers, 26-27; ship's officers dealt with diplomatic personnel during a tour of duty as Asiatic Fleet flagship in the 1930s, 27-28; type of projectiles used for gunnery practice, 38-39

Bahrain, Persian Gulf
Rear Admiral Jack Monroe had to deal with a false report about rioting in Bahrain during the Suez crisis of 1956, 264-266

Barton, USS (DD-722)
Flagship of Destroyer Squadron Two in the mid-1950s, 254; passage through the Suez Canal in September 1956, shortly after it was nationalized by Egypt, 257-261; exercised with the Iranian Navy in the fall of 1956, 261-264; the crew had an enjoyable trip home from the Persian Gulf in early 1957, 271; in 1957, the commanding officer, Ray Peet, received sudden orders to turn over command of the ship in the Mediterranean and go to Washington to become aide to the CNO, 281-283; trip through the Suez Canal with the new skipper, 282-284

Bellino, Joseph, Lieutenant (junior grade), USN (USNA, 1961)
Former Naval Academy football player who served in a minesweeper in the Pacific in the mid-1960s but eventually left the Navy to play professional football, 350

Bennett, Captain Ralph, USNR
Served as technical director of the Naval Ordnance Laboratory during and after World War II, 148-149, 152

Benson, Rear Admiral Roy, USN (USNA, 1929)
Demonstrated an interest in oceanography while serving as Assistant CNO for Administration in the mid-1960s, 368

Bikini Atoll, Marshall Islands
    Role of the destroyer Laffey (DD-724) in doing oceanographic work in connection with the atomic bomb tests in the summer of 1946, 133-134; description of the bomb tests themselves, 134-140, 145-148

Blandy, Vice Admiral William H. P., USN (USNA, 1913)
    Inspected reef at Bikini Atoll from the destroyer Laffey (DD-724) in conjunction with atomic bomb tests in 1946, 133

Blockade
    The light cruiser Memphis (CL-13) was involved in anti-German blockade operations between Brazil and Ascension Island during World War II, 84-85; survivors of abandoned blockade runners, 87-88

Bomb Disposal
    Lieutenant Draper Kauffman learned the techniques in England early in World War II, then returned to the United States to teach new students about bomb disposal, 66-67, 421-422; defuzing of unexploded bombs that the Japanese dropped on Pearl Harbor in December 1941, 76-77

Bombing
    The United States would not give Great Britain the Norden bombsight in the early part of World War II, 41-44; in World War II the Germans had mines equipped with bomb fuzes so they could also be used as bombs, 78-80

Borneo
    Site of a SEATO amphibious exercise in the fall of 1961, 317-319

Brazil
    The light cruiser Memphis (CL-13) was involved in anti-German blockade operations between Brazil and Ascension Island during World War II, 84-85; aircraft operating from Brazil conducted antisubmarine operations against German U-boats in the South Atlantic in 1943, 85-86; role of Vice Admiral Jonas Ingram in dealing with the Brazilians, 87; survivors of abandoned blockade runners headed to Brazil, 87-88; Ingram had an entertaining comment about a talkative Brazilian naval officer in World War II, 103-104; a Brazilian admiral had a most enjoyable visit to Disneyland in the mid-1960s, 354

Brown, Vice Admiral Charles R., USN (USNA, 1921)
    As Sixth Fleet commander in 1957, got principals to provide accounts of an operation against a Soviet submarine, 279; sent a clever message upon completion of a NATO exercise in 1957, 289; liked smart, aggressive maneuvers on the part of Sixth Fleet ships, 289-291

Brumby, Lieutenant (junior grade) Frank H., Jr., USN (USNA, 1932)
Had difficulties paying for fuel following a visit by his ship, the destroyer Tucker (DD-374), to Trinidad in 1937, 32

Bureau of Naval Weapons (BuWeps)
Waters was involved in getting rid of a BuWeps officer who had an alcoholism problem in the early 1960s, 332-333, 339-340; Waters inspected ammunition depots and ordnance plants on behalf of the bureau, 334; Rear Admiral P. D. Stroop's qualities as bureau chief in the early 1960s, 339-340

Bureau of Ordnance (BuOrd)
Operated the Navy's mine disposal school at Washington, D.C., in World War II, 56-57

Burke, Rear Admiral Arleigh A., USN (USNA, 1923)
Helped Vice Admiral Turner Joy with the conduct of the Korean War in the early 1950s, 191; showed personal interest when U.S. destroyers were holding down a Soviet submarine in the Mediterranean in 1957, 278-279; Commander Ray Peet received sudden orders in 1957 to turn over command of the destroyer Barton (DD-722) in the Mediterranean and go to Washington to become aide to Burke, 281-283

Canada
The attack transport USS Glynn (APA-239) provided supply support for the construction of an Air Force radar system in Labrador in 1952, 202-215; Mounted Police made periodic checks on Eskimos in 1952, 213-214

Carpenter, Lieutenant Commander Malcolm Scott, USN
After being one of the original U.S. astronauts in the early 1960s, he became an aquanaut to take part in the Navy's Sea Lab underwater habitat program later in the decade, 397-399

Chilton, Captain William Pierce, USN (USNA, 1927)
As commanding officer of the Naval Mine Depot, Yorktown, Virginia, in the mid-1950s, he was disappointed at not making flag rank and didn't take much interest in the station, 296-297

China, People's Republic of
Supplied mines for use by North Korea against United Nations forces in the Korean War in the early 1950s, 166-168, 363; in the early 1950s the Operational Development Force did experiments aimed at stopping Chinese Communist junks if they tried to invade Formosa, 178-185

China, Republic of
In the early 1950s the Operational Development Force did experiments aimed at stopping Chinese Communist junks if they tried to invade Formosa, 178-185

Civil Service
 Mixture of naval officers and civil servants in the organizational structure of the Naval Ordnance Laboratory, White Oak, Maryland, in the late 1940s, 148-152; many local civilians were employed by the Naval Mine Depot, Yorktown, Virginia, in the late 1950s, 304-307; getting rid of unsatisfactory civil service employees was time-consuming and expensive at the Naval Ordnance Laboratory in the late 1940s, 334-335

Coast and Geodetic Survey, U.S.
 Had a close working relationship with the Naval Oceanographic Office in the late 1960s, 384-385

Coast Guard, U.S.
 Provided a small contingent of volunteers to be trained in the Navy's mine disposal school in Washington, D.C., in World War II, 55, 57; one member of the class, Fred Nichols, took charge of the school in 1943, 81

Coleman, Commander Walter D., USN (USNA, 1932)
 Was involved in a warship habitability study on behalf of the Operational Development Force in the early 1950s, 198-201

Collisions
 The patrol craft USS PC-815 sank in San Diego Harbor in September 1945 as a result of a collision with the destroyer Laffey (DD-724), 120-124; court of inquiry that followed the collision, 124-126

Combat Fatigue
 A number of crew members from the destroyer Laffey (DD-724) sought psychiatric care for combat fatigue after their ship was hit by a kamikaze in 1945, 115-118

Commercial Ships
 The U.S. light cruiser Memphis (CL-13) was involved in blockade operations against German merchant ships between Brazil and Ascension Island during World War II, 84-85, 88; an oil company sent the ice-strengthened tanker Manhattan through the Canadian Arctic around 1970, prior to the construction of the Alaska oil pipeline, 216-220

Communications
 Importance of visual signaling on board the cruiser Augusta (CA-31) in the early 1930s, 27; the USS Vixen (PG-53) had excellent communications facilities while serving as Atlantic Fleet flagship in World War II, 93-94; atmospheric conditions made radio communications difficult during arctic operations in 1952, 204-205

Communism
   During a Suez Canal transit in 1956, Waters stopped until a Yugoslavian was removed from the destroyer Barton (DD-722) because of a prohibition against having pilots from Communist nations on board, 258-261

Congress, U.S.
   Representative Robert Walton Moore promised in 1927 to give Waters an appointment to the Naval Academy, 4; in the late 1960s Senator Warren Magnuson introduced a bill to upgrade the billet of Oceanographer of the Navy from two stars to three, but the proposal died, 382-383

Coral Sea, USS (CVA-43)
   Carrier whose pilots had a tendency to misbehave in the Western Pacific while on liberty in the early 1960s, 321-322

Corregidor
   Trained U.S. mine disposal personnel were captured by the Japanese when this island fortress at Manila was surrendered in 1942, 57

Courts of Inquiry
   Investigation after the patrol craft USS PC-815 sank in San Diego Harbor in September 1945 as a result of a collision with the destroyer Laffey (DD-724), 124-126

Crossroads, Operation
   Role of the destroyer Laffey (DD-724) in doing oceanographic work in connection with the atomic bomb tests at Bikini Atoll in the summer of 1946, 133-134; description of the bomb tests themselves, 134-140, 145-148

Crotty, Lieutenant Thomas J. E., USCG
   Trained mine disposal officer who was captured on Corregidor in 1942 and died in the Bataan death march, 57

Cruise, Rear Admiral Edgar A., USN (USNA, 1922)
   During the Korean War, conducted tests off Tokyo on methods for sinking Chinese junks, 183-184

Damage Control
   Waters received thorough damage control training before taking command of the destroyer Laffey (DD-724) in 1945, 107-108; description of the damage sustained by the Laffey off Okinawa in the spring of 1945, 108-109

Delewski, Gunner's Mate Second Class Lawrence H., USN
   USS Laffey (DD-724) sailor who survived a kamikaze attack in 1945 but then had to leave the ship because of poor teeth, 118

Demobilization
  The rapid release of crew members from the destroyer Laffey (DD-724) at war's end in 1945 reduced the ship's operational readiness, 128-130

Depression
  Conditions were difficult in both the Navy and civilian life in the early 1930s as a result of austerity induced by the national Depression, 19-21; the Navy had top-notch enlisted men in the 1930s because the Depression allowed it to be quite selective in recruiting and retaining quality individuals, 21-22

Destroyer Flotilla One
  This command was highly sought after by up-and-coming flag officers in the early 1960s, 314; makeup of the flotilla, 315; homeported at Yokosuka, Japan, in the early 1960s, 315-316, 320-321, 323-330; support of SEATO exercise in the fall of 1961, 317-319; the flagship tender took local Japanese families out for a cruise in the early 1960s, 327-328

Destroyers
  In 1940 the United States supplied the Royal Navy with 50 destroyers that had outmoded Mark VIII torpedoes, 44-46

Destroyer Squadron Two
  Captain Lot Ensey was relieved hurriedly in 1956 as ComDesRon 2 so he could become Sixth Fleet chief of staff, 253, 256; operations in the Sixth Fleet in 1956, 256-257; passage of the Barton (DD-722) and Soley (DD-707) through the Suez Canal in September 1956, 257-261; exercised with the Iranian Navy in the fall of 1956, 261-264; most of the ships returned to the United States in late 1956 after their Mediterranean deployment, 267-269, 271; operations in 1957, including deployment to the Mediterranean, 271-280, 287-289; fuel shortage was a problem during the return home from the Mediterranean in late 1957, 291-294

DEW
  See Distant Early Warning (DEW) Line

Diplomacy
  The officers of the heavy cruiser Augusta (CA-31) dealt with diplomatic personnel during the ship's tour of duty as Asiatic Fleet flagship in the 1930s, 27-28

Disciplinary Matters
  Errant Naval Academy midshipmen in the early 1930s were punished by being confined on board the ship Reina Mercedes (IX-25), 17-19; Waters had to deal with misbehaving sailors and

aviators while ComDesFlot 1 in the early 1960s, 321-322; Waters was involved in getting rid of a BuWeps officer who had an alcoholism problem in the early 1960s, 332-333, 339-340

Distant Early Warning (DEW) Line
The attack transport USS Glynn (APA-239) provided supply support for the construction of this Air Force radar system in the Arctic in 1952, 202-215

Diving
Individuals trained for mine disposal work by the U.S. Navy in World War II had to be physically qualified for deep-sea diving, 63; training at the Washington Navy Yard, 68; development of scuba equipment during World War II, 82-83; dangerous conditions were involved in the Sea Lab underwater habitat program in the 1960s, 399-401

Dixie, USS (AD-14)
Destroyer tender whose band played "Dixie" when Waters was ComDesFlot 1 in the early 1960s, 315

Downes, USS (DD-375)
Shakedown cruise to South America in 1937, 29-32; Waters, a line officer, was responsible for the supply and disbursing functions, 30-35; hints of trouble with torpedoes in the late 1930s, 35; sent a boarding party to a boat of the Scripps Institute of Oceanography on Christmas Eve in 1937, 36-37

DUKWs
Amphibious trucks that proved useful during radar site construction in the Arctic in 1952 because of their ability to carry cargo ashore, 211

Education
Waters's study in public schools in Virginia the 1910s and 1920s, 2-3, 5; Waters attended Army-Navy Prep in Washington, D.C., in 1927-28, 4-6; curriculum at the Naval Academy in the late 1920s and early 1930s, 13-14, 16; in the mid-1960s, the Navy didn't have a postgraduate course in oceanography, 366; in the late 1960s a master's program in physical oceanography was established at the Naval Postgraduate School, 389; Waters's post-Navy work as a department head at the Florida Institute of Technology in the early 1970s, 417-418

Egypt
Passage of the destroyers Barton (DD-722) and Soley (DD-707) through the Suez Canal in September 1956, shortly after it was nationalized by Egypt, 257-261

Eigell, Chief Gunner's Mate Robert W., USN
Devised a tool known as the Eigell wrench that was used to defuze unexploded bombs at Pearl Harbor at the Japanese attack in 1941, 76-77

Enlisted Personnel
The Navy had top-notch enlisted men in the 1930s because the Depression allowed it to be quite selective in recruiting and retaining quality individuals, 21-22

Ensey, Captain Lot, USN (USNA, 1930)
Was relieved hurriedly in 1956 as ComDesRon 2 so he could become Sixth Fleet chief of staff, 253, 256

Entwistle, Rear Admiral Frederick I., USN (USNA, 1921)
As Commander Operational Development Force in the early 1950s, sent his staff officers to witness Korean War operations firsthand in order to validate the command's work, 190-193; worked with Commander in Chief Atlantic Fleet in the early 1950s on improving warship habitability, 198-201; released Waters in 1952 for command of the attack transport _Glynn_ (APA-239), 202-203

Explosive Ordnance Disposal
Waters served as an observer in England in 1940-41 to acquire knowledge about German magnetic mines, 46-53, 420-422; after the Japanese attack on Pearl Harbor in December 1941, a call went out for bomb and mine disposal personnel to deal with unexploded ordnance, 69-70, 76-77; sweeping of German mines off the U.S. East Coast in 1942, 71-74; defuzing of German bombs dropped on London in World War II, 78-80; cross-pollination of training of U.S. and British EOD personnel in World War II, 80

See also Mine Disposal School, Washington, D.C.

Families of Servicemen
When the cruiser _Augusta_ (CA-31) was reassigned from the Atlantic to the Asiatic Fleet in the early 1930s, married officers were permitted to transfer to other duty, 24

Fechteler, Admiral William M., USN (USNA, 1916)
As Commander in Chief Atlantic Fleet and CNO in the early 1950s, was interested in improving living conditions on board warships, 198-201

Fishing
In 1942 shrimp fishermen near Jacksonville, Florida, used their nets to recover pieces of exploded German mines, 73-74

Football
   As Naval Academy athletic director in the late 1920s, Commander Jonas Ingram was always enthusiastic about the football team, 87; Naval Academy Heisman Trophy winner Joe Bellino served in a minesweeper in the Pacific in the mid-1960s but eventually left the Navy to play professional football, 350

Formosa
   In the early 1950s the Operational Development Force did experiments aimed at stopping Chinese Communist junks if they tried to invade Formosa, 178-185

Fourth Fleet
   Jonas Ingram served as fleet commander in World War II, used the light cruiser Memphis (CL-13) as flagship, 90

France
   Voiced disagreements in the early 1950s over the NATO command structure, 224-225

Freed, Lieutenant Maitland G., USN
   Legal officer who reported on misdeeds of Navy men ashore in the Western Pacific in the early 1960s, 322

French Navy
   Role on the SACLant staff in the mid-1950s, 231-232

Frosch, Robert A.
   As Assistant Secretary of the Navy (Research and Development) in the late 1960s, met with Waters on a regular basis to discuss the operation of the Naval Oceanographic Office, 391-392

Fuel Oil
   Shortage of fuel was a problem when the ships of Destroyer Squadron Two returned from the Mediterranean to the East Coast in late 1957, 291-294

German Air Force
   In World War II equipped mines with bomb fuzes so they could be used also as bombs, 78-80

German Merchant Ships
   The light cruiser Memphis (CL-13) was involved in anti-German blockade operations between Brazil and Ascension Island during World War II, 84-85, 88

German Navy
   Waters served as an observer in England in 1940-41 to acquire knowledge about German magnetic mines, 46-53; the U.S. Navy made copies of German magnetic mines to use for disposal

training, 58; the German Navy used submarines to lay a few mines off the U.S. East Coast in 1942, 71-74; aircraft operating from Brazil conducted ASW operations against German U-boats in the South Atlantic in 1943, 85-86; in 1945 the U.S. Atlantic Fleet staff got reports that the German Navy was experimenting with guided missiles on submarines, 95-97; role of the U.S. Tenth Fleet in combating U-boats in World War II, 97-98; in one instance in 1945, Admiral Jonas Ingram's intuition proved superior to operations analysis in locating a German U-boat in the Atlantic, 99-100

Germany
Following World War II, the U.S. Naval Ordnance Laboratory received a vacuum-driven wind tunnel from Germany and used the design in building its own, 160-162

Glynn, USS (APA-239)
Provided supply support for the construction of an Air Force radar system in the Arctic in 1952, 202-215

Gravity
The Naval Oceanographic Office measured the earth's gravity as part of its overall scientific work in the late 1960s, 387-388

Great Britain
Capabilities in radar and sonar at the outset of World War II, 39-41; the United States would not give Great Britain the Norden bombsight in the early part of World War II, 41-44

See also Royal Navy

Griffin, Vice Admiral Charles D., USN (USNA, 1927)
Liked to get publicity when he was serving as Commander Seventh Fleet in the early 1960s, 316-317, 321-322

Gunfire, Naval
In the late 1960s the Naval Oceanographic Office did surveys off the coast of Vietnam to provide improved navigational information to gunfire support ships, 375-377

Gunnery Practice
The cruiser Augusta (CA-31) didn't use her neatly painted projectiles for target practice in the mid-1930s, 38-39

Habitability
In the early 1950s the Operational Development Command studied ways of improving living conditions on board U.S. warships, 198-201

Hale, Captain Fletcher, USN (USNA, 1937)
Role in keeping Waters informed while serving as chief of staff for Naval Base Los Angeles in the mid-1960s, 360-361

Hall, Vice Admiral John L., USN (USNA, 1913)
Because of his amphibious experience, Hall was an ideal officer to serve as commandant of the Armed Forces Staff College, circa 1950, 171-172

Hanks, Captain Robert J., USN (USNA, 1946)
His essay titled "Against All Enemies" presented a real challenge but won the Naval Institute's 1970 contest, 406-409

Hawaii
Operations in the vicinity by the USS Laffey (DD-724) in the fall of 1945, 126-128

Hiwassee Dam, North Carolina
Used for the testing of an antisubmarine weapon in the late 1940s, 156-157

Hughes, Rear Admiral Francis Massie, USN (USNA, 1923)
As Commandant of the Fifth Naval District in 1960, admired Waters's work at Yorktown, 311-312

Hunters Point Naval Shipyard, San Francisco
Dry-docked the radiation-contaminated destroyer Laffey (DD-724) after her return from Operation Crossroads in 1946, 142-143

Iberian-Atlantic Command (IberLant)
After the formation of the NATO military command in the early 1950s, IberLant was created on only paper because of disagreement over which nation should run the organization, 223-225; the Portuguese wanted the headquarters to be at Lisbon, 224-225; eventually got a U.S. commander, 231

Icebreaking
U.S. Navy icebreakers opened paths for a naval force supporting radar construction in the Canadian Arctic in 1952, 206-207; radar on board the Glynn (APA-239) was valuable for navigation through ice fields in the Arctic in 1952, 212-213; an oil company sent the ice-strengthened tanker Manhattan through the Canadian Arctic around 1970, prior to the construction of the Alaska oil pipeline, 216-220

Indian Head, Maryland
See Naval Powder Factory, Indian Head, Maryland

Ingram, Admiral Jonas, USN (USNA, 1907)
Enthusiastic as Naval Academy athletic director in the late 1920s, 87; leadership and diplomatic qualities, 87; monitored the crew of sunken German blockade runner in the South Atlantic, 87-88; flamboyant leader as Commander South Atlantic Force in World War II, 89; took Waters with him when he became Commander in Chief Atlantic Fleet in 1944, 90-91; in 1945

arranged for Waters to get a destroyer command, 92, 105; had a small staff as Commander in Chief Atlantic Fleet, 92-93; made a colorful statement in 1945 about the possibility of dealing with German missiles, 96-97; in one instance in 1945, Ingram's intuition proved superior to operations analysis in locating a German U-boat in the Atlantic, 99-100; exchange of messages with Admiral Ernest J. King to explain a trip to Miami in World War II, 102-103; anecdote about Ingram's comment on a talkative Brazilian naval officer, 103-104

Intelligence
U.S. naval intelligence lost track of a large part of the Japanese fleet in December 1937, 36-37; Waters served as an observer in England in 1940-41 to acquire knowledge about German magnetic mines, 46-53; in 1945 the U.S. Atlantic Fleet staff got reports that the German Navy was experimenting with guided missiles on submarines, 95-97

Iranian Navy
The U.S. destroyers Barton (DD-722) and Soley (DD-707) exercised with the Iranian Navy in the fall of 1956, 261-264

Italy
In 1929 the Naval Academy midshipman cruise included a stop in Naples, a sight-seeing trip to Rome, and an audience with Pope Pius XI, 11-12

Jacksonville, Florida
Mine disposal personnel were summoned to the area in 1942 after the discovery of German mines laid by submarines, 72-74

Japan
Warlike intentions of the Japanese in the early 1930s led to the reassignment of the heavy cruiser Augusta (CA-31) from the Atlantic to the Pacific, 22-24; many people believed that atomic bombs were not needed against Japan in 1945 because the U.S. mining campaign was so successful, 163; part of Destroyer Flotilla One was homeported at Yokosuka in the early 1960s, 315-316, 320-321, 323-330; the Maritime Self-Defense Force demonstrated a lot of professional capability in the early 1960s, 319-320; sightseeing attractions in the country, 326-327

Japanese Navy
U.S. naval intelligence lost track of a large part of the Japanese fleet in December 1937, 36-37; after the Japanese attack on Pearl Harbor in December 1941, a call went out for U.S. bomb and mine disposal personnel to deal with unexploded ordnance, 69-70, 76-77; types of torpedoes in Japanese midget submarines at Pearl Harbor, 70-71; use of mines and suicide torpedo boats in World War II, 75-76; mines used in World War II were simple and effective but not always safe, 162-163

Joy, Vice Admiral C. Turner, USN (USNA, 1916)
As Commander U.S. Naval Forces Far East during the Korean War, gave Operational Development Force staff officers carte blanche to observe Korean War operations, 191; loyal to his commander when President Harry Truman fired General Douglas MacArthur in April 1951, 194

Kamikazes
Description of the kamikaze damage sustained by the destroyer Laffey off Okinawa in the spring of 1945, 108-109

Kauffman, Draper L., USNR (USNA, 1933)
Officer who was trained in bomb disposal in England early in World War II, then returned to the United States to teach bomb disposal, 66-67, 421-422

King, Admiral Ernest J., USN (USNA, 1901)
Had an exchange of messages with Vice Admiral Jonas Ingram about a trip Ingram made from South America to Miami, Florida, 102-103

Korea, North
Used Russian- or Chinese-supplied mines against United Nations forces during the Korean War in the early 1950s, 166-168, 363

Korean War
The Soviet Union and Red China supplied mines for use by North Korea against United Nations forces, 166-168, 363; Rear Admiral Frederick Entwistle, Commander Operational Development Force in the early 1950s, sent his staff officers to witness Korean War operations firsthand to validate the command's work, 190-193; war operations led to the idea of the usefulness of small gunboats of the type later used in Vietnam, 192-193; reaction in Tokyo to President Harry Truman's firing of General Douglas MacArthur as Far East commander in April 1951, 193-195

Labor Unions
Organizers were unable to unionize the civil service employees at the Naval Mine Depot, Yorktown, Virginia, in the late 1950s, 304-306

Labrador
See Canada

Laffey, USS (DD-724)
Ship's characteristics, 105; Waters received thorough training before taking command in 1945, 106-108; description of the damage sustained by the ship off Okinawa in the spring of 1945, 108-109; hurry-up repairs and provisioning of ship for the planned invasion of Japan in late 1945, 109-115; Waters's

experiences handling the ship at Seattle soon after he took command, 111-112; problems with the steering cables, 113-114; a number of crew members sought psychiatric care for combat fatigue, 115-118; collision with the PC-815 in September 1945 resulted in the sinking of the PC, 120-124; court of inquiry concerning the collision, 124-126; operations around Hawaii in the fall of 1945, 126-128; effect of demobilization on the quality of the crew in 1945, 128-131; emergency repair to turbine bearing, 132; oceanographic work in connection with atomic bomb tests at Bikini Atoll in 1946, 132-134, 144; description of the tests themselves from the perspective of the ship's crew, 134-140, 145-148; radioactive contamination of the ship, 138-143; dry-docked at Hunters Point Navy Yard after return from Bikini, 142-143

Leadership
The crew of the cruiser Augusta (CA-31) had wonderful leadership from various skippers in the early 1930s, 24-26; Vice Admiral Jonas Ingram was a flamboyant leader as Commander South Atlantic Force in World War II, 89

Leave and Liberty
Waters had to deal with disciplinary matters when sailors and aviators were unruly ashore in the Western Pacific in the early 1960s, 321-322

Lee, Commander Paul F., USN (USNA, 1919)
While serving as an observer in Britain in 1940, helped the Royal Navy rectify problems with outmoded torpedoes, 44-46

Lee, Vice Admiral Willis A., Jr., USN (USNA, 1908)
Brought together operational people in 1945 in an effort to find a counter to the Japanese kamikazes, 153

LeMay, Major General Curtis, USA
Many people believed that the use of atomic bombs against the Japanese in 1945 was unnecessary because LeMay's mining campaign was so successful, 163

Leverton, Rear Admiral Joseph W., USN (USNA, 1931)
Might have gone higher in rank than two stars if not for a heart attack, 314

London, England
Damaged in World War II by German mines equipped with bomb fuzes so they could also function as bombs, 78-80

Long Beach
For reasons of business, the city was much more hospitable to the Navy in the 1960s than in the 1930s, 357-358

Los Angeles Naval Base
   In the mid-1960s the base commander worked in conjunction with the Commandant of the 11th Naval District, 351-352; the commander worked out tours for VIPs to visit Disneyland and movie and TV studios, 352-356; Waters's visit to Mayor Sam Yorty of Los Angeles, 356-357; the base had a good relationship with the city of Long Beach, 357-358; construction of a hospital to avoid trips to San Diego for injured personnel, 358-359; construction of breakwater in the 1930s shifted naval activities away from San Pedro to the Long Beach side of the harbor, 359-360; Waters's working routine as a double-hatted commander, 360-361

MacArthur, General of the Army Douglas, USA (USMA, 1903)
   Reaction in Tokyo to President Harry Truman's firing of MacArthur as Far East commander in April 1951, 193-195

Mack, Rear Admiral William P., USN (USNA, 1937)
   Argued for a controversial essay in the Naval Institute's 1970 General Prize Essay Contest, 407

Magnuson, Senator Warren G.
   In the late 1960s introduced a bill to upgrade the billet of Oceanographer of the Navy from two stars to three, but the proposal died, 382-383

Manhattan (Commercial Oil Tanker)
   An oil company sent this ice-strengthened tanker through the Canadian Arctic around 1970, prior to the construction of the Alaska oil pipeline, 216-220

Marine Corps, U.S.
   Many Marines were attached to the Naval Weapons Station, Yorktown, Virginia, for security purposes in the late 1950s, 298, 301, 309

Maynard, Ted
   Civilian who did an impressive job of making a movie as part of a NATO briefing in the mid-1950s, 234-237

McCain, Rear Admiral John S., Jr., USN (USNA, 1931)
   Animation idea for his famous sea power briefings came from SACLant in the mid-1950s, 238

McKeehan, Commander Louis, USNR
   Worked on behalf of the Navy's mine disposal school while serving in the Bureau of Ordnance in World War II, 56-57

McMahon, Captain Bernard, USN (USNA, 1931)
   Relieved Waters as destroyer squadron commodore in the Persian Gulf during the Suez crisis in late 1956, 266-267

McNamara, Secretary of Defense Robert S.
Issued an order in the early 1960s against DoD contracting officers accepting gratuities from defense contractors, 336-337; told flag officers they couldn't fly first class anymore, 342; became interested in the mid-1960s in the potential effectiveness of naval mines for use in the Vietnam War, 342-343

Medical Problems
A number of crew members from the destroyer Laffey (DD-724) sought psychiatric care for combat fatigue after their ship was hit by a kamikaze in 1945, 115-118; a USS Laffey (DD-724) sailor survived a kamikaze attack in 1945 but then had to leave the ship because of poor teeth, 118; doctors on board the Glynn (APA-239) were disappointed during a cruise to the Arctic in 1952 because the lack of germs kept crewmen from getting sick, 208-209

Mediterranean Sea
Operating conditions for Sixth Fleet ships in the relatively confined spaces of the Mediterranean in 1956-57, 274-275; U.S. destroyer operations against a Soviet submarine in 1957, 276-280

See also Sixth Fleet, U.S.

Memphis, USS (CL-13)
Light cruiser whose fire control equipment was outdated by 1943, 83; blockade duty against German ships in the South Atlantic in World War II, 84-85

Middle East Force, U.S.
The U.S. destroyers Barton (DD-722) and Soley (DD-707) exercised with the Iranian Navy in the fall of 1956, 261-264; providing destroyers to the Middle East Force in the late 1950s tied up quite a few ships, 286

Military Sea Transportation Service (MSTS)
Its ships served more effectively for surveying work in the late 1960s than did Navy-manned ships because the MSTS ships spent more time at sea, 373-374

Mine Disposal School, Washington, D.C.
Established at the Naval Gun Factory in mid-1941, then moved to Anacostia, 54-55; trainees were all volunteers, 55-56, 60; operated directly under the Bureau of Ordnance, 56-57; established outlying detachments in 1941, 57; development of new tools and techniques, 58; establishment of Stump Neck annex at Indian Head, Maryland, for training exercises, 59-60; mine disposal had fewer casualties than bomb disposal, 60; types of

individuals sought for training, 61-63; administration of school, 64; number of students trained, 64-65; mine disposal trainees helped form the nucleus of the original underwater demolition teams during World War II, 65-66; necessary to sell people in the Navy on the value of the school prior to World War II, 68-69; importance of not mixing bomb and mine disposal, 421-422

Mine Force, Pacific Fleet
Made preparations in 1964 for dropping naval mines into Vietnamese waters from the air, but the plans were not executed until 1972, 343-349; minesweepers had a limited role in the Pacific Fleet in the mid-1960s, 349-351; the force commander had operational control of the ships, 362; Mine Force pushed for new countermeasures ships, 364; no problem getting quality personnel in the 1960s, 364-365

Mines
Waters served as an observer in England in 1940-41 to acquire knowledge about German magnetic mines, 46-53; the German Navy used submarines to lay a few mines off the U.S. East Coast in 1942, 71-74; in World War II Germany used mines equipped with bomb fuzes so they could also function as bombs, 78-80; research and development projects on mines at the Naval Ordnance Laboratory in the late 1940s, 153-154, 164-166, 169; Japanese mines in World War II were simple and effective but not always safe, 162-163; in the late 1940s, the Naval Ordnance Laboratory had an impressive assembly of scientists and engineers with knowledge of mines, 163-164; the Soviet Union and Red China supplied mines for use by North Korea against United Nations forces in the Korean War in the early 1950s, 166-168, 363; manufacture of at Naval Mine Depot, Yorktown, Virginia, 303-304; Secretary of Defense Robert McNamara became interested in the mid-1960s in the potential effectiveness of naval mines for use in the Vietnam War, 342-343; the Navy made preparations in 1964 for dropping naval mines into Vietnamese waters from the air, but the plans were not executed until 1972, 343-349

See also Mine Disposal School, Washington, D.C.

Minesweepers
Had a limited role in the Pacific Fleet in the mid-1960s, 349-351

Missiles
In 1945 the U.S. Atlantic Fleet staff got reports that the German Navy was experimenting with guided missiles on submarines, 95-97; the Operational Development Force used the former battleship Mississippi (AG-128) for missile testing in the early 1950s, 178, 186; three-T missiles were stored at the Naval Weapons Station, Yorktown, Virginia, in the late 1950s, 297-298

Mississippi, USS (AG-128)
 The Operational Development Force used the former battleship for missile testing in the early 1950s, 178, 186

Monroe, Rear Admiral Jack P., USN (USNA, 1927)
 Was serving as Commander Middle East Force when the destroyers Barton (DD-722) and Soley (DD-707) exercised with the Iranian Navy in the fall of 1956, 261-264; had to deal with a false report about rioting in Bahrain during the Suez crisis of 1956, 264-266; allowed Waters to leave the Persian Gulf when two destroyer squadron commanders were on scene in late 1956, 266-267

Montgomery, Field Marshal Bernard L.
 Involvement in a NATO command post exercise briefing in the mid-1950s, 232-237

Moore, Walton Robert
 Virginia congressman who in 1927 promised Waters an appointment to the Naval Academy, 4

Moorer, Admiral Thomas H., USN (USNA, 1933)
 As Commander in Chief Pacific Fleet in the mid-1960s, he stepped up training of aviators to drop naval mines in Vietnamese waters, 343-344; wrote to Waters in 1972 about the use of mines that year against Vietnam, 345-346; in the late 1960s, as Oceanographer of the Navy, Waters had direct access to CNO Moorer, 381-383, 392-393; as ex-officio president of the Naval Institute, approved publication of a controversial essay in 1970, 407-408

Mountbatten, Admiral Lord Louis, RN
 Demonstrated his thoroughness while attending a NATO briefing in the mid-1950s, 239-240

Movies
 Civilian Ted Maynard did an impressive job of making a movie as part of a NATO briefing in the mid-1950s, 234-237; in the mid-1960s Commander Naval Base Los Angeles helped arrange for visiting VIPs to get tours of movie and TV studios, 352-356

National Oceanographic and Atmospheric Administration (NOAA)
 Involved Waters in a variety of projects during a brief tour of duty in 1970, 412-414

NATO
 See North Atlantic Treaty Organization

Naval Academy, U.S.
Waters was admitted in 1928 through substantiating examinations of his previous work, 6-7; Waters's work on the 1932 yearbook, Lucky Bag, 8; aviation training was substituted for one summer cruise around 1929, 9-11; summer cruises, 1929-31, 11-12; curriculum in the late 1920s and early 1930s, 13-14, 16; social life for midshipmen, 14-15; superintendents, 16; discipline in the early 1930s could include confinement in the Reina Mercedes (IX-25), 17-19; graduation of the class of 1932, 19

Naval Gun Factory, Washington, D.C.
Site of mine disposal school established in mid-1941, 54-55; the Naval Ordnance Laboratory opened a new facility shortly after World War II, moving to White Oak, Maryland, from the Naval Gun Factory in Washington, D.C., 148

Naval Institute, U.S.
Role of board members in the late 1960s, 404-406; difficult judging for 1970 General Prize Essay Contest, 406-409; changes to Proceedings, 409-410

Naval Material Command
Took a number of good officers from material bureaus in the 1960s, 340-342; Vice Admiral William Schoech as chief, 341-342

Naval Mine Depot, Yorktown, Virginia
Physical description of the station in the late 1950s, 295, 298-299, 302-304, 307; served as a manufacturing and storage site for mines and other weapons, 297-299, 303-304; many Marines were attached to the station for security purposes in the late 1950s, 298, 301, 309; name was changed to Naval Weapons Station Yorktown in 1958, 299-300; helped celebrate Yorktown Day in honor of the Revolutionary War battle, 300-301; civil service employees, 304-307; safety precautions, 307-308

See also Naval Weapons Station, Yorktown, Virginia

Naval Oceanographic Office
Had its headquarters at Suitland, Maryland, in the mid-1960s, then moved to Alexandria, Virginia, 367-371; organization of functions, 371-372; role in doing both hydrographic and oceanographic surveying in the late 1960s, 371-381; had a close working relationship with the Army Mapping Service and the Coast and Geodetic Survey in the late 1960s, 384-385; did classified survey work on the ocean bottom for ballistic missile submarines, 385-386; measurements of the earth's magnetic anomalies and gravity, 386-388; relationship with civilian oceanographic organizations, 393; work with small submersibles, 396-397, 401-402; work with the Sea Lab underwater habitat program in the 1960s, 397-401; contact with many other government organizations that have similar or related interests, 402-404

Naval Ordnance Laboratory, White Oak, Maryland
New facility opened shortly after World War II, moving to White Oak from the Naval Gun Factory in Washington, D.C., 148; mixture of naval officers and civil servants in the organizational structure, 148-152; research and development projects on mines in the late 1940s, 153-154, 164-166, 169; work on atomic bomb fuzes, 155; Weapon Able was an antisubmarine rocket developed on a high-priority basis at the laboratory in the late 1940s, 155-158; British personnel on the staff, 158-159; development work on explosives in the late 1940s, 159-160; following World War II, the U.S. Naval Ordnance Laboratory received a vacuum-driven wind tunnel from Germany and used the design in building its own, 160-162; in the late 1940s, NOL had an impressive assembly of scientists and engineers with knowledge of mines, 163-164; getting rid of unsatisfactory civil service employees was time-consuming and expensive, 334-335

Naval Postgraduate School, Monterey, California
In the late 1960s a master's degree program in physical oceanography was established, 389

Naval Powder Factory, Indian Head, Maryland
Stump Neck site used for mine disposal training during World War II, 59-60

Naval Weapons Station, Yorktown, Virginia
Name was changed from Naval Mine Depot Yorktown in 1958, 299-300

<u>See also</u> Naval Mine Depot, Yorktown, Virginia

Navigation
Navy underwater demolition teams did survey work on poorly charted waters in the Canadian Arctic in 1952, 207-208; a young reserve officer on board the <u>Glynn</u> (APA-239) did valuable survey work in the Arcic, 211-212; radar on board the <u>Glynn</u> was valuable for navigation through ice fields, 212-213; the destroyer <u>Barton</u> (DD-722) made a trip through the Suez Canal with a new skipper in 1957, 282-284; Navy hydrographic surveys in the late 1960s, 374-378; classified survey work on the ocean bottom for ballistic missile submarines, 385-386

Nichols, Lieutenant Commander Fred F., USCG
Took command of the Navy's mine disposal school in 1943, 81

Nimitz, Fleet Admiral Chester W., USN (USNA, 1905)
Provided superb leadership to the crew of the cruiser <u>Augusta</u> (CA-31) in the early 1930s, 25-26; while serving in the Bureau of Navigation in the mid-1930s helped find assignments for his officers from the <u>Augusta</u>, 28-29; flag officers on active duty on the West Coast gathered in San Francisco to celebrate his 80th birthday in 1965, 365-366

Norden Bombsight
   The United States would not give Great Britain information on the bombsight in the early part of World War II, 41-44

Norfolk, Virginia
   Mine disposal personnel were summoned to the area after German submarines laid mines off the port in 1942, 71-72; serves as headquarters for the Supreme Allied Commander Atlantic (SACLant) in the NATO organization, 222

North Atlantic Treaty Organization (NATO)
   Officers from various NATO nations made up the planning staff for the Supreme Allied Commander Atlantic (SACLant) in the mid-1950s, 220-223, 231-232, 240-242; after the formation of the NATO military command in the early 1950s, the Iberian-Atlantic command was created only on paper because of disagreement over which nation should run the organization, 223-225; planning for possible use of nuclear weapons, 225-226; declining role for the Royal Navy because of reduction in forces, 227-230; briefings on command post exercises and NATO functions, 232-238, 244-245; SACLant boundary lines dividing national command responsibilities, 242-243; relationship between Supreme Allied Commander Europe and Supreme Allied Commander Europe, 246-249; relationship with the United Nations, 249-251; U.S. political ambassador to NATO, 250-251; NATO policy for dealing with close encounters at sea with the Soviet Navy, 251-252; the Sixth Fleet took part in a NATO exercise in the Mediterranean in 1957, 287-289

Norway
   Challenges in briefing members of the Norwegian Parliament when they visited SACLant headquarters at Norfolk in the mid-1950s, 244-245

Nuclear Weapons
   See Atomic Bombs

OS2U Kingfisher
   Plane that was useful for observation when the light cruiser _Memphis_ (CL-13) was involved in anti-German blockade operations between Brazil and Ascension Island during World War II, 84

Oceanographer of the Navy
   The Naval Oceanographic Office had its headquarters at Suitland, Maryland, in the mid-1960s then moved to Alexandria, Virginia, 367-371; as a result of a reorganization in early 1966, the oceanographer reported directly to the Chief of Naval Operations rather than through an assistant CNO, and various other entities reported to the oceanographer, 368-371, 381-383, 392-393; in the late 1960s Senator Warren Magnuson introduced a

bill to upgrade the oceanographer's billet to three stars, but the proposal died, 382-383; direct relationship with the Assistant Secretary of the Navy (Research and Development), 391-392

Oceanography
Oceanographic work in connection with atomic bomb tests at Bikini Atoll in 1946, 132-134, 144; in the mid-1960s, the Navy didn't have a postgraduate course in oceanography, 366; role of the Naval Oceanographic Office in doing both hydrographic and oceanographic surveying in the late 1960s, 371-381; in the late 1960s a master's program in physical oceanography was established at the Naval Postgraduate School, 389

Oil
An oil company initially sent the ice-strengthened tanker Manhattan through the Canadian Arctic around 1970, prior to the construction of the Alaska oil pipeline, 216-220

Okinawa
Description of the kamikaze damage sustained by the destroyer Laffey off Okinawa in the spring of 1945, 108-109

Operation Crossroads
See Crossroads, Operation

Operational Development Force
Grew out of efforts in 1945 to develop a method of countering Japanese kamikazes, 153; the mission in the early 1950s, as it has been ever since, is the operational testing of new weapons brought out by the technical establishment, 177-178; used the former battleship Mississippi (AG-128) for missile testing in the early 1950s, 178, 186; did experiments aimed at stopping Chinese Communist junks if they tried to invade Formosa in the early 1950s, 178-185; had high-quality, technically trained staff officers in the early 1950s, 188-190; Rear Admiral Frederick Entwistle, Commander of OpDevFor in the early 1950s, sent some of his staff officers to witness Korean War operations firsthand in order to validate the command's work, 190-193; comparison of work in peace and war, 195-196; the command had no direct relationship with the manufacturers of various equipment, 196-197; studied ways of improving habitability on board warships in the early 1950s, 198-201

Operations Analysis
In one instance in 1945, Admiral Jonas Ingram's intuition proved superior to operations analysis in locating a German U-boat in the Atlantic, 99-100

Osborn, Lieutenant James B., USN (USNA, 1942)
As a junior officer in the late 1940s, was a summer student at the Naval Ordnance Laboratory, 154

Ouvry, Lieutenant Commander John, RN
Defused a recovered German magnetic mine in England in 1939, 50

PC-815, USS
Patrol craft that sank in San Diego Harbor in September 1945 as a result of a collision with the destroyer Laffey (DD-724), 120-124

Pay and Allowances
Salaries of naval personnel were cut in the early 1930s because of the Depression, 20-21; because of a shortage of Supply Corps officers in the late 1930s, line officers took on the supply and disbursing functions in destroyers, 30-35

Pearl Harbor, Hawaii
After the Japanese attack in December 1941, a call went out for bomb and mine disposal personnel to deal with unexploded ordnance, 69-70, 76-77

Peet, Commander Raymond E., USN (USNA, 1943)
Received sudden orders in 1957 to turn over command of the destroyer Barton (DD-722) in the Mediterranean and go to Washington to become aide to the CNO, 281-283; was a skilled ship handler, 290

Persian Gulf
The U.S. destroyers Barton (DD-722) and Soley (DD-707) exercised with the Iranian Navy in the fall of 1956, 261-264; Rear Admiral Jack Monroe had to deal with a false report about rioting in Bahrain during the Suez crisis of 1956, 264-266; providing destroyers to the Middle East Force in the late 1950s tied up quite a few ships, 286

Pius XI, Pope
Had an audience at the Vatican with visiting Naval Academy midshipmen in 1929, 12

Planning
Officers from various NATO nations made up the planning staff for the Supreme Allied Commander Atlantic (SACLant) in the mid-1950s, 220-223; planning in the mid-1950s for possible use of nuclear weapons by NATO nations, 225-226; the Navy made preparations in 1964 for dropping naval mines into Vietnamese waters from the air, but the plans were not executed until 1972, 343-349

Portugal
In the early 1950s, when the Iberian-Atlantic command was being established by NATO, the Portuguese wanted the headquarters to be at Lisbon, 223-224

Prairie State, USS (IX-15)
Former battleship <u>Illinois</u> (BB-7) had by World War II been converted to a training ship and was the site of recruiting for the mine disposal program, among others, 61-62

Preminger, Otto
Movie director who got help from Naval Base Los Angeles in staging the premiere of his movie <u>In Harm's Way</u> in the mid-1960s, 355-356

Profanity
Vice Admiral Jonas Ingram had an entertaining comment about a talkative Brazilian naval officer in World War II, 103-104

Projectiles
The cruiser <u>Augusta</u> (CA-31) didn't use her neatly painted projectiles for target practice in the mid-1930s, 38-39

Promotion of Officers
Duty in the Pentagon was considered useful for selection for flag rank in the late 1950s, 295-297; Rear Admiral P. D. Stroop believed responsible duty in the field should be rewarded by promotion, 309-311; Waters's selection for rear admiral in 1960, 310-312, 422-423

Public Relations
In 1945 Admiral Jonas Ingram made a colorful statement to the media about plans to intercept German missiles, 96-97; Vice Admiral Charles Griffin liked to get publicity when he was serving as Commander Seventh Fleet in the early 1960s, 316-317, 321-322; a Navy PR man was overenthusiastic during a SEATO exercise in the fall of 1961, 318-319; in the mid-1960s Commander Naval Base Los Angeles helped arrange for visiting VIPs to get tours of movie and TV studios, 352-356; Waters's visit to Mayor Sam Yorty of Los Angeles, 356-357

Puget Sound Navy Yard, Bremerton, Washington
Hurry-up repairs and provisioning of the destroyer <u>Laffey</u> (DD-724) for the planned invasion of Japan in late 1945, 109-115

Radar
The United States and Great Britain exchanged information on radar technology at the outset of World War II, 40-41; the attack transport U.S. <u>Glynn</u> (APA-239) provided supply support for the construction of the Air Force's DEW Line radar system in the Arctic in 1952, 202-215; radar on board the <u>Glynn</u> was valuable for navigation through ice fields in the Arctic, 212-213

Radio
Atmospheric conditions made radio communications difficult during arctic operations in 1952, 204-205

Radioactivity
See Atomic Bombs

Recruiting
In World War II officer trainees were recruited for possible service in mine disposal, 61-62

Reina Mercedes, USS (IX-25)
Captured Spanish cruiser that was used for many years to confine errant Naval Academy midshipmen, 17-19

Replenishment at Sea
Vice Admiral Charles Brown liked smart, aggressive maneuvers on the part of Sixth Fleet ships during replenishments in the late 1950s, 289-291

Research and Development
Research and development projects on mines at the Naval Ordnance Laboratory in the late 1940s, 153-154, 164-166, 169; work on atomic bomb fuzes, 155; the antisubmarine rocket called Weapon Able was developed on a high-priority basis at NOL in the late 1940s, 155-158; development work on explosives in the late 1940s, 159-160

Revolutionary War
In the 1950s, the Naval Weapons Station, Yorktown, Virginia, helped celebrate annual Yorktown Day in honor of the Revolutionary War battle, 300-301

Roach, Lieutenant John P., USN (USNA, 1932)
Training for mine disposal work in World War II, 55, 62

Rockets
Weapon Able was an antisubmarine rocket developed on a high-priority basis at the Naval Ordnance Laboratory in the late 1940s, 155-158

Royal Navy
At the outset of World War II, British sonar was superior to that used in the U.S. Navy, 39-40; in 1940 the United States supplied the Royal Navy with 50 destroyers that had outmoded Mark VIII torpedoes, 44-46; Waters served as an observer with the Royal Navy in 1940-41 to acquire knowledge about German magnetic mines, 46-53; had to adjust to a declining role in the NATO structure in the 1950s because of a reduction in the number of warships, 227-230; officers were divided in the 1950s into wet and dry lists, 229-230; British officers harbored hard

feelings when the United States did not get involved in the Suez crisis in late 1956, 269-270; relations had improved by 1957, 273; took part in a SEATO amphibious exercise at Borneo in the fall of 1961, 317-319

Safety
Japanese mines in World War II were simple and effective but not always safe, 162-163; precautions taken at the Naval Mine Depot, Yorktown, Virginia, in the late 1950s, 307-308

San Diego, California
Because U.S. naval intelligence lost track of a large part of the Japanese fleet in December 1937, U.S. warships checked all traffic going in and out of San Diego Harbor, 36-37; the patrol craft USS PC-815 sank in San Diego Harbor in September 1945 as a result of a collision with the destroyer Laffey (DD-724), 120-124

Schoech, Vice Admiral William A., USN (USNA, 1928)
Fine officer who served as Chief of Naval Material in the early 1960s, 341-342

Scuba
Steps toward developing underwater breathing apparatus during World War II, 82-83

Security
In the late 1930s there was super secrecy about the magnetic exploders in the Mark XIV torpedoes, 37-39; the United States would not give Great Britain the Norden bombsight in the early part of World War II, 41-44

Scripps Institute of Oceanography
One of its boats was inspected by a boarding party from the destroyer Downes (DD-375) on Christmas Eve 1937, 36-37; worked with the Naval Oceanographic Office in the late 1960s, 393

Sea Lab
Underwater habitat program that the Navy operated in the 1960s, 397-401

SEATO
See Southeast Asia Treaty Organization

Seattle, Washington
Waters's experiences making a landing at Seattle in 1945 soon after taking over command of the destroyer Laffey (DD-724), 111-112

Seventh Fleet, U.S.
Vice Admiral Charles Griffin liked to get publicity when he was serving as fleet commander in the early 1960s, 316-317

Shah of Iran
  Was present when ships of his navy took part in an exercise with the destroyers Barton (DD-722) and Soley (DD-707) in the fall of 1956, 261-264

Ship Handling
  Waters's experiences making a landing at Seattle in 1945 soon after taking over command of the destroyer Laffey (DD-724), 111-112; problems with the steering cables in the Laffey, 113-114; Vice Admiral Charles Brown liked smart, aggressive maneuvers on the part of Sixth Fleet ships in the late 1950s, 289-291

Shore Patrol
  Waters administered local shore patrols while serving as ComDesFlot 1 in the Western Pacific in the early 1960s, 321-322

Sixth Fleet, U.S.
  Captain Lot Ensey was relieved hurriedly in 1956 as ComDesRon 2 so he could become Sixth Fleet chief of staff, 253, 256; destroyer operating patterns in the late 1950s, 256-257; operating conditions for ships in the relatively confined spaces of the Mediterranean in 1956-57, 274-275; U.S. destroyer operations against a Soviet submarine in 1957, 276-280; took part in a NATO exercise in 1957, 287-289; Vice Admiral Charles Brown liked smart, aggressive maneuvers on the part of fleet ships in the late 1950s, 289-291

Snyder, Captain J. Edward, Jr., USN (USNA, 1945)
  As special assistant to the Assistant Secretary of the Navy (R&D) in the late 1960s, provided excellent liaison to the Naval Oceanographic Office, 396

Soley, USS (DD-707)
  Passage through the Suez Canal in September 1956, shortly after it was nationalized by Egypt, 257-261; exercised with the Iranian Navy in the fall of 1956, 261-264; the crew had an enjoyable trip home from the Persian Gulf in early 1957, 271

Sonar
  At the outset of World War II, British sonar was superior to that used in the U.S. Navy, 39-40; conditions in the Mediterranean in the late 1950s for use of sonar, 275-278

Southeast Asia Treaty Organization (SEATO)
  Conducted a large-scale amphibious exercise in the fall of 1961 at Borneo, 317-319

Soviet Navy
NATO policy for dealing with close encounters at sea with the Soviet Navy, 251-252; U.S. destroyer operations against a Soviet submarine in the Mediterranean in 1957, 276-280

Soviet Union
Supplied mines for use by North Korea against United Nations forces in the Korean War in the early 1950s, 166-168

State Department
Objected to the use of naval mines in Vietnamese waters in 1964, 344-345

Stone, Lieutenant Commander Lowell T., USN (USNA, 1929)
Officer in charge of the deep-sea diving school at the Washington Navy Yard early in World War II, 68

Stroop, Vice Admiral Paul D., USN (USNA, 1926)
As Chief of the Bureau of Naval Weapons in 1960, believed that responsible officers in the field should be rewarded with promotion to flag rank, 309-311; qualities of leadership as Chief of the Bureau of Naval Weapons in the early 1960s, 339-340; while serving as ComNavAirPac in 1965, gathered up West Coast flag officers to celebrate Fleet Admiral Chester Nimitz's 80th birthday, 365-366

Submarines
Types of torpedoes in Japanese midget submarines stranded at Pearl Harbor during the attack in December 1941, 70-71; the German Navy used submarines to lay a few mines off the U.S. East Coast in 1942, 71-74; in 1945 the U.S. Atlantic Fleet staff got reports that the German Navy was experimenting with guided missiles on submarines, 95-97; role of the U.S. Tenth Fleet in antisubmarine warfare against U-boats in World War II, 97-98; in one instance in 1945, Admiral Jonas Ingram's intuition proved superior to operations analysis in locating a German U-boat in the Atlantic, 99-100

Suez Canal
Passage of the destroyers _Barton_ (DD-722) and _Soley_ (DD-707) through the canal in September 1956, shortly after it was nationalized by Egypt, 257-261; the United States did not get involved in the military action during the Suez crisis in October-November 1956, 269-271; the destroyer _Barton_ (DD-722) made a trip through the canal with a new skipper in 1957, 282-284

Supply Corps
Because of a shortage of Supply Corps officers in the late 1930s, line officers took on the supply and disbursing functions in destroyers, 30-35

Supreme Allied Commander Atlantic (SACLant)
Officers from various NATO nations made up the planning staff in the mid-1950s, 220-223, 231-232, 240-242; after the formation of the NATO military command in the early 1950s, the Iberian-Atlantic command was created on paper only because of disagreement over which nation should run the organization, 223-225; planning for possible use of nuclear weapons, 225-226; briefings on command post exercises and NATO roles, 232-238, 244-245; boundary lines dividing national command responsibilities, 242-243; liaison officer to the U.S. Navy, 245-246; relationship to Supreme Allied Commander Europe, 246-249

Surveying
Navy underwater demolition teams did survey work in poorly charted waters in the Canadian Arctic in 1952, 207-208; a young reserve officer on board the Glynn (APA-239) did valuable survey work in the Arctic, 211-212; role of the Naval Oceanographic Office in doing both hydrographic and oceanographic surveying in the late 1960s, 371-381; classified contour mapping of the ocean bottom for ballistic missile submarines, 385-386

Sylvester, Captain John, USN (USNA, 1926)
As ops officer for ComCruDesPac in the fall of 1945, was involved in monitoring the readiness of various destroyers during a period of demobilization, 127, 130-131

TFX
Rear Admiral Frederick L. Ashworth testified to Congress in connection with the TFX aircraft investigation in the early 1960s and wound up being promoted, 337-339

Tactics
U.S. destroyer operations against a Soviet submarine in the Mediterranean in 1957, 276-280

Tenth Fleet, U.S.
Role in antisubmarine warfare in the Atlantic in World War II, 97-98

Terrier Missile
The Operational Development Force used the former battleship Mississippi (AG-128) for missile testing in the early 1950s, 178, 186

Thistleton-Smith, Lieutenant Commander Geoffrey, RN
Commanded British mine warfare forces early in World War II, 49

Torpedoes
On board the destroyer Downes (DD-375) in the late 1930s there was a hint of problems to come, 35; in the late 1930s there was super secrecy about the magnetic exploders in the Mark XIV torpedoes, 37-39; in 1940 the United States supplied the Royal Navy with 50 destroyers that had outmoded Mark VIII torpedoes, 44-46; types of torpedoes in Japanese midget submarines at Pearl Harbor, 70-71

Toulouse-Lautrec, Captain Guy de
French naval officer of the 1950s, he was related to the famous artist, 231-232

Training
Program for training junior officers in the cruiser Augusta (CA-31) in the early 1930s, 26-27; Waters served as an observer in England in 1940-41 to acquire knowledge about German magnetic mines, 46-53; the U.S. Navy established a mine disposal school in Washington, D.C., in mid-1941 and subsequently trained hundreds of men in explosive ordnance disposal techniques, 53-83; cross-pollination during World War II of U.S. and British explosive ordnance disposal training, 80; sonar, radio, and damage control training for Waters before he took command of the destroyer Laffey (DD-724) in 1945, 106-108; the Navy trained aviators in 1964 for dropping naval mines into Vietnamese waters from the air, but the plans were not executed until 1972, 343-349

Truman, President Harry S
Reaction in Tokyo to President Truman's firing of General Douglas MacArthur as Far East commander in April 1951, 193-195

Tucker, USS (DD-374)
Difficulties paying for fuel following a cruise to Trinidad in 1937, 32

Underwater Demolition Teams
Bomb disposal and mine disposal trainees formed the nucleus of the original underwater demolition teams during World War II, 65-66; Navy UDTs did survey work on poorly charted waters in the Canadian Arctic in 1952, 207-208

United Nations
Relationship with the North Atlantic Treaty Organization in the 1950s, 249-250

Vietnam War
U.S. naval operations in the Korean War led to the idea of the usefulness of small gunboats of the type later used in Vietnam, 192-193; Secretary of Defense Robert McNamara became interested in the mid-1960s in the potential effectiveness of naval mines

for use in the Vietnam War, 342-343; the Navy made preparations in 1964 for dropping naval mines into Vietnamese waters from the air, but the plans were not executed until 1972, 343-349; the Naval Oceanographic Office ran a rather expensive surveying operation off the coast of Vietnam in the late 1960s to support U.S. naval forces operating there, 375-377

Visual Signaling
Importance of on board the cruiser Augusta (CA-31) in the early 1930s, 27

Vixen, USS (PG-53)
Former private yacht that served as flagship in 1944-45 for Admiral Jonas Ingram, who had a small staff as Commander in Chief Atlantic Fleet, 92-93; excellent communications facilities, 93-94

Walsh, Captain Don, USN (Ret.) (USNA, 1954)
Intelligent naval officer who earned a doctorate in oceanography in the 1960s, then retired in 1975 soon after making captain, 390-391

Waters, Rear Admiral Odale D., Jr., USN (Ret.) (USNA, 1932)
Family background in the state of Virginia, 1-2; education in public schools in Virginia the 1910s and 1920s, 2-3, 5; attendance at business college in 1927, 3; in 1927 received the promise of a Naval Academy appointment, 4; attended Army-Navy Prep in Washington, D.C., in 1927-28, 4-6; admission to the Naval Academy in 1928, 6-7; experiences as a midshipman, 1928-32, 8-19; service from 1932 to 1936 in the heavy cruiser Augusta (CA-31), 19-28; service from 1936 to 1940 in the destroyer Downes (DD-375), 29-40; duty as a naval observer in England in 1940-41, 41-53; in 1941 helped open and run a mine disposal school at the Naval Gun Factory in Washington, D.C., from 1941 to 1943, 53-83; duty as gunnery officer in the light cruiser Memphis (CL-13) in 1943, 83-89; service in 1944 as Fourth Fleet gunnery officer, 90; death of father, 90; assignment to Atlantic Fleet staff in 1944, 90-104; command of the destroyer Laffey (DD-724) in 1945-46, 105-148; duty at the Naval Ordnance Laboratory, White Oak, Maryland, from 1946 to 1950, 148-187; was a student in 1950 at the joint-service Armed Forces Staff College, Norfolk, Virginia, 170-176; served from 1950 to 1952 on the staff of Commander Operational Development Force, 176-202; commanded the attack transport Glynn (APA-239), 1952-1953, 202-220; served in the plans section of the SACLant staff from 1953 to 1956, 221-252, 254-256; commanded Destroyer Squadron Two in 1956-57, 252-254, 256-294; commanded Naval Mine Depot/Naval Weapons Station, Yorktown, Virginia, from 1957 to 1960, 295-313; selection for rear admiral in 1960, 310-312, 422-423; commanded Destroyer Flotilla One from 1960 to 1962, 314-331; served as inspector general in the Bureau of Naval

Weapons, 1962-1964, 331-341; served as Commander Mine Force Pacific Fleet and Commander Naval Base Los Angeles, 1964-65, 342-367; served as Oceanographer of the Navy from 1965 to 1970, 367-404; duties as a member of the board of the U.S. Naval Institute, 404-412; brief assignment in 1970-71 as an adviser with NOAA, 412-414; had second-longest tour as Oceanographer of the Navy to Matthew Fontaine Maury, 414-416; post-Navy work as a department head at the Florida Institute of Technology from 1971 to 1975, 417-418

Weapon Able
Antisubmarine rocket developed on high-priority basis at the Naval Ordnance Laboratory in the late 1940s, 155-158

Weather
The patrol craft USS PC-815 sank in San Diego Harbor in September 1945 as a result of a collision in fog with the destroyer Laffey (DD-724), 120-124; variable weather conditions during arctic operations in 1952, 205-206

Wellings, Lieutenant Commander Joseph H., USN (USNA, 1925)
Provided guidance to junior officers in dealing with the British while serving as a special observer with the Royal Navy in the early part of World War II, 42-44

West Virginia, USS (BB-48)
Work of Chief Gunner's Mate Robert Eigell in defuzing an unexploded Japanese bomb left on board the ship after the attack on Pearl Harbor in December 1941, 77

Wind Tunnels
Following World War II, the U.S. Naval Ordnance Laboratory received a vacuum-driven wind tunnel from Germany and used the design in building its own, 160-162

Withington, Rear Admiral Frederic S., USN (USNA, 1923)
Cultivated Japanese admirals while serving as Commander Naval Forces Japan in the early 1960s, 323

Wonsan, North Korea
The North Koreans effectively mined this harbor during the Korean War to protect against a Marine landing, 167

Wright, Admiral Jerauld, USN (USNA, 1918)
While serving as SACLant in the mid-1950s, wanted to make a big splash in a NATO briefing for Field Marshal Bernard Montgomery, 233-240; emphatically denied Waters an opportunity to serve on the Armed Forces Special Weapons Project in the 1950s, 339

Yokosuka, Japan
Part of Destroyer Flotilla One was homeported there in the early 1960s, 315-316, 320-321, 323-330

Yorty, Sam
Mayor of Los Angeles who arranged an interesting visit for Waters in the mid-1960s, 356-357

Yugoslavia
During a Suez Canal transit in 1956, Waters stopped until a Yugoslavian was removed from the destroyer *Barton* (DD-722) because of a prohibition against having pilots from Communist nations on board, 258-261

www.ingramcontent.com/pod-product-compliance
Lightning Source LLC
Chambersburg PA
CBHW080625170426
43209CB00007B/1515